Taiwan Straits Standoff

D1446767

Taiwan Straits Standoff

70 Years of PRC–Taiwan Cross-Strait Tensions

 5/10/2022

Bruce A. Elleman

A

ANTHEM PRESS

Anthem Press
An imprint of Wimbledon Publishing Company
www.anthempress.com

This edition first published in UK and USA 2022
by ANTHEM PRESS
75–76 Blackfriars Road, London SE1 8HA, UK
or PO Box 9779, London SW19 7ZG, UK
and
244 Madison Ave #116, New York, NY 10016, USA

First published in the UK and USA by Anthem Press in 2021

The thoughts and opinions expressed in this publication
are those of the author and are not necessarily those of the
U.S. government, the U.S. Navy department, or the U.S. Naval War College.

British Library Cataloguing-in-Publication Data
A catalogue record for this book is available from the British Library.

ISBN-13: 978-1-83998-556-0 (Pbk)
ISBN-10: 1-83998-556-9 (Pbk)

This title is also available as an e-book.

Dedicated to my number one fan, my Mom

CONTENTS

ILLUSTRATIONS

Maps

Figure

INTRODUCTION

STALEMATE ALONG THE TAIWAN STRAITS, 1949–2020

Following the Nationalist defeat on the mainland in 1949, Chiang Kai-shek and his followers retreated to Taiwan, reforming the Republic of China (ROC). To many it seemed almost certain that the People's Republic of China (PRC) would attack and take Taiwan, perhaps as early as summer 1950. Control over a number of offshore islands, especially Quemoy (Jinmen) and Matsu (Mazu), became a deciding factor in whether the PRC could invade Taiwan or, conversely, the ROC could invade the mainland. Twice in the 1950s tensions peaked, during the first (1954–55) and second (1958) Taiwan Strait crises. During both events the US government intervened both diplomatically and militarily.

This work provides a short, but highly relevant, history of the Taiwan Strait and its significance today. This small body of water—often compared to the English Channel—separates the PRC and Taiwan and has been the location for periodic military tensions, some threatening to end in war. During the 1950s, the two outbreaks appeared like they might result in a global war. During the evacuation of the Dachen Islands, for example, the US Navy sent seven aircraft carriers and was authorized to nuke three Chinese coastal cities if the PLA tried to interfere.

In the modern era, the Taiwan Strait separates the democratic Taiwan from the authoritarian PRC. This study will discuss the origins of these conflicts, the military aspects of the confrontations, and in particular the complicated and largely secret diplomatic negotiations—including two previously unknown Eisenhower–Chiang secret agreements—going on behind the scenes between the US government and the Nationalist government in Taiwan. This book will end with a short discussion of the ongoing COVID crisis and how the PRC might take advantage of this crisis to extend its political, and eventually military, control over Taiwan.

Chapter 1

THE TWO CHINAS AND THE BATTLE FOR CONTROL OF OFFSHORE ISLANDS

This book will examine the role of offshore islands in twentieth-century East Asian history, and in particular those islands located in the Taiwan Strait that were disputed by the People's Republic of China (PRC) and the Republic of China (ROC) during the 1950s and afterward, and how these apparently insignificant islands impacted Cold War history. The history of the 1945–91 Cold War can be divided into three parts: (1) breaking apart the Sino-Soviet monolith, (2) forging Sino-US cooperation against the USSR, and (3) the two-front destruction of the USSR. The Harry S. Truman Presidential Library and the Dwight D. Eisenhower Presidential Library contain especially pertinent information on the first of these three periods, allowing for a greater understanding of how and why Washington adopted polices with the strategic goal of breaking apart the Sino-Soviet alliance.

For much of this period, from 1950 to 1979, the US Navy (USN) conducted a buffer operation in the Taiwan Strait to neutralize the region. The most important goal of this USN operation was to ensure that neither side attacked the other, an action that might lead to global war. While it is often assumed that the US government's focus was just on the Taiwan Strait, in fact there were equally valid concerns that after "China is Communized, the remainder of Asia and the islands to the south and east will be vulnerable to rapid Communization"; due to East Asia's geography, "there are no natural barriers to the advance of Communism from China to Indo-China, Siam, Burma and thence to Malaya, India, Indonesia and the other islands of the Western Pacific."[1] Because of the enormous Nationalist losses, by late 1949 America's defense line had moved from the China's Pacific Coast to the various islands from the Aleutians, down through the Kurils, Hokkaido, the main Japanese

---

1 Letter from Major General Claire Lee Chennault to John R. Steelman, June 10, 1949, Papers of Harry S. Truman (hereafter PHST), Official File, OF 150, Box 759, File O.F. 150 Misc. (1947–48) [2 of 2], Harry S. Truman Presidential Library (hereafter HSTPL).

islands, Okinawa, Formosa [Taiwan], and the Philippines. In particular, "Formosa is in the direct line—in fact, it is the center of our whole defense."[2]

Seen in this perspective, the defense of Taiwan was essential to the defense of all of East Asia. To better set the stage for this study, this chapter will examine the historical background, the strategic importance of the Taiwan Strait in the creation of the "two Chinas" conflict, the beginning of the Korean War, and how all of these factors contributed to the establishment of the Taiwan Patrol Force. It will also examine in greater detail the location of the various offshore islands, their military and/or strategic importance, and what factors led to their retention by the Nationalists or to their return—either by force or through an orderly withdrawal—to the control of the PRC.

Historical background

The offshore islands between Mainland China and Taiwan have often played an important military role.[3] The Taiwan Strait is a very strategic region, since it lies along the primary north–south sea lane in East Asia. Japanese, Korean, and northern and central Chinese produce and luxury goods flowing primarily from north to south must transit this strait to reach Southeast Asia, just as luxury goods and raw materials flowing from south to north must travel through this region. The Taiwan Strait has long been a choke point, and whichever country dominated both sides of the strait could close these waters to international shipping. Such an action would force commercial vessels to take the longer and more exposed route to the east of Taiwan.

Due to its strategic importance, Taiwan has been fought over many times, including in the seventeenth century by the Dutch, Ming loyalists, the Manchus in the eighteenth century opposing a local rebellion, and during the 1880s' Sino-French War. As a result of the first Sino-Japanese War, China ceded Taiwan to Japan in perpetuity in the 1895 Treaty of Shimonoseki. Japan maintained sovereignty over Taiwan for 50 years, until Japan's surrender in 1945, at which point—according to the terms of the Cairo and Potsdam agreements—Taiwan was returned to "China," which at this stage meant "Nationalist China" since it was the internationally recognized government.

---

2 Letter from Senator Homer Ferguson to Harry S. Truman, December 13, 1949, PHST, Official File, OF 150-G, Box 761, Formosa, HSTPL.

3 Anti-Manchu forces used the various offshore islands to attack and take Taiwan from the Dutch beginning in 1661. Two decades later, in 1683, Qing forces also used the offshore islands to defeat the Ming loyalists and retake Taiwan. 杨志本 [Yang Zhiben, ed.], 中国海军百科全书 [*China Navy Encyclopedia*], vol. 2 (Beijing: 海潮出版社 [Sea Tide Press], 1998), 1912–14.

The division of China into ROC and the mainland-based PRC was a direct outcome of World War II and the Chinese civil war. During World War II, the US government encouraged the Nationalists and Communists to form a coalition government. As Nationalist rule imploded, the Communists orchestrated an increasingly effective campaign to rally popular support. It looked like the USSR might attack. President Truman decided it was not worth billions of dollars and millions of men defending China. On July 26, 1946, Fleet Admiral William D. Leahy, Chief of the Joint Chief of Staff (JCS), reported to Truman that if there was Soviet attack in China all US troops would immediately withdraw "southward" and would be evacuated out of the Chinese city of Tsingtao (Qingdao).[4]

The US government refused to get involved in the Chinese civil war. As early as November 14, 1945, Congressman Ellis E. Patterson wrote to Truman condemning "intervention on our part" on the side of any Chinese faction.[5] After assigning General Marshall to find a solution in China, on December 18, 1945, Truman wrote to Secretary of Commerce Henry A. Wallace, telling him that his instructions to Marshall including using US influence "to the end that the unification of China by peaceful democratic methods may be achieved as soon as possible." With regard to extending US credits or technical assistance, both of an economic and military type, Marshall told them that "a China disunited and torn by civil strife could not be considered realistically as a proper place for American assistance." Truman then ordered Wallace to suspend all ongoing talks with Chinese officials "which might encourage the Chinese to hope that this Government is contemplating the extension of any type of assistance to China, except in accordance with the recommendations of General Marshall."[6] Although the Marshall mission was widely considered a failure, Maurice Votaw cautioned that Marshall had "all the cards stacked against him in advance, so [...] Marshall could not have possibly brought about a settlement."[7]

On June 2, 1947, the Department of State warned that Nationalist troop morale in Manchuria was so poor that "there is a possibility of a sudden military debacle which would lay all Manchuria open to the Communists."[8]

---

4 Memorandum for the President, TOP SECRET, July 26, 1946, PHST, SMOF-Naval Aide, Box 22, State Department Briefs File, HSTPL.
5 Letter from Ellis E. Patterson to Harry S. Truman, November 14, 1945, PHST, Official File, OF 148-A, Box 757, File O.F. 150 (1945–46), HSTPL.
6 Letter from Harry S. Truman to Henry A. Wallace, December 18, 1945, PHST, Official File, OF 148-A, Box 757, File O.F. 150 (1945–46), HSTPL.
7 Letter from Maurice Votaw to Charles G. Ross, April 9, 1947, PHST, Official File, OF 150, Box 759, File O.F. 150 Misc. (1947–48) [1 of 2], HSTPL.
8 Summary of Telegrams, TOP SECRET, June 2, 1947, PHST, SMOF-Naval Aide, Box 22, State Department Briefs File, HSTPL.

During September 1947, in fact, the Communists were able to shift to the offensive in Manchuria. They pushed the retreating Nationalist troops into a small triangle, bounded by the cities of Jinzhou, Changchun, and Mukden. On February 9, 1948, William C. Bullitt, the former US Ambassador to Moscow, warned President Truman that "If Manchuria falls to the Communists, their sweep south to the Yangtze River will be rapid, and they may then be able to conquer all China; and you, Mr. President, will, thereafter, have to account to the American people for the consequences to them and to the world of control of China by Stalin."[9]

By May 1948, the People's Liberation Army (PLA) had cleared most of the Nationalist troops from Manchuria. In November 1948, the Communists wiped out another 100,000 Nationalist troops. Finally, on December 15, 1948, after 63 days of fighting, the Communists took Xuzhou, opening the road south to the Yangzi River and to Nanjing.[10] The US Army had a small number of troops—60 officers and 4,000 men—stationed in Qingdao, Shandong, and during November 1948 the JCS for the first time discussed withdrawing them.[11] At the same time, US military advisers in China were "unanimous in the view that short of the actual employment of US troops in China no amount of military assistance can now save the Chiang Kai-shek regime in the face of the present political, military and economic deterioration."[12] Even Chiang's personal secretary called the defeat in Manchuria a "shameless debacle."[13]

Although they lost North China, the Nationalists retained their traditional power base in South China. As early as November 29, 1948, no less a personage than the Mayor of Boston, James M. Curley, wrote to Truman to say that "our most important ally in the event we should have trouble with Russia should prove [to be] China, with its tremendous natural resources and enormous population [...] the powerhouse of Russia's war industries is located in the vicinity of Siberia and the nearest approach to Siberia is from China."[14] A year later, Frederick C. McKee argued: "China is the key to the

---

9 Letter from William C. Bullitt to President Truman, February 9, 1948, PHST, Official File, OF 150, Box 759, File O.F. 150 Misc. (1947–48) [1 of 2], HSTPL.

10 Bruce A. Elleman, "Huai-Hai," in Jeremy Black, ed., *The Seventy Great Battles of All Time* (London: Thames & Hudson, 2005), 279–81.

11 Memorandum for the President, TOP SECRET, November 4, 1948, PHST, President's Secretary's File, Box 189, P.S.F. Subject File, HSTPL.

12 Summary of Telegrams, TOP SECRET, November 8, 1948, PHST, SMOF-Naval Aide, Box 23, State Department Briefs File, HSTPL.

13 Summary of Telegrams, TOP SECRET, November 9, 1948, PHST, SMOF-Naval Aide, Box 23, State Department Briefs File, HSTPL.

14 Letter from Boston Mayor James M. Curley to Harry S. Truman, November 29, 1948, PHST, Official File, OF 150, Box 759, File O.F. 150 Misc. (1947–48) [2 of 2], HSTPL.

defense of Asia [...] if we help the Chinese to hold West China, its airfields could be our closet bases for counter attack on the Soviet Atom Bomb plants North of Lake Baikal."[15]

On January 6, 1949, members of the National Assembly of the Republic of China wrote to Truman begging for assistance in their "campaign against totalitarian rule in defense of freedom and democracy."[16] Bullitt accused Truman and Marshall of not doing enough to stop the communists: "Mr. President, you and your Secretary of State, General Marshall, would go down in history as having been unintentional patrons of the Soviet campaign for destruction of the United States and domination of the world."[17] On June 10, 1949, Major General Claire Lee Chennault sent a letter to the White House warning "that all of South East Asia will rapidly go Communist once China has fallen."[18]

But on August 3, 1948, a CIA assessment of the Nationalists concluded: "Chiang's position is steadily deteriorating, and his Government is in such precarious situation that its collapse or overthrow could occur at any time."[19] Only four months later, an updated report concluded that Chiang might be "removed from his position as President of the Republic of China at any time," and that "his removal would be brought about by forced resignation or a coup d'etat, possibly including his assassination."[20] According to Ambassador Stuart, "any effort to keep Chiang in power through American aid would not only be undemocratic but would also arouse greater sympathy for the Communist cause and create violent anti-American feeling."[21]

Many foreign commentators assumed that China would now be divided into a North and South. For example, Irving Zuckerman wrote to Clark Clifford

15 Letter from Frederick C. McKee to Harry S. Truman, November 29, 1949, PHST, Official File, OF 150, Box 759, File O.F. 150 Misc. (1947–48) [1 of 2], HSTPL.

16 Letter from Members of the National Assembly of the Republic of China to Harry S. Truman, January 6, 1949, PHST, Official File, OF 150, Box 758, File O.F. 150 (1947–49), HSTPL.

17 Letter from William C. Bullitt to President Truman, February 9, 1948, PHST, Official File, OF 150, Box 759, File O.F. 150 Misc. (1947–48) [1 of 2], HSTPL.

18 Letter from Major General Claire Lee Chennault to John R. Steelman, June 10, 1949, PHST, Official File, OF 150, Box 759, File O.F. 150 Misc. (1947–48) [2 of 2], HSTPL.

19 Central Intelligence Agency, Prospects for a Negotiated Peace in China, SECRET, August 3, 1948, PHST, President's Secretary's File, Box 216, P.S.F. Intelligence Reports, ORE 12–48, HSTPL.

20 Central Intelligence Agency, Possible Development in China, SECRET, November 19, 1948, PHST, President's Secretary's File, Box 216, P.S.F. Intelligence File, ORE 27–48, HSTPL.

21 Summary of Telegrams, TOP SECRET, December 23, 1948, PHST, SMOF-Naval Aide, Box 23, State Department Briefs File, HSTPL.

at the White House on November 30, 1948, to advise: "It is quite possible that peace in China may be almost immediately possible by <u>letting the Red Chinese have the northern part of China (Manchuria), with Chiang having the southern part of China</u>," thus making it "easier to administer."[22] Ambassador Stuart reported on November 26, 1948, that the Nationalists would make an "all-out effort to contain the Communists north of the Yangtze River."[23] The CIA determined that if the Nationalists relocated to South China, US "aid in the form of capital, food, equipment, and intelligent direction could probably give the National Government reasonable chance of carrying on effective anti-Communist resistance from South China," although ultimately there would be "little future safeguard from eventual defeat and collapse."[24]

To many, the Yangzi River could act as the new boundary for a China divided equally between a Communist north and a Nationalist south. Stalin reportedly ordered Mao not to cross the Yangzi River.[25] The US embassy reported on January 31, 1949, that "the Kremlin planners are fearful that the Communists may be able to develop too strong and independent a state."[26] But on February 25, 1949, the Nationalist flagship, *Chongqing*, mutinied. This symbolized the waning Nationalist mandate to rule. The Secretary of State Dean Acheson even referred to this event at a National Security Council (NSC) meeting, commenting that "The defection to the Communists of the only cruiser in the Chinese fleet is symptomatic of the uncertainties in the present situation, particularly with respect to political conspiracy and 'deals' in the higher echelons."[27] By the end of April 1949, much of the rest of the Nationalist fleet guarding the Yangzi River also defected. On April 20, 1949, Communist forces crossed the Yangzi to overrun Nanjing three days later. Thereafter, the PLA quickly consolidated control over all of mainland

---

22 Letter from Irving Zuckerman to Clark Clifford, November 30, 1948, PHST, Official File, OF 150, Box 759, File O.F. 150 Misc. (1947–48) [2 of 2], HSTPL; underlining in original.
23 Summary of Telegrams, TOP SECRET, November 26, 1948, PHST, SMOF-Naval Aide, Box 23, State Department Briefs File, HSTPL.
24 Central Intelligence Agency, Limitations of South China as an Anti-Communist Base, SECRET, June 4, 1948, PHST, President's Secretary's File, Box 216, P.S.F. Intelligence File, ORE 30–48, HSTPL.
25 S. C. M. Paine, *The Wars for Asia, 1911–1949* (New York: Cambridge University Press, 2014), 276.
26 Summary of Telegrams, TOP SECRET, January 31, 1949, PHST, SMOF-Naval Aide, Box 23, State Department Briefs File, HSTPL.
27 Secretary of State Dean Acheson, Speech to the 35th National Security Council Meeting, SECRET, March 3, 1948, PHST, President's Secretary's File, Box 179, P.S.F. Subject File, HSTPL.

China, taking Shanghai and Wuhan in May, Xi'an and Changsha in August, Guangzhou in October, and the Nationalist wartime capital of Chongqing in November 1949.[28]

The PLA rapid advance southward forced the remaining Nationalist units to retreat to Taiwan. According to one CIA analysis dated October 19, 1949, the 681,000 Nationalist combat forces had lost the "will to fight." There were six major reasons given for this loss:

(1) army politics, which keep incompetent officers in positions of high command; (2) general professional incompetence in the armed forces; (3) the personal interference of Chiang Kai-shek in tactical operations; (4) Chiang's refusal to supply money and materiel to commanders on the mainland; (5) inadequate pay, food, clothing, and equipment for the troops; and (6) chronic graft and corruption practiced by senior officers at the expense of the men.[29]

By contrast, the PLA experienced enormous growth from an estimated half a million in mid-1945, to 1.3 million in mid-1946, 2 million in mid-1947, to 2.8 million by mid-1948, and 4 million by early 1949.[30] American officials at this time considered the Chinese Communists to be little better than Soviet puppets. According to Secretary of State Dean Acheson: "This Chinese Government is really a tool of Russian imperialism in China." The most important thing to avoid was adopting "any course of action that would solidify the Chinese people behind the Communist regime."[31] Later, Acheson explained that "conflict would eventually develop between China and the USSR," and when this happened "we should seek to take advantage of this conflict when it developed and meanwhile avoid actions which would deflect Chinese xenophobia from Russia to ourselves."[32]

---

28 Bruce A. Elleman, "The *Chongqing* Mutiny and the Chinese Civil War, 1949," in Christopher M. Bell, Bruce A. Elleman, eds., *Naval Mutinies of the Twentieth Century: An International Perspective* (London: Frank Cass, 2003), 232–45.

29 Central Intelligence Agency, Survival Potential of Residual Non-Communist Regimes in China, SECRET, October 19, 1949, PHST, President's Secretary's File, Box 218, P.S.F. Intelligence File, ORE 76–49, HSTPL

30 Bruce A. Elleman and S. C. M. Paine, *Modern China: Continuity and Change 1644 to the Present* (New York: Prentice Hall, 2010), 343–44.

31 Supplemental Notes on Executive Session, Senate Foreign Relations Committee, October 12, 1949, PHST, President's Secretary's File, Box 140, P.S.F. Subject File, HSTPL.

32 Memorandum for the President, TOP SECRET, December 30, 1949, PHST, President's Secretary's File, Box 188, P.S.F. Subject File, HSTPL.

Chiang Kai-shek and his advisors officially moved the Nationalist government to Taiwan on December 8, 1949, the eighth anniversary of Japanese attack on Pearl Harbor to continue their anti-Communist struggle.[33] Even after relocating his government to Taipei, Chiang claimed that the ROC remained the legitimate government of all of China. Meanwhile, in late September 1949, Mao Zedong assembled a new Political Consultative Conference that elected him chairman of the central government and once again made Beijing the capital. On October 1, 1949, Mao officially proclaimed the creation of the PRC. Concerned about the strategic weakness of Hong Kong, Great Britain, the main US ally in Europe, extended official recognition to the PRC government on January 6, 1950.

During the summer and fall 1949, Nationalist forces fiercely defended their hold over numerous offshore islands. The Nationalists initially kept one regiment of marines on the Miao Islands north of Shandong Peninsula to blockade the Bo Hai Gulf and the northern ports, while they fortified Zhoushan and the Saddle islands to blockade the Yangzi River. Meanwhile, the Tachens (Dachens), Matsu (Mazu), Quemoy (Jinmen), and the Pescadores (Penghu) islands near Taiwan, Lema and Wan Shan islands near Guangzhou, and Hainan Island, 15 miles off the southern coast, blockaded the rest of China. After their retreat from the mainland in 1949, the Nationalist government in Taiwan used these offshore islands to conduct a naval blockade of the PRC.

The Nationalist blockade strategy

While the Nationalists were forced to retreat, they were not defeated. Instead, Chiang shifted from a land-based offensive to a naval offensive, by supporting a blockade strategy against the PRC. China had also agreed to purchase "all surplus property owned by the United States in China and on seventeen Pacific Islands and bases."[34] China was charged only $95,500,000 for equipment valued at $1,079,300,000.[35] The Nationalists controlled a total of 824 vessels

---

33 While December 7, 1941 is remembered in the United States, Japan was across the international dateline so it was December 8. This timing perhaps emphasized to Western audiences that the Nationalist struggle against communism was a continuation of their alliance with the United States during the Pacific War. Tacit acknowledgment of this perhaps occurred a year later, when the United States adopted a full strategic embargo of the PRC on December 8, 1950.

34 Statement by the President, December 18, 1946, PHST, Official File, OF 148-A, Box 757, File O.F. 150 (1945–46), HSTPL.

35 Summary of United States Government Economic and Military Aid Authorized for China Since 1937, PHST, Official File, OF 150, Box 758, File O.F. 150 (1950–53) [1 of 2], HSTPL.

of various types. By 1947, the Nationalist Navy had grown to almost 40,000 men, and by October 31, 1948, it reached 40,859, including a total of 8,062 officers.[36] The Nationalist Navy was comparatively large, estimated in late 1949 to include 30,000 men and approximately 150 ships, but morale was low and "it is possible that many units might defect."[37] To conduct their blockade against the PRC, the Nationalists worked with a number of autonomous guerrilla movements located on offshore islands not far from China's coast. Later, the USN provided military assistance—especially aircraft—that made air patrols of the blockade possible. The Nationalist blockade lasted from 1949 through 1958.[38]

With its navy both equipped and manned, in 1947 the Nationalists attempted to halt Soviet shipments to the Chinese Communists in Manchuria via Port Arthur and Dalian by adopting a naval blockade, albeit mainly a paper blockade. Beginning on June 18, 1949, the Nationalists announced that any Chinese port not under their control would be closed to trade as of midnight on June 25. Because Manchuria's ports were already closed to most foreign shippers, the blockade of Port Arthur and Dalian (together called Lüshun) elicited no complaints from the foreign powers. But a July 1949 report by the Admiralty's Intelligence Division warned that if the Nationalists lost the Miao Islands and the entire Zhoushan area including Dinghai, the blockade would have no effect north of the Yangzi River, only a "limited and sporadic" effect on trade entering and leaving the Yangzi River, and the "Nationalist blockade could only be effective south of Fuzhou."[39]

As the Nationalists retreated from their northern bases, therefore, the focus of the naval blockade moved further and further southward. The Nationalist retreat to Taiwan was a major maritime undertaking, during which the Nationalist Navy and other ships impressed into service transported approximately 2 million civilians and 600,000 soldiers to Taiwan. On August 6, 1948, the CIA argued that US bases on the Ryukyu (Okinawa) islands would "give the US a position from which to operate in defense of an unarmed post-treaty Japan and US bases in the Philippines and other Pacific

36 "Intelligence Briefs: China," *ONI Review*, January 1949, 39.
37 Central Intelligence Agency, Survival Potential of Residual Non-Communist Regimes in China, SECRET, October 19, 1949, PHST, President's Secretary's File, Box 218, P.S.F. Intelligence File, ORE 76–49, HSTPL
38 Bruce A. Elleman, "The Nationalists' Blockade of the PRC, 1949–58," in Bruce A. Elleman and S.C.M. Paine, eds., *Naval Blockades and Seapower: Strategies and Counter-Strategies, 1805–2005* (London: Routledge, 2006), 133–44.
39 "Appreciation of the Ability of the Chinese Nationalist Navy to Effect a Blockade of Communist Territorial Waters (Secret)," Intelligence Division, Naval Staff, Admiralty, July 9, 1949, The National Archives, Kew, FO 371 75902.

Islands."[40] Taiwan was a key part of the island chain running from the Aleutians through Hokkaido to Japan, and then to Okinawa and Taiwan to the Philippines. Assuming Taiwan fell to the Chinese Communists, the PLA could use it as a base from which to invade other islands in the chain, as well as to interfere with international shipping.

On March 14, 1949, the CIA suggested that supporting Taiwan might strengthen the "will to resist Communism in Japan, in Korea, in the Philippines and elsewhere throughout the Far East," in particular if an American aid program "were developed in such a way as to secure local stability and contentment in Taiwan."[41] On October 26, 1949, the NSC included Taiwan in what it called its "first line of strategic defense" and argued that this "minimum position will permit control of the main lines of communication necessary to United States strategic development of the important sections of the Asian area."[42] On November 21, 1949, the Department of State opined that "the resources of that island [Taiwan] appear adequate, if resolute steps are taken to utilize them effectively, to achieve our objective of denying the island to the Communists by political and economic means." However, what Taiwan really needed was a "spiritual regeneration" that would need to create new leadership able to "devote themselves with determination to their cause and which would revitalize their followers."[43]

General Omar N. Bradley, Chairman of the JCS, vocally supported protecting Taiwan. On July 27, 1950, he submitted a four-page "Memorandum on Formosa," written by Douglas MacArthur on June 14, 1950, to the Secretary of Defense discussing the importance of the Pacific island chain running from the Aleutians to the Philippines: "Geographically and strategically Formosa is an integral part of this offshore position which in the event of hostilities can exercise a decisive degree of control of military operations along the periphery of Eastern Asia." In particular, during times of conflict Taiwan's position would give US forces the "capability to interdict the limited means of communication available to the Communists and deny or materially reduce

---

40 Central Intelligence Agency, The Ryukyu Islands and their Significance, SECRET, August 6, 1948, PHST, President's Secretary's File, Box 216, P.S.F. Intelligence File, ORE 24–48, HSTPL.

41 Central Intelligence Agency, Probable Developments in Taiwan, SECRET, March 14, 1949, PHST, President's Secretary's File, Box 218, P.S.F. Intelligence File, ORE 39–49, HSTPL.

42 National Security Council (hereafter NSC), The Position of the United States with Respect to Asia, DRAFT For NSC Staff Consideration Only, TOP SECRET, October 25, 1949, PHST, President's Secretary's File, Box 180, P.S.F. Subject File, HSTPL.

43 Summary of Telegrams, TOP SECRET, November 21, 1949, PHST, SMOF-Naval Aide, Box 23, State Department Briefs File, HSTPL.

the ability of the USSR to exploit the natural resources of East and Southeast Asia." Calling Taiwan an "unsinkable aircraft carrier and submarine tender," MacArthur emphasized how it was at "the very center of that portion of our [defensive] position now keyed to Japan, Okinawa, and the Philippines."[44]

During fall 1949, a Communist attack on the Nationalist-held base on Jinmen was bitterly opposed by Nationalist troops, and the PLA failed to take the island during October 1949. According to one view: "The armored division, which is under the Generalissimo's son, is doing a splendid job, as was shown in the battle of Kingman (sic) [Jinmen] with a loss of approximately 10,000 Communist soldiers and an additional 12,000 Communists captured."[45] The loss of a number of strategic islands in the north effectively narrowed the blockade to central and southern China. During 1950, the PLA advanced toward the southern coastline. Communist forces, in spite of naval and air inferiority, succeeded in overwhelming the Nationalist base on Hainan Island during February–May 1950, the Zhoushan Archipelago during May 1950, and Tatan Island as late as July 1950. By the summer of 1950, therefore, the Nationalists had lost their crucial island bases in the Bo Hai Gulf, off the mouth of the Yangzi River, and on Hainan Island. These losses cut the Nationalist blockade's reach by over half.

Traditionally, offshore islands had acted as "stepping stones" to support an invasion of Taiwan. Thus, Nationalist control of the offshore islands was considered critical to deter the Communists from launching an invasion of Taiwan. By spring 1950, the Communist forces seemed to be ready to invade. April and May were considered to be the best months to attack, since it was unusual to encounter typhoons.[46] The PLA concentrated thousands of junks in the port cities along the Taiwan Strait in preparation for a massive amphibious invasion.[47] The Communists could assemble "7,000 ships and craft" and "200 aircraft" to transport 200,000 troops across the Strait.[48] To

44 General Omar N. Bradley, Chairman of the Joint Chiefs of Staff, Memorandum for the Secretary of Defense, TOP SECRET, July 27, 1950, PHST, President's Secretary's File, Box 181, P.S.F. Subject File, HSTPL.

45 Letter from Edward C. Spowart to Harry S. Truman, January 5, 1950, PHST, Official File, OF 150-G, Box 761, Formosa, HSTPL.

46 National Intelligence Estimate, Chinese Communist Capabilities and Intentions with Respect to Taiwan, SECRET, April 10, 1951, PHST, President's Secretary's File, Box 215, P.S.F. Intelligence File, HSTPL.

47 He Di, "The Last Campaign to Unify China," in Mark A. Ryan, David M. Finkelstein, and Michael A. McDevitt, eds., *Chinese Warfighting: The PLA Experience since 1949* (Armonk, NY: M.E. Sharpe, 2003), 73–90.

48 Edward J. Marolda, "Hostilities along the China Coast During the Korean War," in Robert W. Love Jr., Laurie Bogle, Brian VanDeMark, and Maochun Yu, eds., *New Interpretations in Naval History* (Annapolis, MD: Naval Institute Press, 2001), 352.

foil such an invasion attempt, the Nationalists retained control over the large island bases of Jinmen and Mazu, right off the coast of Fujian Province, and the Penghu Islands in the Taiwan Strait halfway between the mainland and Taiwan. The Nationalists turned to "guerrillas" located on offshore islands along China's southeastern coastline to help the Nationalists blockade about two-thirds of China's southeastern coastline.

Nationalist-Supported Guerrilla movements

Rather than fortifying all of these offshore islands themselves, the Nationalists worked with groups of anti-Communist guerrillas. The degree to which the Nationalists interacted and controlled their guerrilla allies was intentionally left unclear. For example, in the Dachens, naval interdiction was carried out only by guerrillas, which allowed the Nationalists to avoid any blame for the guerrillas' actions. To motivate the guerrillas, it was decided early on that the crew of each blockading vessel would share in the prize money from capturing blockade running ships. Following China's intervention in the Korean War, for the first time during mid-January 1951 the NSC recommended to the US government: "Furnish now all practicable covert aid to effective anti-communist guerrilla forces in China."[49]

Not surprisingly, the Nationalists largely depended on guerrillas in distant locations like the Dachen Islands to enforce the blockade. The Nationalists portrayed these guerrilla bands as anti-Communist fighters. But to many foreign shippers, the pro-Nationalist guerrillas appeared little better than modern-day "pirates." As reported by one British official in 1952, "Indications are that most of the piracies are done by Nationalist guerrillas not under the effective control of Taipei. The border line is obscure. In 1948 it was respectable for bandits to masquerade as Communist Liberation forces; in 1952 it is respectable for pirates to masquerade as the Nationalist Navy."[50] Unlike regular Nationalist troops, these guerrillas were more interested in their own financial gains—either by taking bribes or by confiscating the foreign shipments. As the USN's Office of Naval Intelligence (ONI) reported: "Actually, even though the Nationalists have the capability, they probably do not wish to suppress the guerrilla activities because it would undoubtedly lose them the guerrilla support in the coastal islands."[51]

---

49 NSC, U.S. Action to Counter Chinese Communist Aggression, TOP SECRET, January 15, 1951, PHST, President's Secretary's File, Box 182, P.S.F. Subject File, HSTPL.
50 "Report on Visit to Hong Kong, 15–21 February, 1952," (Secret), by D. F. Allen, The National Archives, Kew, ADM 1/23217.
51 "The Southeast China Coast Today," *ONI Review*, February 1953, 51–60.

Beginning in January 1951, the US government adopted a policy of assisting the Chinese guerrillas. NSC estimates were that 700,000 guerrillas were in China, half of them owing allegiance to the Nationalists. Supporting bands in China's interior would require making air drops, with a high likelihood that many supplies would be lost. Supplying bands along the coast was "relatively simple." The benefits of supporting the guerrillas were potentially great: "Successful guerrilla action should eliminate the physical aspects of communist support in Indochina, occupy the attention within China of the major part of the CCF [Chinese Communist Forces, or PLA], and counter the myth of communist invincibility." While the Nationalist troops on Taiwan were numerous, this report concluded: "The optimum use of the Nationalist forces under present conditions appears to be in support of guerrilla operations on the mainland."[52]

On the Lower Dachen Island, the CIA-sponsored Western Enterprises Incorporated (WEI) sent US advisors to train the guerrillas. The first mention of creating a Military Advisory Group (MAAG) in China dated to February 26, 1946.[53] On July 16, 1946, Truman had also authorized the USN to "detail not more than one hundred officers and two hundred enlisted men of the United States Navy or Marine Corps to assist the Republic of China in naval matters."[54] As the civil war led to greater chaos in China, however, the NSC warned that "units of the U.S. fleet should not now be stationed at or off Formosan ports in support of the political and economic measures" on Taiwan.[55]

US plans to support the Nationalists never went fully into effect until the early 1950s on Taiwan, however, due to the chaos of the Chinese Civil War. Once the Nationalists lost the mainland, they did ask Washington for permission to "employ as a matter of immediate urgency a small group of American advisors composed of civilian, economic, industrial, agricultural and military advisors." This group of 130–150 advisors would be used to build up defenses to save Taiwan from Communist invasion, which "would greatly strengthen the resistance forces on the mainland [and] would give new courage to millions of Chinese who are opposed to communist domination and control."[56]

---

52 NSC, Statement of the Problem, TOP SECRET, January 17, 1951, PHST, President's Secretary's File, Box 182, P.S.F. Subject File, HSTPL.
53 Letter from James F. Byrnes to Harry S. Truman, February 26, 1946, PHST, Official File, OF 148-A, Box 757, File O.F. 150 (1945–46), HSTPL.
54 Executive Order signed by Harry S. Truman, July 16, 1946, PHST, Official File, OF 150, Box 758, File O.F. 150 (1947–49), HSTPL.
55 NSC, Supplementary Measures with Respect to Formosa, TOP SECRET, March 1, 1949, PHST, President's Secretary's File, Box 179, P.S.F. Subject File, HSTPL.
56 Letter from William D. Pawley to the Secretary of State, November 7, 1949, PHST, Official File, OF 150, Box 758, File O.F. 150 (1947–49), HSTPL.

By 1951, the number of American advisors on Taiwan totaled about 650, with half of these associated with the MAAG, and the other half with a variety of smaller organizations, including one called "Western Enterprises" (WEI) that appeared to be engaged in "guerrilla training and psychological warfare."[57] At any one time, about half of this number—or from 250 to 300—were concentrating on assisting the Nationalist Navy. Lon Redman, a WEI advisor, even attempted to bulldoze an airstrip on the Dachens so that C-46 cargo planes could land, but this plan had to be abandoned once it became clear that they "could not clear a strip long enough to permit a C-46 to land unless he bulldozed down almost to sea level."[58]

Contested control over offshore islands

By 1953, the Nationalists controlled 25 offshore islands. On July 30, 1953, a USN report entitled "Security of Offshore islands Presently Held by the Nationalist Government of the Republic of China" divided 20 of these into three categories. In Category I were four offshore islands off Fuzhou, including Mazu, and four islands off Xiamen, including Jinmen, which "could be used to counter Chinese Communist invasion operations."[59] Retaining these eight islands was considered militarily desirable, but for defensive purposes only, since Xiamen and Fuzhou were "natural harbors for the staging of a sea invasion of Formosa." If these islands were invaded by the PRC, however, their "function could largely be replaced by an increased use of naval craft which could blockade these two harbors."[60]

The Nationalists hoped to use these offshore islands to return to the mainland. But, this region was mountainous, which meant there were "few means of communication" with the interior or China, so a Nationalist invasion south of Xiamen or north of Fuzhou "would be more appropriate."[61] Meanwhile,

57 "American Military Activity in Taiwan (Secret Guard)," Naval Liaison Office, British Consulate, Tamsui, October 5, 1951, The National Archives, Kew, FO 371/92300.

58 Frank Holober, *Raiders of the China Coast: CIA Covert Operations during the Korean War* (Annapolis, MD: Naval Institute Press, 1999), 113–14.

59 Appendix to "Security of the Offshore Islands Presently Held by the Nationalist Government of the Republic of China," Memorandum from CNO, ADM Robert B. Carney, to Join Chiefs of Staff (Top Secret), July 30, 1953, Strategic Plans Division, NHHC Archives, Box 289.

60 Preliminary Draft of Possible Statement of Position for Communication to the Republic of China, SECRET, April 7, 1955, Dulles, J.F., W.H. Memo, Box 2, Offshore April–May 1955 (4), 7, Dwight D. Eisenhower Presidential Library (hereafter DDEPL).

61 Dulles Draft "Formosa" Paper to Eisenhower, SECRET, April 8, 1955, Dulles, J.F., W.H. Memo, Box 2, Offshore April–May 1955 (3), 9, DDEPL.

defending them "minimizes rather than maximizes the usefulness of our [U.S.] sea strength," whereas US sea power would be "particularly effective in defending Taiwan."[62] Seen in strategic terms alone, the offshore islands were a net liability, especially for an already overextended USN. Category II included two islands in the Dachen group and were not considered important to the defense of Taiwan and the Penghu Islands.

Category III had ten smaller offshore islands, mainly important in defending the 10 islands in Categories I and II. As for the other offshore islands under Nationalist domination, USN planners concluded they "are not now being utilized for important operations and are not considered worth the effort necessary to defend them against a determined attack." Still, as one USN report was quick to point out, none of the offshore islands could be called "essential" to the defense of Taiwan and the Penghus in the sense of being "absolutely necessary" militarily. Their importance to the Nationalists was mainly for "psychological warfare purposes," as well as their "pre-invasion operations, commando raiding, intelligence gathering, maritime resistance development, sabotage, escape and evasion"[63] (see Map 1).

China's southern coast was especially tense during the early 1950s. Both sides fiercely defended their positions on offshore islands in the hopes of changing the strategic balance. The legal status of the offshore islands was unclear. On March 19, 1955, Secretary of State John Foster Dulles explained that since Jinmen and Mazu islands were indisputably considered to be "parts of China" and since the US government recognized the Nationalists as the "Government of China," the Nationalists had a "better title" to these offshore islands than the PRC.[64] According to Dulles, "for the United States, the offshore islands were of no intrinsic importance except in the context of an attack on Formosa," but he did acknowledge that these islands could be used as "stepping stones for such an attack."[65] Later, the NSC confirmed this when it suggested that the number one reason the PRC wanted to claim

---

62 Dulles Draft "Formosa" Paper to Eisenhower, SECRET, April 8, 1955, Dulles, J.F., W.H. Memo Box 2, Offshore April–May 1955 (3), 7, DDEPL.

63 Appendix to "Security of the Offshore Islands Presently Held by the Nationalist Government of the Republic of China," Memorandum from CNO, ADM Robert B. Carney, to Join Chiefs of Staff (Top Secret), July 30, 1953, Strategic Plans Division, NHHC Archives, Box 289.

64 John Foster Dulles Letter to Lew Douglas, PERSONAL, March 19, 1955, DDE Ad Series 12, Douglas, Lewis W. (3), DDEPL.

65 Telegram from UK Embassy, Washington, to Foreign Office (secret), February 9, 1955, The National Archives, Kew, PREM 11/867.

NATIONALIST HELD ISLANDS OFF THE CHINA COAST

★ Islands within 12 miles of China Coast

Map 1 Nationalist-controlled offshore islands.

Quemoy and Mazu was to remove the Nationalists' "stepping stones toward the mainland."[66]

By spring 1950, the two Chinas faced each other across the Taiwan Strait. To many it appeared that the PLA was planning to replicate its successful invasion of Hainan Island by organizing a massive maritime attack against Taiwan. Due to the Truman administration's disillusionment with Chiang Kai-shek and his exiled Nationalist government, it seemed highly unlikely that the US government would intervene openly on the side of Taiwan. On October 6, 1949, the NSC reported that while the Nationalists had sufficient supplies to "hold out on Formosa for at least two years," the biggest problem was the "transfer to the Island of the ills and malpractices that have characterized the Kuomintang in China."[67]

Trying to defend the weak Nationalist regime would be too costly, therefore, and General Marshall concluded "that Chiang's government is both hopelessly corrupt and Fascist in character."[68] Secretary of State Dean Acheson described the Nationalist government as "corrupt and incompetent."[69] On October 26, 1949, Truman wrote to Senator Elbert D. Thomas of Chiang Kai-shek's failure that "Corruption and inefficiency caused that blow up."[70] Six months later, on March 27, 1950, Truman told Senator Arthur B. Vandenberg that the "unfortunate situation in the Far East [...] came about as a result of the corrupt Chinese Nationalist government."[71]

Others disagreed. On November 25, 1945, Colonel C. A. Seoane told Brigadier General Harry H. Vaughan: "Russia's plans now clearly unfolding are to arm and organize this communist group [in China] with a view of having them come into possession of China proper in order that communism shall become definitely established there with its spreading thru Korea and

---

66 U.S. and Allied Capabilities for Limited Military Operations to July 1, 1961, TOP SECRET, May 29, 1959, WH Office, OSANSA, Records 1952–61, NSC Series, Policy Paper Subseries, Box 22, A6 NSC 5724-Gaither Report (1), C3, DDEPL.

67 NSC, the Position of the United States with Respect to Formosa, TOP SECRET, October 6, 1949, PHST, President's Secretary's File, Box 180, P.S.F. Subject File, HSTPL.

68 Letter from Senator Glen H. Taylor to President Truman, March 5, 1948, PHST, Official File, OF 150, Box 759, File O.F. 150 Misc. (1947–48) [1 of 2], HSTPL.

69 Secretary of State Dean Acheson, Current Position of the United States with Respect to Formosa, TOP SECRET, August 5, 1949, PHST, President's Secretary's File, Box 180, P.S.F. Subject File, HSTPL.

70 Letter from Harry S. Truman to Elbert D. Thomas, October 26, 1949, PHST, Official File, OF 150, Box 758, File O.F. 150 (1947–49), HSTPL; copy in Box 826.

71 Letter from Harry S. Truman to Senator Arthur H. Vandenberg, March 27, 1950, PHST, Official File, OF 150, Box 758, File O.F. 150 (1950–53) [2 of 2], HSTPL.

even Japan, thus ousting us eventually from the Pacific, both as to position as well as influence."[72] On January 4, 1950, Hollington K. Tong warned Truman that "Once the Communists get into Formosa, there would be no way to prevent Soviet Russia from basing its fleet and submarines in Formosan naval bases—among the best in the world." This in turn would allow Russian agents to "stand at the gates of Japan and the Philippines."[73] Finally, Senator H. Alexander Smith told Truman on May 5, 1950: "My trip to the Far East last fall made it very clear to me that what has happened in China has been the conquest by Russia of that unfortunate country through the Russian method of infiltration and boring from within."[74]

Others had a more nuanced view. H. T. Goodier, a retired American Consul, wrote on January 2, 1950 to the White House that the US government should not "give any kind of <u>aid</u> to Chiang, political, economic or otherwise," even though Chiang should "occupy Formosa, pending the conclusion of a peace treaty with Japan and the formation of an autonomous Formosan Chinese state."[75] Many Taiwanese wanted an independent Formosa, with one group telling Truman:

> Formosa is neither the personal property of Chiang Kai-shek nor the colony of the Communists and inhabitants of Formosa should have a chance and right to determine their own destiny and form of govt; hope this [American] govt will support their demands for the U.N. to send its police forces to take up jurisdiction of Formosa until plebiscite is held for decision as to status of Formosa, and that Formosa remain a permanent, neutral, independent nation under the security of the U.N.[76]

All of this changed with the beginning of the Korean War in June 1950, when the political importance of Taiwan suddenly increased.

---

72 Letter from Colonel C. A. Seoane to Brigadier General Harry H. Vaughan, November 25, 1945, PHST, Official File, OF 150, Box 758, File O.F. 150 Misc. (1945–46) [1 of 2], HSTPL.

73 Letter from Hollington K. Tong to Harry S. Truman, January 4, 1950, PHST, Official File, OF 150, Box 759, File O.F. 150 Misc. (1947–48) [1 of 2], HSTPL.

74 Letter from Senator H. Alexander Smith to Harry S. Truman, May 5, 1950, PHST, Official File, OF 150, Box 758, File O.F. 150 (1950–53) [1 of 2], HSTPL.

75 Letter from H. T. Goodier to Harry S. Truman, January 2, 1950, PHST, Official File, OF 150-G, Box 761, Formosa, HSTPL; underlining in the original.

76 Letter from Thomas W. Liao, President, and Frank S. Sins, Chief of Political Affairs, Formosan Democratic Independence Party, to Harry S. Truman, August 9, 1950, PHST, Official File, OF 150-G, Box 761, Formosa, HSTPL.

Conclusions

On January 5, 1950, President Harry S. Truman issued a press statement clarifying that since the "United States had no predatory designs on Formosa or on any other Chinese territory," it "will not provide military aid or advice to Chinese forces on Formosa."[77] Meanwhile the United States and its Allies had "accepted the exercise of [Nationalist] Chinese authority over the island" of Taiwan, but it did not want to establish a base on Taiwan and so does not have "any intention of utilizing its armed forces to interfere in the present situation," including not becoming involved in the "civil conflict in China" and not providing "military aid or advice to Chinese forces on Formosa (Taiwan)." Secretary of State Acheson clarified later that same day that "in the unlikely and unhappy event that our forces might be attacked in the Far East, the United States must be completely free to make whatever action in whatever area is necessary for its own security."[78]

According to one first-hand report, "American personnel"—most likely not directly associated with the US Army—were helping the Nationalists repair and recondition their American-made equipment.[79] Between 1937 and November 1, 1949, the US government had given China $3,523,000,000: $2,422,000,000 in grants and $1,101,000,000 in credits.[80] Most of this ample aid had been wasted due to "giving aid without proper supervision."[81] But much of this American money did go for weapons and ammunition, so the Nationalists on Taiwan had military supplies.

If the PLA had initiated a spring or summer cross-strait attack, then Taiwan might have been incorporated into China during 1950. But the Nationalists' naval dominance in the Taiwan Strait meant that they retained the capability to carry out an offensive policy, including capturing cargoes destined for Chinese ports, using the offshore islands to mount raids against the Chinese mainland,

---

77 Statement by Harry S. Truman, January 5, 1950, PHST, Official File, OF 150, Box 758, File O.F. 150 (1947–49), HSTPL; copy in Box 761.

78 "Commitments and Problems of the United States to the Republic of China, Including any Divergencies between the Two Governments, and Chinese Problems with Other Asian Nations (Other Than Military)," TOP SECRET, undated (probably summer 1954), DDE WHO, OSANSA, Spec. Assist., Presidential Subseries, Box 2, Presidential Papers, 1954 (13), 2–3, DDEPL.

79 Letter from Edward C. Spowart to Harry S. Truman, January 5, 1950, PHST, Official File, OF 150-G, Box 761, Formosa, HSTPL.

80 Summary of United States Government Economic and Military Aid Authorized for China Since 1937, PHST, Official File, OF 150, Box 758, File O.F. 150 (1950–53) [1 of 2], HSTPL.

81 Letter from Major General Claire Lee Chennault to John R. Steelman, June 10, 1949, PHST, Official File, OF 150, Box 759, File O.F. 150 Misc. (1947–48) [2 of 2], HSTPL.

and procuring valuable intelligence on mainland areas. On May 23, 1950, Sun Li-Jen, Commander in Chief, Chinese Army, told President Truman that "Taiwan must be held against the Communists at all costs [as] a beacon light to the suffering people on the mainland of China, who are being trampled upon by the Communists."[82] Soon afterward, the Korean War broke out in June 1950. Suddenly, Taiwan's continued existence became both politically and militarily important, since the war in Korea could always spread south to include a naval invasion of Taiwan. If the PRC invaded Taiwan, it could cut off a major sea line of communication (SLOC) bringing UN troops and supplies to the Korean theatre. This two-pronged PRC military strategy had to be avoided at all costs.

---

82 Letter from Sun Li-Jen, Commander-in-Chief Chinese Army to Harry S. Truman, May 23, 1950, Papers to HST, Official File, OF 150, Box 758, O.F. 150 (1950–53) [1 of 2], HSTPL; summary copy in Box 826.

Chapter 2

PRESIDENT HARRY S. TRUMAN'S DECISION TO PROTECT TAIWAN

With the beginning of the Korean War in June 1950, the USN was tasked to create the Taiwan Strait Patrol to neutralize the strait and protect Taiwan from a PRC attack. On August 27, 1950, President Truman wrote to Congressman Warren R. Austin to emphasize that

> the action of the United States was an impartial neutralizing action addressed both to the forces on Formosa and to those on the mainland. It was an action designed to keep the peace and was, therefore, in full accord with the spirit of the Charter of the United Nations. As President Truman has solemnly declared, we have no designs on Formosa, and our action was not inspired by any desire to acquire a special position for the United States.

Furthermore, as a result of this US policy "Formosa is now at peace and will remain so until someone resorts to force."[1]

On September 21, 1950, Secretary of State Dean Acheson addressed a letter to the Secretary General of the United Nations explaining the US government's policy toward Taiwan and certain offshore islands, like the Penghus. He began by citing the December 1, 1943, Cairo declaration stating Formosa would be returned to "Republic of China."[2] Thereafter, the July 1945 Potsdam declaration confirmed Cairo's terms and in General Order No. 1 the Japanese forces in Formosa were ordered to surrender to "Generalissimo Chiang Kai-shek." From 1945 onward, the Republic of China retained administrative control over Formosa, the Penghus, plus a number of other offshore islands. On April 28, 1952, Japan signed a peace treaty renouncing its claim to Formosa and the Penghus, although "in whose favor Japan was

---

1 Letter from Harry S. Truman to Congressman Warren R. Austin, August 27, 1950, PHST, Official File, OF 150-G, Box 761, Formosa, HSTPL.
2 Letter to Dulles, February 1, 1955, Dulles, J.F., W.H. Memo, Box 2, W.H. Memo 1955, FS (2), DDEPL.

renouncing was not stipulated." Thereafter, Japan and the ROC signed their own peace treaty, effective August 5, 1952, where Japan repeated this renunciation, but again without saying which state it was ceding its rights to.[3]

While title over Formosa and the Penghus might be vague, the ROC had occupied these areas continuously since 1945: "There is no question that the Republic of China is today and at all times since the effective date of the Japanese Peace Treaty, has been in effective possession of and exercising administrative control over Formosa and the Pescadores."[4] Dulles cautioned Lew Douglas that the title to Formosa and the Penghus was still not 100 percent binding: "I am not quite clear as to why, from a legal standpoint, we are on strong ground as regards Formosa, where the title of the Republic of China is incomplete, than in relation to Quemoy and Matsu where the legal title is complete." Counterintuitively, Dulles argued that if the PRC was recognized as the "lawful government of China," then "the legal position of the Chinese Nationalists becomes better in relation to Formosa than in relation to Quemoy and Matsu."[5] As for the PRC taking the islands by force, Dulles told the UN General Assembly: "Also I do not ignore the fact that the Offshore Islands are physically close to Mainland China. But we can scarcely accept the view that nations are entitled to seize territory by force just because it is near at hand." If one regime tried to take territory that "has long been under the authority of another government," then "that is a use of force which endangers world order."[6] This issue became particularly important once the Korean War expanded to include China.

The Korean War

Immediately after the outbreak of the Korean War, President Truman decided that the Communist occupation of Taiwan would directly threaten the security of the entire Pacific region. On June 27, 1950, Truman ordered the Seventh Fleet to intervene to prevent any attack on Taiwan. He also tasked the USN to ensure that the Nationalists "cease all air and sea operations against the mainland." On July 19, 1950, Truman told Congress: "The present military

---

3 Letter to Dulles, February 1, 1955, Dulles, J.F., W.H. Memo, Box 2, W.H. Memo 1955, FS (2), DDEPL.

4 Letter to Dulles, February 1, 1955, Dulles, J.F., W.H. Memo, Box 2, W.H. Memo 1955, FS (2), DDEPL.

5 John Foster Dulles Letter to Lew Douglas, PERSONAL, March 19, 1955, DDE Ad Series 12, Douglas, Lewis W. (3), DDEPL.

6 Address by the Honorable John Foster Dulles Secretary of State of the United States of America before the United Nations General Assembly, September 18, 1958, D-H 10, Dulles September 1958 (1), 2, DDEPL.

neutralization of Formosa is without prejudice to political questions affecting that island. Our desire is that Formosa not become embroiled in hostilities disturbing to the peace of the Pacific and that all questions affecting Formosa be settled by peaceful means as envisaged in the Charter of the United Nations."[7] For this reason Truman's attitude toward China and Taiwan was called the neutralization policy.

The Taiwanese government wanted to solidify relations with the United States. One CIA report had concluded that the Nationalists would use Taiwan as a "bargaining point":

Aware of US interest in that island, they will present themselves as a means and perhaps the sole means of preventing its communization, and will offer various inducements and assurances in return for US aid and US moral support for a regional Chinese regime. They will also argue the legality of such a Chinese administration despite the fact that Taiwan's status has not been formalized by conclusion of a peace treaty with Japan.[8]

Taipei had strong opinions on the neutralization policy. While there were no secret agreements, per se, the Nationalist government presented four conditions of its own for cooperating with the neutralization policy:

First, pending the conclusion of the treaty of peace on Japan, the Government of the United States of America may share with the Government of the Republic of China the responsibility for the defense of Taiwan.

Secondly, that Taiwan is a part of the territory of China is generally acknowledged by all concerned Powers. The proposals of the United States of America as contained in the above mentioned *aide memoire* should in no way alter the status of Formosa as envisaged in the Cairo Declaration, nor should it in any way affect China's authority over Formosa.

---

7 "Commitments and Problems of the United States to the Republic of China, Including any Divergencies between the Two Governments, and Chinese Problems with Other Asian Nations (Other Than Military)," TOP SECRET, undated (probably summer 1954), DDE WHO, OSANSA, Spec. Assist., Presidential Subseries, Box 2, Presidential Papers, 1954 (13), 3, DDEPL.

8 Central Intelligence Agency, Probable Developments in Taiwan, SECRET, June 16, 1949, PHST, President's Secretary's File, Box 218, P.S.F. Intelligence File, ORE 45–49, HSTPL.

Thirdly, the aforesaid proposals and the policies outlined in President Truman's statement dated June 27 are emergency measures adopted to cope with the critical situation as existing on the mainland and in the Pacific region where a number of states have been threatened by or become the victims of aggressive International Communism. The Chinese Government may succeed in the suppression of the aggression of International Communism within a reasonably short time, but should these measures prove to be inadequate, the Chinese Government, in conjunction with other governments concerned, will have to seek for more effective measures in resisting such aggression.

Fourthly, in accepting the American proposals, the Government of the Republic of China does not intend to depart from its dual policy of resistance against the aggression of International Communism and the maintenance of the territorial integrity of China.[9]

The USN assigned a number of ships to form the Taiwan Patrol Force. At any one time, one or more USN ships patrolled the strait to ensure that the PRC did not attempt to invade Taiwan. From 1950 through early 1953, the Truman Administration had ordered the Taiwan Patrol Force to stop attacks from either side of the strait. In this operation, USN ships were intended to play a neutral role and act as a buffer between the PRC and Taiwan. The neutralization order, however, specifically did not include the many offshore islands controlled by the Nationalists. On October 7, 1950, it was clarified in Operation Order 7–50 that the Seventh Fleet forces would not participate in the "defense of any coastal islands held by the Nationalist Chinese nor will they interfere with Nationalist Chinese operations from the coastal islands."[10]

Shortly after Dwight D. Eisenhower won the 1952 presidential election, the focus of the Taiwan Patrol Force began to change. Eisenhower heeded hardliners' call to "unleash Chiang Kai-shek."[11] A Gallup poll from early 1953 showed that 61 percent of Americans in a nationwide survey support "the

---

9 "Commitments and Problems of the United States to the Republic of China, Including Any Divergencies Between the Two Governments, and Chinese Problems with Other Asian Nations (Other Than Military)," TOP SECRET, undated (probably summer 1954), DDE WHO, OSANSA, Spec. Assist., Presidential Subseries, Box 2, Presidential Papers, 1954 (13), 4, DDEPL; citing *China Handbook 1951* (Taipei, Taiwan: China, 1951), 115.

10 U.S. Navy Operation Order, ComCruDivONE No. 7–50, October 7, 1950, NHHC Archives, Post-1946 Operation Plans, Task Force 72.

11 http://www.globalsecurity.org/military/ops/quemoy_matsu.htm (accessed on December 14, 2010).

United States supplying more warships to Free China for use in blockading the China mainland coast and more airplanes for use in bombing the China mainland."[12] On February 2, 1953, Eisenhower announced in his "State of the Union" address that there is "no longer any logic or sense in a condition that required the United States Navy to assume defensive responsibilities on behalf of the Chinese Communists." As for the offshore islands, Assistant Secretary of State Allison clarified that they were not included in the original order "or in the contemplated amendment of the order."[13]

This policy change opened a new peripheral theatre in the south so as to put pressure on Beijing to sign a peace treaty ending the Korean War.[14] On April 5, 1951, the JCS had concluded: "Preparations should be made immediately for action by naval and air forces against the mainland of China."[15] As early as July 31, 1951, Senator Harry P. Cain wrote to Truman to support Nationalist attacks in the south as a "potentially powerful means of strengthening our own hand in the truce negotiations and may, if adequately supported, force some Communist withdrawals from the Korean front."[16] In 1954, a Top Secret study admitted that this new policy "represented the then need for diversionary threats."[17] Two years later, Dulles would even suggest reusing this diversionary strategy, when he suggested "that it might be preferable to slow up the Chinese Communists in Southeast Asia by harassing tactics from Formosa and along the seacoast which would be more readily within our natural facilities than actually fighting in Indochina." The transcript of the conversation then states: "The President indicated his concurrence with this general attitude."[18]

---

12 "U.S. to Send 100 Thunderjets, Warships to Free China," from "Free China Information" service, February 4, 1953, The National Archives, Kew, FO 371/105272.

13 "Commitments and Problems of the United States to the Republic of China, Including any Divergencies between the Two Governments, and Chinese Problems with Other Asian Nations (Other Than Military)," TOP SECRET, undated (probably summer 1954), DDE WHO, OSANSA, Spec. Assist., Presidential Subseries, Box 2, Presidential Papers, 1954 (13), 8, DDEPL.

14 For more on opening new peripheral theatres, see Bruce A. Elleman and S. C. M. Paine, eds., *Naval Power and Expeditionary Warfare: Peripheral Campaigns and New Theatres of Naval Warfare* (London: Routledge, 2011).

15 General Omar N. Bradley, The Joint Chiefs of Staff, Military Action in Korea, TOP SECRET, April 5, 1951, PHST, President's Secretary's File, Box 183, P.S.F. Subject File, HSTPL.

16 Letter from Senator Harry P. Cain to Harry S. Truman, July 31, 1951, PHST, Official File, OF 150, Box 758, File O.F. 150 (1950–53) [1 of 2], HSTPL.

17 Report on US Government Policies in Relation to China, TOP SECRET, undated, Dulles, J.F., White House Memorandum, Box 2, 1954, Formosa Straits (1), 4, DDEPL.

18 Memorandum of Conversation with the President, March 24, 1954, Dulles, J.F., W.H. Memo, Box 1, Meetings 1954 (4), DDEPL.

After the Chinese Communists intervened in the Korean War, the JCS recommended a stronger Taiwan policy to the Secretary of Defense: "a. Maintain the security of the off-shore defense line: Japan—Ryukyus—Philippines." They then added: "b. Deny Formosa to the Communists."[19] Three days later, a Top Secret NSC report went a step further when it stated: "Send a military training mission and increase MDAP to the Chinese on Formosa."[20] On March 22, 1952, the JCS had developed five points in support of Taiwan:

1. Take such measures as may be necessary to deny Formosa to any Chinese regime aligned with or dominated by the USSR;
2. In its own interests, take unilateral action if necessary, to ensure the continued availability of Formosa as a base for possible US military operations;
3. Continue that part of the mission presently assigned to the Seventh Fleet relative to the protection of Formosa until such time as conditions in the Far East permit the Chinese Nationalists on Formosa to assume the burden of the defense of that island;
4. Support a friendly Chinese regime on Formosa, to the end that it will be firmly aligned with the United States; and
5. Develop and maintain the military potential of that Chinese regime on Formosa.

The goal of these five points was to achieve the primary goal: "The denial of Formosa to communism is of major importance to United States security interests, and is of vital importance to the long-term United States position in the Far East."[21]

On February 2, 1953, Eisenhower lifted the USN's previous orders to restrict the Nationalist forces. At this time, Eisenhower described the neutralization policy as helping the Communists, saying "in effect, that the United States Navy was required to serve as a defensive arm of Communist China."[22] According to a US government statement, the US Seventh Fleet will

---

19 Joint Chiefs of Staff, Courses of Action Relative to Communist China and Korea, TOP SECRET, January 12, 1951, PHST, President's Secretary's File, Box 182, P.S.F. Subject File, HSTPL.
20 NSC, U.S. Action to Counter Chinese Communist Aggression, TOP SECRET, January 15, 1951, PHST, President's Secretary's File, Box 182, P.S.F. Subject File, HSTPL.
21 NSC, The Joint Chiefs of Staff, On Formosa, TOP SECRET, March 24, 1952, PHST, President's Secretary's File, Box 186, P.S.F. Subject File, HSTPL.
22 "Memorandum by the Attorney General on Congressional Attitude to Formosa Defense," undated but probably summer 1954, DDE WHO OSANSA Spec. Assist. Series, President Subseries, Box 2, Presidential Papers, 1954 (7), DDEPL.

"no longer be employed as a shield for the mainland of China."[23] However, a report by the Attorney General later clarified that this new order was not "evidence of any understanding that the President's announcement meant that the United States would defend the off-shore islands controlled by the Nationalists in addition to defending Formosa and the Pescadores."[24]

One immediate result of this policy change was that the Commander, Seventh Fleet, was ordered to remove the requirement that the Taiwan Patrol Force prevent the use of Taiwan and the Penghu Islands as a Nationalist base for operations against the China mainland.[25] This change led to the revision of previous orders. In particular, on paper copies of operation order 20–52, entitled "Special Patrol Instructions," the line "Large forces moving from Formosa toward the mainland will be reported to CTG 72.0." was scratched out.[26] Most Congressmen agreed with this change of policy, but Senator Sparkman did point out that the previous policy never "prevented 'pin-prick' raids from Quemoy or the off-shore islands," so that the new order could be seen as a "medium for enlarging the war."[27]

During April 1953, talks were held in Taipei between Adlai Stevenson and Chiang Kai-shek. During this meeting Chiang promised Stevenson that with continued US military support his forces would be ready to return to the mainland within "three years at the latest," and that once they returned to China they would gain a significant domestic following within "three to six months."[28] The US government agreed to support this plan. One reason later given by Dulles to the British Ambassador was to "make a diversionary threat at a time when fighting was going on in Korea so as to cause the Chinese Communists to transfer forces away from Korea towards Formosa."[29]

---

23 UK Embassy, Washington, to Foreign Office (Secret), January 30, 1953, The National Archives, Kew, PREM 11/867.

24 "Memorandum by the Attorney General on Congressional Attitude to Formosa Defense," undated but probably summer 1954, DDE WHO OSANSA Spec. Assist. Series, President Subseries, Box 2, Presidential Papers, 1954 (7), DDEPL.

25 U.S. Navy Operation Order, CTF 72 No. 2-A-53, May 1, 1954, NHHC Archives, Post-1946 Operation Plans, Task Force 72.

26 U.S. Navy Operation Order, CTG. 72.0 No. 20–52, December 3, 1952, NHHC Archives, Post-1946 Operation Plans, Task Force 72; there is no way to know when this line was marked out, but most likely it was during January–March 1953.

27 "Memorandum by the Attorney General on Congressional Attitude to Formosa Defense," undated but probably summer 1954, DDE WHO OSANSA Spec. Assist. Series, President Subseries, Box 2, Presidential Papers, 1954 (7), DDEPL.

28 John Foster Dulles Papers, Princeton University, Reel 204/205, April 8, 1953, 88851.

29 Telegram from UK Embassy, Washington, to Foreign Office (Secret), October 18, 1954, The National Archives, Kew, CAB 21/3272.

The Nationalists seemed eager to carry out this new policy. The first raid mounted directly from Taiwan was against Dongshan Island, which had been taken from the Nationalists on May 11, 1950, after PLA forces assaulted the island with over 10,000 troops. In mid-July 1953, the Nationalists tried to retake the island with approximately 6,500 guerrillas, marines, and paratroopers. Eisenhower's decision to open a peripheral campaign in the Taiwan Strait played an important role in PRC's decision to open talks in Korea. After the armistice was signed on July 27, 1953, the PRC immediately began to move troops to the south, stationing them across from Taiwan. This led to escalation on both sides of the Taiwan Strait.

America's Pacific allies and Great Britain

Spurred on by war on the Korean peninsula, the USN's patrols of the Taiwan Strait "neutralized" the Strait. They also discouraged the Nationalists from mounting a major attack of the Chinese mainland. The goal was to limit the possible spread of the Korean conflict further to the south, which might then escalate into a World War between the United States and the USSR. Later, tensions were increased along the Taiwan Strait to act as a diversion, drawing troops away from the north. Dulles even told a New Zealand delegation that "unleashing Chiang" would "encourage the Chinese [Communists] to retain substantial forces opposite Formosa."[30] By opening a new military theatre in the south, Beijing would feel compelled to reduce the number of PLA troops in Korea. While America's Pacific Allies generally supported this policy, Great Britain opposed it.

The US government had to be concerned about its Pacific allies. As Dulles warned in March 1955: "if Formosa were lost, that would almost surely involve such a major breach of the offshore island chain that the whole position would be lost and the Pacific defense of this continent would be forced back close to our own Pacific Shores." Should this happen, then "the situation in Australia and New Zealand would become virtually untenable."[31] Later that same month, Eisenhower wrote to Churchill that "the loss of Formosa would doom the Philippines and eventually the remainder of the region," and that in his "contacts with New Zealand and Australia, we have the feeling that

---

30 "Extract of New Zealand Delegation's Record of Discussions of Anzus Council Meeting in Washington, September 1953 (Secret)," The National Archives, Kew, FO 371/105272.

31 Summary of Remarks of the Honorable John Foster Dulles at Cabinet Meeting Ottawa, TOP SECRET, March 18, 1955, DH 5, Dulles, J.F., March 1955, 2, DDEPL.

we encounter a concern no less acute than ours."[32] For all of these reasons, keeping Taiwan out of Communist hands was considered vital.[33]

Australia and New Zealand were usually counted as part of a much longer anti-Communist defense line in the Pacific: "Japan-Ryukyus-Philippines-Australia and New Zealand."[34] In 1955, Australian Prime Minister Menzies put it more succinctly: "From the point of view of Australia and, indeed, Malaya, it would be fatal to have an enemy installed in the island chain so that by a process of island hopping Indonesia might be reached and Malaya and Australia to that extent exposed to serious damage either in the rear or on the flank."[35] A year later, Foreign Minister Shigemitsu told the US Ambassador in Tokyo that "Japan would consider the fall of Taiwan to the Communists as a threat to its interests and therefore supports the U.S. policy of preventing such an eventuality."[36]

Coming to some kind of arrangement with the UK was more difficult. While the US and Britain fought side by side with each other in Korea, the British traded more fully with the PRC, while the United States did not. During early 1951, largely in response to China's armed intervention in the Korean War, but with due consideration for the Nationalist blockade, the British government considered limiting trade with the PRC. But it would "undoubtedly suffer severely from any stoppage and would have difficulty in finding alternative employment." Not only could such a stoppage lead to the permanent loss of shipping company land in the PRC, but without sufficient advanced warning—certainly a minimum of five days but preferably ten— many British ships might be stuck in PRC ports, thus risking confiscation by China. At any one time there could be as much as 120,000 tons of British-owned shipping in Chinese ports, which "reinforces the absolute need for notice if British tonnage is to be saved from falling into Chinese hands."[37]

---

32 Eisenhower Letter to Churchill, EYES ONLY-TOP SECRET, DDE Diary Series 10, DDE Diary March 1955 (1), 2, DDEPL.

33 "Meeting of Prime Ministers: The Strategic Importance of Formosa; Memorandum by the United Kingdom Chiefs of Staff (Top Secret)," signed by Fraser, P.S. Slessor, and W.J. Slim, January 6, 1951, The National Archives, Kew, PREM 8/1408.

34 NSC, United States Objectives, Policies and Courses of Action in Asia, TOP SECRET, May 17, 1951, PHST, President's Secretary's File, Box 183, P.S.F. Subject File, HSTPL.

35 "Formosa and Off-shore Islands, Note by the Prime Minister of Australia (Secret)," Meeting of Commonwealth Prime Ministers, February 8, 1955, The National Archives, Kew, PREM 11/867.

36 John Foster Dulles Papers, Princeton University, Reel 212/213, December 2, 1956, 94413.

37 Effect on British Shipping of stoppage of trade with China, January 16, 1951, The National Archives, Kew, FO 371/92273.

Another consideration was the long-term future of British trade with China. Considering its large share in the China market, British shippers felt compelled to continue to trade. But this meant British ships had to challenge the Nationalist Navy's blockade policy. This blockade included using the offshore islands to mount attacks against the mainland ports and Communist-held islands, and against Communist-led convoys escorted by junks armed with small artillery pieces, mortars, and automatic weapons. Whenever possible, Nationalist ships would attack, surround, and sink the convoys. The economic impact of the Nationalist blockade operation was significant, since, in combination with the US embargo on strategic goods, the Nationalist blockade intercepted a high percentage of all of China's international trade. Between 1950 and 1952, the Nationalists halted and searched some 90 ships heading for Communist ports, two-thirds of them British-flagged ships registered in Hong Kong. The British government was particularly vocal in protesting the seizure of cargo, arguing that these ships were complying with US limits on strategic goods and so were carrying "only nonstrategic cargoes."[38]

During the early 1950s, the United States and the UK carried out near-continuous discussions on what to do about China and Taiwan. On February 10 and March 22, 1949, meetings were held between US and British officials regarding putting controls on foreign exports to China.[39] On August 1, 1949, the US Embassy in London was told to tell the British government that "We feel that the failure to demonstrate effective western control over exports of key importance to China's economy would represent abandonment of the most important single instrument available for the defense of western interests in the Far East." As such, it asked London to back restrictions on both restricted and prohibited lists, "since the mutual security interests of the west must be considered as much in terms of political and economic strategy as in terms of direct military factors."[40]

In November 1949, a report commissioned by Dean Acheson, the US Secretary of State, stated that "We have been reluctant thus far to impose unilaterally new controls over exports to China because of the possibility that such action would handicap our negotiations with the British." After "pointing out that such controls would represent the most important single instrument available for use vis-à-vis the Chinese Communists" the British finally agreed to control "1A list exports to China," provided that the other major powers

---

38 "The Southeast China Coast Today," *ONI Review*, February 1953, 51–60.
39 Dean Acheson to Sidney W. Souers, Implementation of NSC 41, TOP SECRET, April 14, 1950, PHST, President's Secretary's File, Box 182, P.S.F. Subject File, HSTPL.
40 Summary of Telegrams, TOP SECRET, August 1, 1949, PHST, SMOF-Naval Aide, Box 23, State Department Briefs File, HSTPL.

also agreed to do so, plus put limits on petroleum sales, and to "observe and to exchange information with the United States of on the movement of 1B goods to China with a view to joint consultation regarding corrective measures if it appeared that the flow was excessive or injurious to our common interests."[41] A complete embargo of China would devastate Hong Kong's commercial enterprises, since approximately 45 percent of all of Hong Kong's exports went to China. According to the governor of Hong Kong, without this trade the "thriving, trading, financial and insurance entrepot of the Colony" would quickly become "an economic desert."[42]

To avoid undermining Anglo-American relations, it was eventually decided to rely more on the US embargo of strategic goods, with help from the Nationalist Navy to enforce the embargo, to put economic pressure on China. With tacit US support, the Nationalist forces tightened the blockade throughout 1949 and into 1950. Following the beginning of the Korean War, and in particular after the PRC intervention during fall 1950, the US government even considered instituting a total naval blockade of its own against mainland China. The British had to be especially concerned about the fate of their colony of Hong Kong. At any point, the PRC could send in troops and take Hong Kong by force. Hong Kong's vulnerability led to the British decision to recognize the PRC on January 6, 1950, and to adopt a more liberal trade policy with China. But in 1958, British Foreign Secretary Selwyn Lloyd reaffirmed that the UK and the United States shared the view that there was a "Communist menace in the Far East," and that the "containing line" had to be drawn to include Japan, South Korea, Okinawa, Taiwan, Hong Kong, South Vietnam, and Malaya.[43]

US-led strategic Embargo of the PRC

A full US naval blockade of the PRC was politically infeasible due to the possible retaliation of the USSR, on the one hand, and to Hong Kong's sensitive strategic position, on the other hand. Beginning in December 1950, the US government instead began to impose an embargo on strategic goods to the PRC. On December 16, 1950, it was announced that the US government

41 Dean Acheson to Sidney W. Souers, US Policy Regarding Trade with China, TOP SECRET, November 4, 1949, PHST, President's Secretary's File, Box 182, P.S.F. Subject File, HSTPL.

42 "Sanctions against China. Probable economic political and strategic consequences in Hong Kong, Malaya and South East Asia generally." Draft Memorandum (Top Secret), undated (but most likely written in December 1950), The National Archives, Kew, FO 371/92276.

43 Letter from Selwyn Lloyd to John Foster Dulles (Top Secret), September 11, 1958, CAB 21/3272.

was "issuing regulations to prohibit ships of United States registry from calling at Chinese Communist ports until further notice," as part of an ongoing effort to halt all exports "to Communist China from the United States without validated export licenses."[44] President Truman signed an Executive Order adopting the Export Control Act. This policy was widened into a trade control regime called the Coordinating Committee for Multilateral Export Controls (COCOM), which had previously been adopted in January 1950.

Americans largely supported this embargo. On December 1, 1950, a telegram from San Francisco arrived at the White House addressed to Major General Harry H. Vaughan. In it, an ordinary citizen wrote:

> Thirty-one cases automobile ignition parts on pier thirty-one in San Francisco consigned to Communist China will move by Pacific Transport Lines ship China Bear about December 3. Handed by Hawaiian freight forwarders. This shipment is valuable as war material. Customs authorities claim they cannot stop. As a former member of 129 field artillery and supporter of President Truman I urgently request Presidential Order to hold this shipment or do you suggest another Boston tea party.

Six days later, Major General Vaughan wrote to thank the sender and to report: "Immediately upon receipt, we contacted the Commerce Department; and today we have been advised that they were successful in stopping the shipment of the parts you described in your telegram."[45]

On May 18, 1951, the United Nations adopted a selective embargo prohibiting the sale of "arms, ammunition and implements of war, atomic energy materials, petroleum, transportation materials of strategic value, and items useful in production of arms, ammunition and implements of war." Due to all of these programs, the participating countries had "instituted and maintained controls on strategic trade with Communist China that are much more severe and sweeping than the system applicable to Soviet Russia and the rest of the Soviet bloc."[46] Although less effective than a full naval blockade,

---

44 Department of State, Control of United States Economic Relationships with Communist China, December 16, 1950, PHST, President's Secretary's File, Box 182, P.S.F. Subject File, HSTPL.

45 Telegram from George O. Kelly to Harry H. Vaughan and reply by letter, December 1 and December 7, 1950, PHST, Official File, OF 150, Box 758, File O.F. 150 (1950–53) [1 of 2], HSTPL.

46 Letter from John Foster Dulles to J. Bracken Lee, Governor of Utah, December 30, 1953, D-H-2, Dulles Dec (53), DDEPL.

the US government worked closely with the Nationalists to help enforce the strategic embargo.

The 15-country COCOM group was composed of the United States, all of the NATO countries, minus Iceland, and then also Japan. To convince other countries to conform to these proscriptions against China, Congress adopted the "Mutual Defense Assistance Control Act of 1951." Commonly called the "Battle Act," after its sponsor Congressman Laurie C. Battle, this legislation would terminate economic and military aid to "countries which fail to cooperate in the control program."[47] After China intervened in the Korean War, the restrictions became even tighter. During fall 1952, China Committee (CHINCOM) controls were instituted that were even tighter, embargoing industrial machinery, steel mill products, and metal of all types. Meanwhile, the US embargo was also broadened to include more countries in COCOM and CHINCOM, such as Greece and Turkey in 1953, and bolstered by pledges of "cooperation from important neutral countries, notably Sweden and Switzerland."[48] The United States shouldered the lion's share of the financial burden to enforce this sanction's program, however, including an estimated $1.7 billion in outright aid every year to various East Asian countries "designed to secure our own vital defense arc in the Far East stretching from the Aleutians to Southeast Asia."[49]

On January 12, 1951, the JCS agreed to "continue and intensify now an economic blockade of trade with China."[50] They also advised the Secretary of Defense

that the neutralization of Formosa would not meet United States military strategic needs since it would improve the strategic position of the Communists by releasing their forces for build-up, and would reduce the strategic position of the United States and restrict freedom of action in the event the military situation required an armed attack against the Chinese Communists on the Mainland.[51]

---

47 "The Southeast China Coast Today," *ONI Review*, February 1953, 51–60.

48 "Intelligence for Economic Defense," Sherman R. Abrahamson, CIA Historical Review Program,. https://www.cia.gov/static/5803efc7ba6c6412056efd616bfea01c/Intel-for-Economic-Defense.pdf

49 The Case for Maintaining a Meaningful China Trade Control Differential, SECRET, [undated], DDE U.S. Council on For Econ Policy, Randall Series, Trips Subseries Box 2, Far East Trip [December 1956], Background Papers (2), 1, DDEPL.

50 Joint Chiefs of Staff, Courses of Action Relative to Communist China and Korea, TOP SECRET, January 12, 1951, PHST, President's Secretary's File, Box 182, P.S.F. Subject File, HSTPL.

51 Joint Chiefs of Staff, China Lobby, General, SECRET, January 2, 1951, PHST, President's Secretary's File, Box 140, P.S.F. Subject File, HSTPL.

General Walter B. Smith, Director of Central Intelligence, told Truman on September 24, 1952, that "building up a Chinese Nationalist force on Formosa was perfectly safe because they will be unable to go anywhere unless we release the trigger in the form of air and naval support."[52]

An early study of the sanctions program pointed out that what the USSR wanted from the West were "items having a high skilled labor content." While it would be too costly to cut all such trade items to Russia, the situation in China was different because "China's trade is so vulnerable to the disruption of its sea communications," which meant:

> Because of the nature of China and the advance state of military activities in that area, our program of economic warfare should be more extensive than in Europe [and] we should be less reluctant to take necessary all-out measures. An important objective would be the attainment of multilateral agreement among the Western Nations on a complete quarantine of China from the technology of the West.

To enact such a quarantine, "careful consideration should be given to an informal merchant shipping embargo of Chinese ports."[53]

There was an important second side of this coin: even while limiting the Soviet Bloc countries' imports, the United States should assist the economic growth of Western-aligned countries. On April 26, 1951, a brand new section was added to the NSC 48/3 report. In addition to helping East Asian countries with their security concerns and economic relations, which was point 5(d), this new point stated: "h. In accordance with 5(d) above, take such current and continuing action as may be practicable to maximize the availability of the material resources of the Asian area to the United States and the free world generally, and thereby correspondingly deny these resources to the communist world."[54]

A CIA report later concluded that free world "controls have somewhat retarded the development of China's economic potential." After discussing the possibility of adopting a full naval blockade to cut China's sea lines of communication, or using air attacks on crucial inland lines of communication, this report warned that the first policy might result in conflict with the USSR

---

52 Memorandum for the President, TOP SECRET, September 24, 1952, PHST, President's Secretary's File, Box 189, P.S.F. Subject File, HSTPL.

53 Economic Cooperation Administration, Trade of the Free World with the Soviet Bloc, SECRET, February 1951, PHST, President's Secretary's File, Box 183, P.S.F. Subject File, HSTPL.

54 NSC, United States Objectives, Policies and Courses of Action in Asia, TOP SECRET, April 26, 1951, PHST, President's Secretary's File, Box 183, P.S.F. Subject File, HSTPL.

over Russian access to Port Arthur and Dalian. There was also a chance that China might retaliate by "seizing Hong Kong and Macao."[55] For these reasons, adopting either plan seemed highly unlikely. Instead, more effort had to be made to tighten the strategic embargo by broadening its reach. One report even suggested: "Encourage the countries of Southeast Asia to restore and expand their commerce with each other and with the rest of the free world, and stimulate the flow of the raw material resources of the area to the free world."[56]

Although a confidential 1955 USN report admitted that the strategic embargo was "not complete" and that "China actually obtains differential goods through triangular deals and transshipments," the overall success of the embargo was shown by the fact that "Chinese procurement has been hampered and the total amount of goods purchased is reduced as a result of higher costs."[57] A 1955 report to Eisenhower persuasively argued that by keeping "the Chinese Communist regime under economic (and other) pressures [...] Such pressures add to the strains which can ultimately lead to disintegration." This was particularly true with regard to the PRC's foreign commitments to its allies, since a failure to grow at a rapid pace would mean Beijing could not fund these commitments: "This kind of dilemma tends to lead to a breakdown."[58]

Impact of the American-led embargo

The only way the embargo would be effective is if Washington convinced most of the other Western trading nations to join it. By and large, America's allies also backed the strategic embargo, at least in part. For example, a British report from the China Association to the British Foreign office dated February 1951 had concluded that the US sanctions program was quite effective and had produced a "great shock to [the mainland] Chinese economy."[59] The Swedish Ambassador

---

55 Central Intelligence Agency, Probable Effects of Various Possible Courses of Action with Respect to Communist China, TOP SECRET, June 5, 1952, PHST, President's Secretary's File, Box 186, P.S.F. Subject File, HSTPL.

56 NSC, United States Objectives, Policies and Courses of Action in Asia, TOP SECRET, June 25, 1952, PHST, President's Secretary's File, Box 186, P.S.F. Subject File, HSTPL.

57 "Memorandum of Information for the Secretary of the Navy," by W. K. Smedberg, Director, Politico-Military Policy (Confidential), October 13, 1955, Strategic Plans Division, NHHC Archives, Box 326.

58 Maintenance of Economic Pressures against Communist China, SECRET, DDE WHO OSANSA, Spec. Assist. Series, Pres. Subseries, Box 2, Presidential Papers 1955 (5), DDEPL.

59 Letter from the China Association, London, to J.S.H. Shattock, Foreign Office, London, February 26, 1951, The National Archives, Kew, FO 371/92276.

to China likewise confirmed during June 1951 that the strategic embargo was having the desired effect, since international "shipping was the Achilles heel of China," and that "a very effective squeeze could be placed" on China.[60]

One problem was the difficulty in estimating how effective the strategic embargo was. In other words, how to calculate the various costs the program put on China, including those not measurable in dollars, such as political and psychological costs. In late 1956, an estimate of these various costs put the US part of the embargo as $100–$150 million per year in trade losses to China, plus another $100 million in financial assets frozen in US banks. With regard to the 15 CHINCOM members, the estimate was between $115 and $154 million. Together, this meant estimated losses in the $215–$304 million range, which accounted for a 13–18 percent reduction in China's strategic imports. A large percentage of these added costs, perhaps as much as a third, was due to increased transportation costs, mainly via the Trans-Siberian railway, which put added pressure on the PRC's diplomatic relations with the USSR.[61]

In addition to financial costs, there were a large number of other benefits accrued from the sanctions program. For example, by means of the sanction program, the PRC lost access to convertible foreign currencies, it imposed "serious and costly delays in Communist Chinese economic planning and implementation," and it put a heavy strain on China's "existing equipment and facilities," in particular related to transportation. Finally, putting additional sanctions on the PRC above and beyond those put on the rest of the Communist bloc made China a "pariah" state, which added even more "political, psychological, and prestige 'costs' to Communist China."[62]

When discussing reducing completely, or perhaps simply partially, the economic and trade sanctions put on China, a number of the hidden costs had to be taken into account. First, it would mean an "enormous loss of prestige" (read face) to the United States, especially in East Asia, if the controls were changed. Second, many neutral countries might move closer to the PRC. Third, it might stimulate even greater "Communist subversive activities throughout Asia." Fourth, it might lead to losing important US bases in the region. Fifth, it might lead to the PRC's admission to the United

---

60 Summary of Telegrams, TOP SECRET, June 5, 1951, PHST, SMOF-Naval Aide, Box 24, State Department Briefs File, HSTPL.
61 The Case for Maintaining a Meaningful China Trade Control Differential, SECRET, [undated], DDE U.S. Council on For Econ Policy, Randall Series, Trips Subseries Box 2, Far East Trip [December 1956], Background Papers (2), 4, DDEPL.
62 The Case for Maintaining a Meaningful China Trade Control Differential, SECRET, [undated], DDE U.S. Council on For Econ Policy, Randall Series, Trips Subseries Box 2, Far East Trip [December 1956], Background Papers (2), 5, DDEPL.

Nations, perhaps even "displacing Free China on the Security Council." Sixth, it might reduce the chance for "securing the release of Americans imprisoned in Communist China." Seventh, it would mean the "loss without adequate recompense of an important bargaining weapon in the cold war in the Pacific." And eighth, it would entail a "fundamental undermining of our moral position against aggression and oppression." In short: "Removal of the China trade differential would therefore relieve Communist China of a very onerous and costly burden."[63]

The very effectiveness of the embargo had a negative impact on British trade with China, however, which led to a sharp increase in Anglo-American tensions. During bilateral talks, the British disagreed with the Americans on what should be considered strategic trade. Accordingly, by late 1956 "the British have seriously suggested to us, at responsible levels, that the only 'defensible' criterion for classifying exports to Red China as 'strategic', is whether or not they could contribute directly to thermo-nuclear warfare." Meanwhile, other CHINCOM partners decried the use of just a "stick" and sought to offer China "carrots": "There are important government officials and elements of public opinion among them who believe that the closer the Free World countries can get to the Red Chinese, the better the chance of converting them from their [aggressive] designs on Asia."[64]

In October 1952, the British government was considering making changes to its export control policies. As a direct response to the Nationalist blockade, beginning in 1953 Royal Navy vessels were ordered to protect British commercial ships by forming its own "Formosa Straits Patrol." To some, this shift in British policy appeared contradictory. On June 18, 1953, for example, Roger Makins told John Foster Dulles that the British government would agree to maintain economic pressure on the PRC, in particular because it provided potential "trading ground at a [future] Korean political conference."[65] One major difference, therefore, was over what political objectives each country had vis-à-vis Beijing.

The number of Nationalist attacks gradually decreased following the creation of the Royal Navy's Formosa Straits Patrol. During 1953–54, the

63 The Case for Maintaining a Meaningful China Trade Control Differential, SECRET, [undated], DDE U.S. Council on For Econ Policy, Randall Series, Trips Subseries Box 2, Far East Trip [December 1956], Background Papers (2), 5–7, DDEPL.
64 The Case for Maintaining a Meaningful China Trade Control Differential, SECRET, [undated], DDE U.S. Council on For Econ Policy, Randall Series, Trips Subseries Box 2, Far East Trip [December 1956], Background Papers (2), 2, DDEPL.
65 Memorandum from John Foster Dulles to President Eisenhower (Secret), June 19, 1953, DH 1, Dulles John, June 1953 (1), DDEPL.

Nationalist blockade gradually shifted away from patrol vessels to using more air power, mainly provided by the United States. In April 1953, Taipei also adopted more stringent shipping regulations, largely in line with those already promulgated by the US Maritime Shipping Association, which would "prohibit any government-chartered foreign vessel from proceeding to any country behind the Iron Curtain within a 60-day period after it had discharged its cargo at ports in Free China."[66] Chiang Kai-shek wrote to President Eisenhower on April 15, 1953, that it was time to "gradually take away the political and military initiative from the Communist world."[67]

During late July 1954, the PRC shot down a Cathay Pacific airliner. When Eisenhower was told the British were playing it down, and accepting that it was an accident, the President replied: "I wonder if old John Bull will take that."[68] The USN sent two aircraft carriers to the scene. Initially, pilots were told not to invade Chinese airspace, even if engaged in "hot pursuit" of the enemy. At Dulles's urging, Eisenhower changed this policy. USN ships and planes could now take "all necessary measures to protect themselves," including pursuing an enemy ship or plane into Chinese sovereign waters.[69] On July 26, Dulles informed Eisenhower that two American search planes had been shot down near Hainan, prompting the president to respond: "Well, it didn't take long for that to happen." Coordinating official protests to the PRC with the British government was all important, since "If we adopt a stiff one and the British not, it will cause more friction between our countries."[70]

Such concerns were not fiction. During September 1954, the State Department told Eisenhower that Sam Watson, a member of the British Labor Party Delegation to Moscow, was warning that an attack on Taiwan would be geared for the "single strategical aim of splitting West" in order to shatter "US-United Kingdom-French cooperation." Furthermore, in a conversation with Zhou Enlai, Watson was told that liberating Taiwan was the PRC's "most important problem," equal if not greater than "feeding, clothing, and housing

---

66 John Foster Dulles Papers, Princeton University, Reel 204/205, April 23, 1953, 88971.
67 Letter from Chiang Kai-shek to President Eisenhower, April 15, 1953, DH 1, Dulles April 1953, DDEPL.
68 Dulles phone call with Eisenhower, July 23, 1954, DDE Diary Series 7, Phone Calls, June–December 1954 (3), DDEPL.
69 "Memorandum of Telephone Conversations," by Dulles with Radford, Wilson, and Eisenhower, July 25, 1954, Dulles, J.F., Tel Conv., Box 10, July–October 1954 (2), DDEPL.
70 President's comments to Dulles, July 26, 1954, DDE Diary Series 7, Phone Calls, June–December 1954 (3), DDEPL.

their millions" of citizens.[71] During 1954, for example, there were a total of 32 incidents in which the Nationalist air force attacked British shipping.[72]

Conclusions

In 1951, a full US blockade of the PRC was discussed by USN planners, but fear of undermining the Anglo-American alliance both in Europe and in Korea overshadowed any possible benefits. During late 1953 and early 1954, therefore, the US government provided the Nationalists with better equipment to enforce the blockade from the air. But the British were upset by US support for the Nationalist blockade of China. Britain's colony in Hong Kong was a major reason. Eisenhower reminded Churchill, however, the United States did not have colonies to worry about: "We have no possessions in that immediate area. Consequently, we cannot be accused of any support of colonialism or of imperialistic designs."[73] This echoed a June 13, 1946, letter from Truman to no less a figure than the American author Pearl Buck, in which he assured her that after the war in Asia "we have asked for no territory and we have asked for no reparations."[74] By contrast, Truman accused the Chinese people of being "deceived into serving the ends of the Russian colonial policy in Asia."[75]

In fact, Eisenhower had tried, and failed, to convince Churchill that "colonialism was ended," and that "the British colonies should be given a chance to stay or leave the British Empire."[76] Rather than being a colonial issue, if fighting over the offshore islands ever broke out it would be "primarily a fight between the Chinese Nationalists and the Chinese Communists, and not a fight between the 'white' Western and the 'yellow' Chinese worlds,"

71 Memorandum of Conversation with Sam Watson, Member of British Labor Party Delegation to Moscow and Peking, September 6, 1954, DH 4, Dulles September 1954 (2), DDEPL.

72 "China: Interference with British Merchant Shipping (Secret)," 1955, The National Archives, Kew, ADM 116/6245.

73 Eisenhower letter to Churchill, TOP SECRET, March 22, 1955, DDE Diary Series 10, DDE Diary March 1955 (1), 3, DDEPL.

74 Letter from Harry S. Truman to Pearl S. Buck, June 13, 1946, PHST, Official File, OF 148-A, Box 757, File O.F. 150 (1945–46), HSTPL; summarized copy in OF 220, Box 964.

75 Statement by the President, November 30, 1950, PHST, Official File, OF 150, Box 758, File O.F. 150 (1950–53) [1 of 2], HSTPL.

76 Conversations with Malcolm Muir about Colonialism, May 25, 1955, DDE Papers 5, ACW Diary May 1955 (2), DDEPL.

so that it would "not take on the appearance of a struggle between races."[77] But Whitehall feared that too strict an embargo might spark a war with the PRC.[78] Because Great Britain had recognized the PRC, the "British people as a whole look on the offshore islands as belonging to Red China, and consider that we are foolish to be supporting Chiang even indirectly in possession of those areas."[79]

An even greater British concern was that increasing Anglo-American friction "might prejudice world-wide defence cooperation between the United Kingdom and United States, with possibly serious consequences to the security of Western Europe, the United Kingdom and, ultimately, the United States."[80] There was always a chance that China would reject monolithic Communism. As long as the PRC could expect to obtain certain supplies from the West, "she would not be completely dependent on the Soviet Union and the East European satellites to meet her needs."[81] In 1954–55, during the so-called "first" Taiwan Strait crisis, one of the PRC's most important objectives was to force the Nationalists to end their blockade of the Chinese coast.

---

77 Preliminary Draft of Possible Statement of Position for Communication to the Republic of China, SECRET, April 7, 1955, Dulles, J.F. W.H. Memo, Box 2, Offshore April–May 1955 (4), 12, DDEPL.

78 Edward J. Marolda, "The U.S. Navy and the Chinese Civil War, 1945–1952," PhD Diss., The George Washington University, 1990, 372.

79 Notes dictated by the President regarding his conversation with Sir Anthony Eden, held Sunday, July 17, in the afternoon, July 19, 1955, DDE Diary Series 11, DDE Diary July 1955 (1), DDEPL.

80 "Strategic Implications of the Application of Economic Sanctions against China," Annex (Top Secret), undated (but most likely written in February 1951), The National Archives, Kew, FO 371/92276.

81 A. A. E. Franklin, "Control of Exports from Hong Kong to China," January 15, 1951, The National Archives, Kew, FO 371/92274.

Chapter 3

THE FIRST TAIWAN STRAIT CRISIS, 1954–55

By the summer of 1953, the Korean conflict stalemated. Stalin's death on March 5, 1953, helped break the negotiating deadlock. The Korean armistice was finally signed on July 27, 1953. Military pressure from the south, directed from Taiwan by means of the offshore islands, was crucial for bringing about the armistice. Soon afterward, the PRC began to redeploy troops from north to south. Tensions gradually grew throughout the south, particularly in the Taiwan Strait region. Soon after the first crisis ended, Secretary of State Dulles describing it as equivalent to "living over a volcano."[1]

On August 11, 1954, Zhou Enlai declared that the PRC must liberate Taiwan. On September 3, 1954, PLA forces began to bombard the offshore islands of Jinmen and Mazu. This renewed focus on reclaiming the offshore islands by force showed Mao Zedong's independence from Moscow. Another important PRC goal was to interrupt the Nationalist blockade. During November 1954, PRC leaders had explained to Jawaharlal Nehru, the visiting Indian Prime Minister, that the Nationalists from their offshore bases were conducting "nuisance raids and interference with shipping." Upon his return, Nehru met with the British High Commissioner in India to warn him that China was "determined not to tolerate this situation any longer."[2]

The shelling of Jinmen and Mazu was also used as a cover to attack other Nationalist-controlled islands, in particular the most northerly of the Nationalist-held offshore island groups, the Dachens. In this overcharged political climate, the US government signed a security pact with Taiwan plus, later in January 1955, proclaimed the Formosa Resolution. After convincing Chiang Kai-shek to evacuate the Dachens, the USN provided the ships, training, and protection during the evacuation operations. This

---

1 Breakfast Discussion with Secretary-of-State John Foster Dulles (Top Secret), July 22, 1955, The National Archives, Kew, PREM 11/879.
2 U.K. High Commissioner in India Report of Meeting with Prime Minister Nehru (Secret), November 10, 1954, The National Archives, Kew, FO 371/110238.

limited the Nationalist-controlled offshore islands to a much smaller area that encompassed Jinmen to the south and Mazu to the north.

The beginning of the 1954–55 Taiwan Strait crisis

Tensions over the offshore islands led to a crisis during fall 1954. In August 1954, Chiang Kai-shek had ordered additional deployments to Jinmen and Mazu. These actions had all of the outward appearances of supporting a future Nationalist invasion of mainland China. Certainly, the PRC leaders were sufficiently concerned to authorize PLA attacks against the Nationalist-held offshore islands, and in particular the northernmost islands of Yichiang and the Dachens. By late 1953, immediately before tensions erupted over control of Jinmen and Mazu islands, the Nationalists held only 25 offshore islands, down from 32 the year before.[3] This trend made the Nationalist position more vulnerable.

On May 22, 1954, a lengthy meeting was held between Eisenhower and his top advisors, including both John Foster Dulles and his brother Allen W. Dulles, plus Anderson and Radford. The main topic was what attitude to take on the offshore islands. In June 1950, the US government had promised to defend Formosa plus the Penghu islands. However, no such guarantees were extended to Jinmen island. When the *New York Times* asked the State Department press officer McDermott on July 25 whether Jinmen was included he said no. A day later, the Nationalist Ambassador Wellington Koo met with Rusk and Dulles and confirmed that the United States "would not help to fight off Communist attacks on the 'Quemoy islands'."[4]

If attacked by the Communists, however, Admiral Radford "pointed out that it might not be necessary to report such an attack." He acknowledged that US airplanes were "quite frequently attacked […] yet neither side had reported these events." After the meeting was over, it was clarified exactly what the policy of air control would entail:

If our Fleet on a patrolling mission, such as has been described, or if engaged in defending outlying islands against attack, was drawn into conflict with the Chinese enemy attacking such islands, our planes

---

3 "The Struggle for the Coastal Islands of China," *ONI Review Supplement*, December 1953, I–IX.
4 "Memorandum by the Attorney General on Congressional Attitude to Formosa Defense," undated but probably summer 1954, DDE WHO OSANSA Spec. Assist. Series, President Subseries, Box 2, Presidential Papers, 1954 (7), DDEPL; underlining in original.

would not be justified in striking at targets on the Chinese Mainland. If, however, the Chinese Reds made an attack from the mainland on our carrier fleet, perhaps 100 or more miles at sea, then our security would permit us to follow such an attack in hot pursuit to the mainland bases.

As per the president's orders, however, US forces should not "offensively attack the mainland of China in defending Formosa and the outlying islands, unless the security of our forces should require such an attack."[5]

During the June–September 1954 period, a series of Top Secret reports by General James A. Van Fleet were sent to President Eisenhower. Van Fleet's assignment was to visit the various East Asian countries allied with the United States to assess their political, economic, and military readiness to fight communism. On June 3, 1954, he sent a "preliminary" report of the findings of his mission. In this 13-page document he examined the current US policies in the Far East, and he submitted his assessments of Japan, Korea, Okinawa, and Formosa, some brief observations, and then a plan for future work. According to Van Fleet, at the heart of the US National Security Policy in the Far East was fighting to protect "South Korea and the offshore island chain (Japan, the Ryukyus, Formosa, Philippines, Australia and New Zealand) from attack by communist forces." This did not include "offensive action forcibly to overthrow the Chinese Communist regime or to unite Korea," although the US government did indirectly support "raids against the mainland and seaborne commerce of Communist China."[6]

When discussing Nationalist China, Van Fleet reported that its policy goals included the "reconquest of all territories it formerly held or claimed (including ultimately Tibet, Sinkiang and Outer Mongolia) through the maximum mobilization of Chinese manpower on the island, with U.S. air, naval and logistic support." Although its own troop strengths were inadequate, if the Nationalists could obtain a foothold on the mainland then "wholesale defections of Communist troops" would allow them to return to power. Strategically, one of Taiwan's strongest assets, and the one Van Fleet mentioned first, were the offshore islands, calling them: "A vital link in the chain of offshore island bases. Offensively, the single most important springboard for the launching of all manner of operations against the mainland of China." Assuming the Nationalist forces were to be trained for such an offensive operation, Van Fleet

---

5 Conference with the President, May 22, 1954, Dulles J.F., W.H. Memo, Box 1, Meetings 1954 (3), 1.
6 Preliminary Report of Van Fleet Mission to the Far East (Japan, Korea, Okinawa, and Formosa), TOP SECRET, June 3, 1954, DDE WHO Spec. Assist., Presidential Subseries, Box 2, President's Papers, 1954 (15), DDEPL.

estimated "about two years" would be required for the full development of its "military potential."[7]

Beijing was fearful of a successful Nationalist attack. After the PRC had completed the task of relocating hundreds of thousands of troops from north to south following the reduction of tensions in Korea, the PRC began to shell Jinmen Island on September 3, 1954. Two American military personnel were killed during the barrage, and another 14 had to be evacuated. Acting Secretary of Defense Robert B. Anderson sent a Top Secret message to President Eisenhower, who was at the summer White House in Denver, Colorado, reporting on a split paper written by the JCS. In it, the chairman of the JCS, supported by the Air Force and the USN, recommended that "National Policy should be changed to permit U.S. Naval and Air Forces to assist in the defense of 10 selected off-shore islands. Quemoy is included among the 10." The majority of the JCS, however, felt that "the Nationalist held off-shore islands near the mainland are important but not essential to the defense of Formosa from a military standpoint." Anderson even warned Eisenhower that if the situation escalated and the USN and Air Force were asked to assist the Nationalists to retain the offshore islands, it "will in all probability, require some action by U.S. Forces against selected military targets on the Chinese mainland." As a short-term measure, the "CINCPAC has been alerted and directed to move carrier forces into a position from which support could be rendered, or a rescue mission undertaken, if directed."[8]

The Communist attacks on Jinmen also led to a series of discussions on whether the offshore islands could be held or not: Radford said yes, Ridgway said no. Eisenhower acknowledged that if the United States did intervene, then its "prestige is as stake. We should not go in unless we can defend it [Jinmen]." What made intervention so difficult was that Jinmen was so close to the mainland that it was within easy artillery range of shore, even while it was "impossible for our vessels to maneuver between island and mainland." Intervention of any kind implied a US commitment, which meant putting US prestige on the line. According to the president: "My hunch is that once we get tied up in any one of these things our prestige [read "face"] is so completely involved."[9]

---

7 Preliminary Report of Van Fleet Mission to the Far East (Japan, Korea, Okinawa, and Formosa), TOP SECRET, June 3, 1954, DDE WHO Spec. Assist., Presidential Subseries, Box 2, President's Papers, 1954 (15), DDEPL.

8 Top Secret message from Acting Secretary of Defense Robert B. Anderson to President Eisenhower, September 3, 1954, DH-4, Dulles, September 1954 (2), DDEPL.

9 Telephone Call from General Smith to President Eisenhower, September 6, 1954, DDE Diary Series 7, Phone Calls, June–December 1954 (2), DDEPL.

The orders to the US forces were clear, however, and Anderson instructed them that once they had arrived they should "get into position for reconnaissance and not to be aggressive." Eisenhower, in a relieved tone, replied: "We are not at war now."[10]

On September 8, 1954, the CIA produced a 33-page Top Secret assessment of the situation entitled "The Chinese Offshore Islands." It described how in just five hours on September 3 approximately six thousand 120mm and 155mm artillery shells were aimed at Jinmen, Little Jinmen, and Nationalist ships at anchor. Accuracy was high, leading to unsubstantiated reports that "the Communists pinpointing was due to Communist agents on Quemoy who directed the Communist shelling." The US and ROC reaction was rapid, and by the morning of September 5 there were "three carriers, a cruiser and three destroyer divisions of the Seventh Fleet [...] patrolling the waters in the Formosa Straits at a distance of several miles from Quemoy." Nationalist counterattacks by naval and air forces against mainland China during September 6–7, 1954, reportedly destroyed five out of fourteen 120mm and 155mm artillery guns being used by the Communists.[11]

After listing Nationalist troop strength—34,000 on Jinmen and another 4,500 on the neighboring island of Little Jinmen—the CIA study detailed the disposition of Nationalist troops, their artillery and mortar armaments, plus the air, naval, and logistical support. The Nationalists' naval assets were particularly important to protect future resupply convoys. While the Nationalist navy had a total of "56 major vessels," the CIA's estimate of what could be tasked to defend Jinmen included "2 destroyers, 3 destroyer-escorts, 2 patrol gunboats, 2 smaller patrol vessels, and about 10 armored junks." While Taiwan had about 850 aircraft, of which 415 were combat aircraft, most of them were "obsolete World War II" planes that could only be used in daylight: "its capacity for night interception and strategical bombing is nil." The CIA estimated that 15 days' supplies were already on the islands, and that Taiwan could provide another 45 days' worth if required.[12] This dire situation led to a series of NSC discussions on how best to respond to the crisis.

---

10 Telephone Call from Acting Secretary of Defense Anderson to President Eisenhower, September 4, 1954, DDE Diary Series 7, Phone Calls, June–December 1954 (2), DDEPL.

11 Central Intelligence Agency, "The Chinese Offshore Islands," September 8, 1943, TOP SECRET, DDE AWF Int. Series 9, Formosa (1), 33 pages, DDEPL.

12 Central Intelligence Agency, "The Chinese Offshore Islands," September 8, 1943, TOP SECRET, DDE AWF Int. Series 9, Formosa (1), 33 pages, DDEPL.

The US NSC discussions

Soon after the Taiwan Strait crisis broke out, the US government focused on what strategy to adopt. On September 12, 1954, the NSC submitted a Top Secret paper discussing the crisis. It was divided into three sections: prowar, antiwar, and recommendations. On the prowar side it pointed out that "Quemoy cannot be held <u>indefinitely</u> without a general war with Red China in which the Communists are defeated." While the PRC might allow Taiwan its independence, it would never allow the "alienation of the off-shore islands like Quemoy." Therefore, if Eisenhower wanted a war with China, then "Quemoy can be made to provide the issue." However, Congress would almost certainly oppose any such action, in particular since "for four years" the various offshore islands "have not been included in the area the [Seventh] Fleet is ordered to defend." A war with China would also "alienate world opinion and gravely strain our alliances, both in Europe and with Anzus."[13]

When discussing the no-war option, the NSC predicted—quite accurately as it would later turn out—that: "It does not seem that any all-out Chicom assault [of the off-shore islands] is likely in the near future because of (a) early adverse weather conditions; and (b) uncertainty as to US reaction." The longer the United States aided the Nationalists, however, the greater would be "the loss of US prestige,"—just another word for "face"—"if the Island is later lost while the US stands by." Therefore, the basic problem, "if we want to avoid all-out war with China, is to do so on terms that will avoid a serious loss of Chinat morale and US prestige."[14] Later, a memorandum from the Department of State's Policy Planning Staff specifically warned Dulles that the US government was "drifting by degrees into a situation in which our prestige will be committed to the retention of the islands."[15]

On April 5, 1955, Eisenhower sent a memorandum to Dulles warning against committing "United States military prestige to a campaign under conditions favorable to the attacker."[16] With regard to "losing face," Dulles warned Eisenhower of the problems associated with committing American prestige to the defense of the offshore islands:

---

13 NSC Talking Paper, TOP SECRET, September 12, 1954, JFD Papers, W.H. Memo 8, Gen For Pol (4), DDEPL; all underlining in original.

14 NSC Talking Paper, TOP SECRET, September 12, 1954, JFD Papers, W.H. Memo 8, Gen For Pol (4), DDEPL; all underlining in original.

15 Robert R. Bowie, Department of State, Policy Planning Staff, Memorandum for the Secretary, TOP SECRET, March 28, 1955, Dulles, J.F., W.H. Memo, Box 2, Offshore April–May 1955 (2), DDEPL.

16 Memorandum For the Secretary of State, TOP SECRET, April 5, 1955, Dulles, J.F., W.H. Memo, Box 2, Offshore Islands April–May 1955 (2), 1, DDEPL.

It is in the interest of the Republic of China, as well as in our own, that the Republic of China not commit its prestige to the defense of these perhaps indefensible positions so deeply that, if they should be lost, all future possibilities now represented by the Republic of China would also be lost. The lesson of Dien Bien Phu should not be forgotten. Originally conceived to be an outpost of transitory value, it gradually became converted into a symbol, so that when it fell, all else fell with it. The same mistake should not be repeated in regard to Quemoy and Matsu, islands which without U.S. aid are probably indefensible, and even with it may not be defensible except by means which would defeat the large common purpose.

Eisenhower concluded that "militarily and politically we and the Chinese Nationalists would be much better off if our national prestige were not even remotely committed to the defense of the coastal islands."[17] One way to shield American prestige was to turn to the United Nations.

Requesting United Nations intervention

After extensive discussions at NSC meetings, it was decided to "explore the possibility of a US appeal to the [UN] Security Council." The purpose of the appeal would be to "charge the Chinese Communists with aggression against Quemoy and threatened aggression against Formosa," which would be a breach of Article 39 of the United Nations Charter. With UN support, a directive could be sent to the Chinese Communists to "refrain, for a stipulated period, from military action directed against areas which have been held by the Republic of China since the close of the Second World War." But if no action was taken, the Nationalists might have to withdraw from the offshore islands, which would be a serious blow to the morale of the Chinese Nationalists on Formosa and to the prestige of the United States in the Far East, and it would raise the question as to whether the United States was really prepared to stand anywhere in the East.[18]

Following the PRC attack, Washington immediately tried to get the United Nations involved. For example, on September 9, 1954, the Acting Secretary of State Dulles reported that while on a trip to London he met with Anthony Eden and the New Zealand High Commissioner to see if the UN Security Council could meet and, under the provisions of Chapter VI, order the PRC

17 Dulles Draft "Formosa" Paper to Eisenhower, SECRET, April 8, 1955, Dulles, J.F., W.H. Memo, Box 2, Offshore April–May 1955 (3), 12–13, DDEPL.
18 NSC Talking Paper; Top Secret Memo, May 16, 1954, JFDP, W.H. Memo 8, Gen For Pol (4), DDEPL.

to suspend its attacks on the offshore islands. New Zealand was not only a member of the Security Council, but since it was also an Asian country, it "gives it a legitimate interest in the situation." These plans were being carried out with the "utmost secrecy."[19]

One major consideration in its UN action was undermining Russian support for China. When evaluating possible courses of action, the NSC suggested going to the Security Council since "action against Quemoy is avowedly part of a program to take Formosa by force," making the situation "not purely domestic, civil war." Asking for a vote under Article 40 might split apart the USSR and PRC, since to veto the move would impair the ongoing Soviet "peace offensive." But if the "Soviets did not veto, the Chicoms could react adversely," perhaps even defying the UN and becoming an "international outcast."[20]

In addition to giving the US leverage over China, turning to the UN might have other subsidiary effects, some negative but others potentially quite positive for the US government. First, if the Communists were restrained in their attacks on the offshore islands, then the Nationalist attacks on the mainland might also end. Second, this "might end the embargo on Red China to the extent that it exceeds the restrictions against strategic goods to the Soviet Union." Third, if the Communists rejected the UN then the moral "sanction" of the "free world against the Communist world would be reinstated," while if they backed it then one "probable ultimate outcome of UN intervention, if the Soviet Union permitted it, would be independence of Formosa and the Pescadores."[21]

On September 29, 1954, Bedell Smith called Eisenhower to tell him that the State Department had backed the proposal that New Zealand should present the case under Chapter VI, and the "President agreed."[22] On October 5, 1954, Eisenhower told Dulles to be careful not to discuss it with "anyone who might allow it to leak to the public," so just before the UN meeting they should "notify Senator Knowland of our position."[23] On October 12, 1954, Dulles could report to the President: "After difficult negotiations, we have a

---

19 Top Secret Telegram from Acting Secretary of State Dulles to the White House, September 9, 1954, DH-4, Dulles September 1954 (1), DDEPL.

20 NSC Talking Paper, TOP SECRET, September 12, 1954, JFD Papers, W.H. Memo 8, Gen For Pol (4), DDEPL; all underlining in original.

21 NSC Talking Paper, TOP SECRET, September 12, 1954, JFD Papers, W.H. Memo 8, Gen For Pol (4), DDEPL; all underlining in original.

22 Telephone Call from Bedell Smith to President Eisenhower, September 29, 1954, DDE Diary Series 7, Phone Calls, June–December 1954 (2), DDEPL.

23 Phone Conversation between Eisenhower and Dulles, October 5, 1954, DH 4, Dulles, J.F., October 1954.

very complete and definite understanding with the United Kingdom and New Zealand."[24]

Taiwanese support would be crucial if the UN intervention were to succeed. On December 18, 1954, Eisenhower met with the Taiwanese Foreign Minister Dr. George Yeh. It was anticipated that Yeh would ask for a continuation of US logistical support for "the defense of the off-shore islands." In response, Eisenhower referred to the recent NSC decision (NSC 5429/4) that stated:

> For the present, seek to preserve, through United Nations action, the status quo of the Nationalist-held off-shore islands; and, without committing U.S. forces except as militarily desirable in the event of Chinese Communist attack on Formosa and the Pescadores, provide to the Chinese Nationalist forces military equipment and training to assist them to defend such off-shore islands, using Formosa as a base.[25]

After New Zealand did make this proposal to the UN, however, the PRC flatly rejected it, with Zhou Enlai even stating that "if the New Zealand idea was to discuss these islands, then that constituted intervention in China's internal affairs." When the British official, Trevelyan, tried to convince Zhou to agree to let the Security Council discuss the dispute, he reassured Zhou that the "New Zealand proposal would be merely that the Security Council should discuss the serious situation existing in the area of the islands, since this was the immediate point of danger." Eisenhower had further promised that the "Chinese Government should be present at the discussion." Zhou turned all of these offers down, reaffirming the disputed islands "were Chinese, and the Chinese would liberate them."[26]

Time was rapidly slipping by. In late February 1955, Eisenhower warned Dulles that if the UN-sponsored ceasefire did not start soon then it might be difficult to stop Chiang Kai-shek from taking action. At Dulles's suggestion, Eisenhower decided it was best to tell the British government that time was running short:

> I agree that it would be wise to inform Eden that unless we soon arrive at a cease fire, we cannot much longer insist that the present policy be

---

24 Message from Dulles to Eisenhower, TOP SECRET EYES ONLY, October 12, 1954, DH 4, Dulles, J.F., October 1954, DDEPL.

25 Memorandum for the President, December 18, 1954, DH 4, Dulles, J.F., December 1954 (2), DDEPL.

26 Mr. Trevelyan's Conversation with Chou-en-Lai on January 28, 1955, TOP SECRET, DDE AWF, Int. Series 10, Formosa Area, U.S. Mil. Ops. (1), DDEPL.

observed which permits major Communist build up or attacks without Chiang reaction. I believe that you should tell him that we do not intend to blackmail Chiang to compel his evacuation of Quemoy and the Matsus as long as he deems their possession vital to the spirit and morale of the Formosan garrison and population. On the contrary we expect to continue our logistic support of Chiang's forces as long as there is no mutually agreed upon or tacit cease fire. Finally, if we are convinced that any attack against those islands is in fact an attack against Formosa, we should not hesitate to help defeat it. Possibly you should tell him too that because of the continuing build-up of Chicom forces, we cannot tell when any of these emergencies might arise.

But Eisenhower clarified that the authority to order American troops to assist Chiang was his and his alone: "Any offensive military participation on our part will be only by order of the President."[27]

On February 25, 1955, Dulles reported that Eden had convinced him it was best not to continue to press for a ceasefire in the UN. Rather, Eden would try to convince the PRC to agree to not "seek a violent solution of Formosa matter." Eden's draft message to Beijing read:

I, therefore, wish to inquire whether the Chinese Government would state, privately or publicly, that, while maintaining their claims, they do not intend to prosecute them by force. If they were prepared [to] give such assurance, we would be ready so to inform the US Government and approach them with, we believe, a good hope of finding basis for a peaceful settlement of the situation in the coastal islands.

In turn, Dulles promised: "I therefore told him that we would agree to suspend for a further brief period request for a cease-fire resolution so as to permit this other initiative of his to have best chance of success."[28] By early March 1955, however, in discussions between Dulles and Chiang Kai-shek, Dulles clarified that while the US government did not expect Taiwan to support the ceasefire resolution, "I must, however, request with the greatest possible strength and earnestness that if such a resolution came to a vote he [Chiang] would not

---

27 Eisenhower Telegram to Dulles, TOP SECRET, February 21, 1955, DH 4, Dulles, J.F., February 1955 (1), DDEPL; responding to Dulles Telegram to Eisenhower, TOP SECRET, February 21, 1955, DH 4, Dulles, J.F., February 1955 (1), DDEPL.

28 Telegrams from Dulles to Eisenhower, TOP SECRET, February 25, 1955, DH 4, Dulles, John Foster, February 1955 (1), DDEPL; underlining in the original.

veto it but would let the Soviets veto it." Chiang laughed and agreed that "actually he would prefer to let the Soviets veto it."[29]

When discussing his recent visit to Taiwan during a trip to Canada, Dulles explained that he had told the Canadian Cabinet that Washington had convinced Chiang Kai-shek to accept the following four points:

1. Limited our Treaty to Formosa and the Pescadores.
2. Secured his agreement not to attack the mainland from any position without our prior agreement.
3. Secured his evacuation of the Tachens and Pishan.
4. Sought a ceasefire for the Formosa Straits which he felt would be a death blow to his hopes.

When discussing further concessions that Chiang could be asked to make, however, Dulles warned: "I did not know whether we could make him take any more bitter medicine at this time without disastrous consequences."[30]

As part of America's attempts to negotiate a ceasefire in the Taiwan Strait, Dulles also worked with a number of countries attending the Bandung conference. These countries put pressure on Zhou Enlai to negotiate. According to Dulles, this had pushed Zhou to "follow a pacific rather than belligerent course." In late April 1955, Dulles told a number of US senators, including Knowland, Hickenlooper, and Smith, that "we should be prepared to talk with the Chinese Communists merely to the extent of ascertaining whether they would make a 'cease-fire'." To refuse to agree to such talks might alienate the friendly countries at Bandung, since "a complete turn-down by the United States would alienate our Asian non-Communist friends and allies." To this, Senator Knowland responded that "we could not trust a cease-fire agreement and that the Armistices in Korea and Indochina were already being broken."[31] At about the same time, Dulles suggested to the Soviet Foreign Minister Molotov that a six-power conference be convened to discuss the Taiwan Strait, so as to create "a situation where as in Germany, Korea and Vietnam, it was agreed that unification would not be sought be force."[32]

29 Dulles Discussions with Chiang Kai-shek, TOP SECRET, March 4, 1955, DDE AWF, Int. Series 10, Formosa (China), 1952–57 (4), DDEPL.
30 Summary of Remarks of the Honorable John Foster Dulles at Cabinet Meeting Ottawa, TOP SECRET, March 18, 1955, DH 5, Dulles, J.F., March 1955, 2, DDEPL.
31 Memorandum of Meeting with the Senators, April 27, 1955, TOP SECRET, April 28, 1955, Dulles, J.F., Gen Cor. Box 1, Memos J-K (2), DDEPL.
32 Telegram from Dulles to the President from Vienna, TOP SECRET, May 14, 1955, DH 5, JFD May 1955, DDEPL.

During the late spring, the PRC attempted to send offers to negotiate to Washington by means of Pakistan and India. For example, in early May, Mir Khan from Pakistan told Ambassador Lodge that in his opinion "the Chinese Communists want to climb down, that they are willing to acknowledge the present status quo in the Formosa area for ten or twenty years." According to this communication, the PRC was now willing to release 11 American airmen it was holding. Importantly, this would not be a tit for tat with any side agreement to allow the PRC in the United Nations.[33] In June 1955, U Nu from Vietnam relayed a message that the Chinese Communists were ready to "sit down directly and negotiate a cease-fire."[34]

In addition to Mir Khan and U Nu, Zhou Enlai told India's Krishna Menon that while the PRC could not agree to a formal ceasefire with Taiwan, so long as there "was evidence of substantial withdrawals" of Nationalist troops from Jinmen and Mazu then "there need be no particular time limit for the standstill in hostilities." As part of such an arrangement the Nationalists would not need to "surrender" the islands to the Communists, so long as they did not carry out a "scorched earth policy such as had been carried out in the Tachens."[35] By mid-July, Menon had visited Eisenhower two times to ask whether talks could be established with the PRC, and in return for talks captured US airmen in China would be released. But the president stood firm that "the American people will not consider using the lives and freedom of their own citizens as a bargaining" chip, and that Washington would only be willing to deal with Beijing "in good faith until after they have released these prisoners."[36] On July 18, 1955, John Foster Dulles sent a memorandum to Eisenhower listing 38 American civilians plus 11 airmen being held by China.[37]

Washington was now hearing signals from at least three different sources: "They agreed this is a typical Chinese trick—they will take whoever has the most to offer—which negotiator is most successful."[38] However, as

---

33 Memorandum from Ambassador Lodge to Dulles, SECRET, May 4, 1955, Dulles, J.F., Tel Conv. Box May 4–August 1955 (8), DDEPL.

34 Telephone Call from Allen Dulles, July 1, 1955, Dulles, J.F., Tel Conv., Box 4, May–August 1955 (4), DDEPL.

35 Memorandum Citing Mr. Krishna Menon's discussions with Zhou Enlai, SECRET AND PERSONAL, June 9, 1955, Dulles, J.F., W.H. Memo, Box 3, Meet Press 1955 (4), 2–3, DDEPL.

36 Notes on Eisenhower Discussion with Menon, DDE Papers 6, ACW Diary July 1955 (3), DDEPL; underlining in original.

37 Memorandum for the President: Americans Imprisoned or Detained in Communist China, July 18, 1955, DH 5, JFD July 1955, DDEPL.

38 Telephone Call from Allen Dulles, July 1, 1955, Dulles, J.F., Tel Conv., Box 4, May–August 1955 (4), DDEPL.

Washington's lengthy, and largely unsuccessful, negotiations with Chiang Kai-shek throughout March and April had shown, Chiang was determined not to withdraw from the offshore islands under any circumstances. The only option the US government had was to increase its military aid to Chiang, largely on his terms.

Discussions over new US–ROC security arrangements

The immediate political impact in Washington of the Communist attack on Jinmen was contrary to PRC expectations. Rather than push the United States and Taiwan further apart, this crisis resulted in renewed discussions concerning a new US–Taiwan security treaty. As early as June 7, 1953, in a letter to President Eisenhower, Chiang Kai-shek had mentioned concluding "bilateral or multilateral security pacts" with the United States and other East Asian countries, notably South Korea, Thailand, and Indochina.[39] However, all previous US–ROC discussions on signing such a pact had ended in failure. This new agreement, while reaffirming the pledges made earlier by Truman and Eisenhower to defend Taiwan and the Penghus against Communist attack, was deliberately vague about the security status of the other offshore islands. Previous USN operation orders had clarified that while the term "enemy forces" included all forces attacking Taiwan or the Penghus, it did not include forces attacking other offshore islands held by the Nationalists.[40]

The US government had to tread softly. Public opinion in the UK opposed a war with China. Churchill, in a private letter to Eisenhower, warned him that "a war to keep the coastal islands for China would not be defensible here."[41] The British Ambassador further emphasized that since the UK had recognized the PRC, it legally "recognized that these [offshore] islands were part of China." This made it highly unlikely that Britain could support the United States in any fight over the offshore islands. This greatly concerned the British government, since if war broke out: "The Western alliance might be split." The British Ambassador even asked: "Were these islands really worth it?"[42]

---

39 Letter from Chiang Kai-shek to President Eisenhower, June 7, 1953, DH-1, Dulles June 1953 (1), DDEPL.

40 U.S. Navy Operation Order, CTF 72 No. 2-A-53, May 1, 1954, NHHC Archives, Post-1946 Operation Plans, Task Force 72.

41 Cited in a letter from Harold Macmillan to John Foster Dulles (Top Secret), September 5, 1958, The National Archives, Kew, CAB 21/3272

42 UK Ambassador, Washington, to Foreign Office (Secret), January 29, 1955, The National Archives, Kew, PREM 11/867.

Taking into consideration the differing views of its allies, the US government adopted an intentionally ambiguous policy of keeping the Communists guessing about the true defense status of the offshore islands.[43] This ambiguous wording gave the president maximum flexibility, since there was "no unconditional Presidential decision to defend the coastal positions."[44] According to one press report:

> The pact will be deliberately vague about how the U.S. might react if the Reds were to invade any of the other Nationalist-held islands off the China coast. The U.S. doesn't want the Reds to know which it will defend, and which it will simply write off. It prefers to keep them guessing.[45]

After lengthy negotiations, the two sides agreed to very specific wording. The treaty stated that the US security guarantee was also "applicable to such other territories as may be determined by mutual agreement."[46] This wording deferred any decision on whether the offshore islands would be included in the treaty.

A Top Secret report discussing the US–Taiwan mutual security treaty stated that it should cover "Formosa and the Pescadores, but not the offshore islands." The treaty should be "defensive in nature," similar to the German renunciation of "force to unite Germany" or to Korea, where the US government opposes "the use by Rhee of force to unite Korea."[47] The resulting US–ROC Mutual Defense Treaty, which was signed on December 2, 1954, contained this ambiguous wording. Interestingly, prior to China's attacks the US government had hesitated finalizing this treaty, because of the "inherent difficulty of concluding a purely defensive pact with a country engaged in actual hostilities," especially since Washington hoped to "avoid direct United States involvement."[48] Once Eisenhower agreed to the treaty,

43 George W. Anderson, Jr., *Reminiscences of Admiral George W. Anderson, Jr.* Oral History 42, 272.

44 Preliminary Draft of Possible Statement of Position for Communication to the Republic of China, SECRET, April 7, 1955, Dulles, J.F. W.H. Memo, Box 2, Offshore April–May 1955 (4), 9, DDEPL.

45 "Pressure and a Pact," *Newsweek*, December 13, 1954.

46 Hungdah Chiu, *China and the Taiwan Issue* (New York: Praeger, 1979), 160.

47 Report on U.S. Government Policies in Relation to China, TOP SECRET, undated, Dulles, J.F., W.H. Memo, Box 2, 1954, Formosa Straits (1), 5, DDEPL.

48 "Commitments and Problems of the United States to the Republic of China, Including any Divergencies between the Two Governments, and Chinese Problems with Other Asian Nations (Other Than Military)," TOP SECRET, undated (probably summer

however, he insisted on an exchange of separate notes giving the United States veto power over a Nationalist attack. This would avoid Chiang calling the shots.

The US government did not want to give Chiang the power to declare war. A secret agreement was signed to make sure this would not happen. Dulles explained during a telephone call on December 22, 1954, that "there is an exchange of notes which more or less gives us the power to control any offensive operations from Formosa, etc."[49] Two months later, Eisenhower told Churchill that in this secret agreement Chiang promised he would not "conduct any offensive operations against the mainland either from Formosa or from his coastal positions, except in agreement with us." In addition, the Nationalists were limited in "their right to take away from Formosa military elements, material or human, to which we had contributed if this would weaken the defense of Formosa itself."[50]

Chiang Kai-shek later confirmed this promise in a March 4, 1955, discussion with Dulles: "Now that the Mutual Security Treaty was in force, he wished to assure me that he would take no independent action insofar as the use of force was concerned, and would undertake no large-scale military operations against the Mainland without full consultation with the US."[51] Eisenhower further explained to Churchill that the secret agreement would allow Washington to stop Chiang from using his offshore bases to continue the "sporadic war against the mainland" or to support an "invasion of the mainland of China." According to Eisenhower, the secret agreement with Chiang showed that the US government has "done much more than seems generally realized."[52] One of the most important concessions Eisenhower convinced Chiang to make was the evacuation of the Dachen Islands (see next chapter).

1954), DDE WHO, OSANSA, Spec. Assist., Presidential Subseries, Box 2, Presidential Papers, 1954 (13), 11, DDEPL.

49 Telephone Call from Mr. Hagerty, December 22, 1954, Dulles, J.F., Telephone Conv., Box 10, November–February 1955 (2), DDEPL.

50 Message for Transmittal to the Prime Minister, TOP SECRET, February 19, 1955, DDE Diary Series 9, DDE Diary, February 1955 (1), DDEPL; underlining in original.

51 Dulles Discussions with Chiang Kai-shek, TOP SECRET, March 4, 1955, DDE AWF, Int. Series 10, Formosa (China), 1952–57 (4), DDEPL.

52 Letter from President Eisenhower to Prime Minister Churchill (Top Secret), February 19, 1955, The National Archives, Kew, PREM 11/879, underlining in original document.

Negotiating the Formosa Resolution

PRC attacks on the Dachen Islands during January 1955 led to Eisenhower's request that Congress give him special powers to defend Taiwan. It was decided to sign a second document, unofficially called the Formosa Resolution, to extend certain US guarantees to Taiwan to defend the offshore islands. This idea was perhaps first proposed by Dr. George K. C. Yeh, the Nationalist Foreign Minister, in a December 20, 1954, meeting with President Eisenhower. During this meeting, Yeh quoted Chiang Kai-shek: "With respect to the off-shore islands, the Generalissimo recognized that the Treaty did not cover these, but felt that it would be a good psychological warfare move for the U.S. to give some form of assurance that it would provide logistic support for Chinese forces engaged in their defense." In reply, Eisenhower said that while Washington was not "indifferent as to these islands," it would be better to handle the offshore islands on a "case by case" basis, "each on its merits."[53]

On January 20, 1955, Secretary of State Dulles met with six Senators, six Congressmen, and Admiral Radford, the Chairman of the JCS, to discuss what he called "a sounder defensive concept" to handle tensions in the offshore islands.[54] Dulles explained that an evacuation of the Dachen Islands was the president's preferred policy, but that the president thought the administration should have "some authority from Congress to use the armed forces of the United States in the area for the protection and security of Formosa and the Pescadores."[55] Dulles then argued that if "the Formosan treaty were ratified, and the President were given these powers, there will be a realization that we have reached the point that we are not going to retreat more and it possibly will have a stabilizing effect." Not to take this action would, in his mind, make the "risk of war" greater.[56]

However, the important thing to understand about the resolution, according to a telephone conversation between Eisenhower and Dulles, was that the wording of the resolution would include possible "enlargement of the area described in the treaty."[57] On January 25, 1955, Eisenhower wrote a

---

53 Memorandum of Conference with the President, December 20, 1954, DDE Papers 3, ACW Diary, December 1954 (2), DDEPL.

54 Meeting of Secretary with Congressional Leaders, Personal and Private, SECRET, January 20, 1955, Dulles, J.F., Box 2, W.H. Memo 1955, FS (3), 1, DDEPL.

55 Meeting of Secretary with Congressional Leaders, Personal and Private, SECRET, January 20, 1955, Dulles, J.F., Box 2, W.H. Memo 1955, FS (3), 4, DDEPL.

56 Meeting of Secretary with Congressional Leaders, Personal and Private, SECRET, January 20, 1955, Dulles, J.F., Box 2, W.H. Memo 1955, FS (3), 5, DDEPL.

57 Dulles and Eisenhower Telephone Conv., January 22, 1955, DDE Diary Series 9, Phone Calls, January–July 1955 (3), DDEPL.

TOP SECRET letter to Churchill responding to the British concern that the United States might get drawn into a "Chinese war." Eisenhower explained his reasoning:

> It is probably difficult for you, in your geographical position, to understand how concerned this country is with the solidarity of the Island Barrier in the Western Pacific. Moreover, we are convinced that the psychological effect in the Far East of deserting our friends on Formosa would risk a collapse of Asiatic resistance to the Communists. Such possibilities cannot be lightly dismissed; in our view they are almost as important, in the long term, to you as they are to us.

Reassuring Churchill that he was working for the "preservation and strengthening of the peace," Eisenhower said: "But I am positive that the free world is surely building trouble for itself unless it is united in basic purpose, is clear and emphatic in its declared determination to resist all forceful Communist advance, and keeps itself ready to act on a moment's notice, if necessary."[58]

On January 28, 1955, a concise transcript of a two-and-a-half-hour interview between the British official in Beijing, Trevelyan, and the Chinese foreign minister, Zhou Enlai, made the Chinese views clear. Divided into six points, Zhou (1) accused the president of sending a "war message" to Congress: (2) he denounced Washington for using the UN as a cover "for aggression against China," (3) the UN had no right to discuss the offshore islands since they were a matter of "internal sovereignty," (4) the offshore islands dispute could not be separated from Taiwan's status, (5) the PRC would never cut a "deal" on the offshore islands but planned to "liberate" them, and finally (6) the Chinese government was "not afraid of war threats and would resist if war was thrust on them." Trevelyan described Zhou's attitude during their lengthy meeting as "tense and absolutely uncompromising."[59]

On January 29, 1955, the "Formosa Resolution" was passed by the Congress.[60] This resolution stated that only the president could judge if a PRC attack on the offshore islands was part of a more general assault on

---

58 Letter from Eisenhower to Churchill, TOP SECRET, January 25, 1955, DDE Diary Series 9, DDE Diary, January 1955 (1), DDEPL.

59 Formosan Straits, Substance of a message dated January 28 from Mr. Trevelyan in Peking, SECRET, January 28, 1955, DH 4, Dulles, J.F., January 1955, DDEPL.

60 The full name of the "Formosa Resolution" is "U.S. Congressional Authorization for the President to Employ the Armed Forces of the United States to Protect Formosa, the Pescadores, and Related Positions and Territories of That Area."

Taiwan. This vague wording concerned Chiang Kai-shek. On January 29, 1955, Ambassador Rankin telegrammed to Washington to report that a very "nervous" Chiang had expressed his hope that there would be a specific US statement that it intended to help defend Jinmen and Mazu. While admitting that he did not know the details, Rankin told Chiang that perhaps a vague resolution, without "mentioning them [the islands] by name," would have the added "advantage of not implying all other islands being written off."[61]

Dulles met with Yeh on January 28, 1955. Yeh requested that a "joint announcement [on] Quemoy and Matsu" be announced publicly. But the Secretary informed the Foreign Minister "orally and confidentially" that under the present circumstances the United States considered Jinmen and Mazu important to the defense of Formosa:

> Secretary said any formal Chinese statement should avoid implication of agreement or commitment between United States and Chinese Governments. United States responsibilities as to "related area" were unilateral. There was no agreement as to related area, and United States might have to deny any implications to contrary. Chinese unofficial sources could speculate, but there should be no official statement on either side as to understanding re defense of related area. Secretary felt impossible to draw absolute geographical line or to specify which island were important to defense of Formosa and which were not important. Relative defensive importance of islands could change. Any significant Communist buildup in area would be regarded by United States with concern.[62]

It was best not to state this publicly, argued Dulles, since by the terms of the Formosa Resolution it was up to the president to decide what the term "related area" actually meant. Accordingly, the best option was to be ambiguous.

The day after the Formosa Resolution was signed, on January 30, 1955, US Ambassador Rankin warned of an extremely "difficult situation" with regard to Chiang Kai-shek. In what appeared to be an ultimatum, which was one of his standard negotiating tactics, Chiang informed Rankin that "his government would not request assistance in withdrawing from Tachens until US position re Kinmen [Jinmen] and Matsu clarified. Failure to insist on this

---

61 Ambassador Rankin to Secretary of State, January 29, 1955, DDE AWF, Int. Series 10, Formosa Area, U.S. Mil. Ops. (3), DDEPL.

62 Telegram from Washington to Taipei, TOP SECRET, January 29, 1955, DDE AWF, Int. Series 10, Formosa Area, U.S. Mil. Ops. (3), DDEPL.

would betray China." Chiang's understanding of events was that three things should happen:

1. After approval of resolution by Congress, two governments would issue simultaneous and complementary statements on offshore islands.
2. Above statements would provide for US assistance in evacuation of Tachens.
3. At same time, it would be made clear US was extending protection to Kinmen [Jinmen] and Matsu.

Chiang explained that he considered this a matter of "honor," and in order not to "lose face" Chiang was willing to lose everything: "He said Tachen and forces there might be lost, that Formosa where he and his people were prepared to die might also be lost, but that if China's honor were preserved for posterity it would be worthwhile." He ended by reminding Washington that it should realize that "in relation with his government [...] it was not dealing with children."[63]

In early March 1955, Dulles flew to Taiwan and met with Chiang Kai-shek. He started by apologizing for any confusion about the status of Jinmen and Mazu and acknowledged that he "was prepared to take full responsibility." However, Dulles then went on to explain to Chiang that "the matter had developed in the US in such a way that the authority to use the Armed Forces of the US outside of the treaty area had to be left to the future judgment of the President of the US and that therefore there could not be any actual present commitment" to Jinmen and Mazu.[64] From this point on, the policy of "strategic ambiguity" was applied to the status of the offshore islands.

This policy was not just effective against China. There was a very real threat in Washington too that a small conflict in the Taiwan Strait could expand into a World War. For example, Senator Mundt, a long-time member of the House Foreign Affairs Committee, wrote to Eisenhower on May 12, 1955, to suggest that if a Communist attack appeared "beyond the capacity of the Nationalists to repel" it, then the United States should use its "air and sea power" to attack the mainland "so that in 72 hours we could bring great destruction on the Mainland." After this "fierce attack" the Senator suggested dropping leaflets over the mainland "stating the war—started by Communists—was over unless

---

63 Telegram from Taipei, TOP SECRET, January 30, 1955, DDE AWF, Int. Series 10, Formosa Area, US Mil. Ops. (3), DDEPL.
64 Dulles Discussions with Chiang Kai-shek, TOP SECRET, March 4, 1955, DDE AWF, Int. Series 10, Formosa (China), 1952–57 (4), DDEPL.

they attacked again."[65] It was just this kind of no-win scenario that Eisenhower was actively seeking to avoid.

Conclusions

In a show of force, the PRC initiated the first Taiwan Strait crisis during early September 1954. Scholars have argued that the PRC's primary motivation was to test "American resolve."[66] On April 26, 1955, former US Ambassador to the USSR, William C. Bullitt, agreed with this view, writing to Eisenhower:

> From Japan to Germany, the most serious men—even our devoted friends—have begun to doubt that we will have the intelligence and moral character to resist the Communist threat *in time*. The drift away from us is world-wide. If you defend Matsu and Quemoy, you will stop the rot in our world position. If you let them go, you will accelerate our decline and fall.[67]

Communist forces successfully overran Yichiang Island and attacked the Dachen Islands. During this period Washington repeatedly urged Taipei to withdraw from all the offshore islands, but Chiang Kai-shek refused. Not only would complete abandonment force Chiang to lose face, but so long as the Nationalists held these islands right off China's coast the Communists could not proclaim total victory over the mainland. In addition, Chiang argued that Chinese history had shown that the Nationalists could always stage a future mainland invasion from their offshore bases, thereby using the disputed islands as stepping stones to retake control of China.

From purely a strategic viewpoint the PRC's attacks backfired. In December 1954, Taiwan and the United States signed a mutual security pact reaffirming that the   United States would defend Taiwan and the Penghu Islands. As part of a secret pact, Chiang Kai-shek promised that no offensive operations were to take place against the mainland "without American agreement." Recounting this discussion four years later during October 1958, Dulles said that Chiang "had maintained that limitation and honourably maintained it."[68]

---

65 Memorandum to the President regarding Senator Mundt's letter, May 12, 1955, DDE Papers 5, ACW Diary May 1955 (5), DDEPL.

66 Thomas J. Christensen, *Useful Adversaries: Grand Strategy, Domestic Mobilization, and Sino-American Conflict, 1947–1958* (Princeton, NJ: Princeton University Press, 1996), 195.

67 Personal Letter from William C. Bullitt to President Eisenhower, Personal, April 26, 1955, DDE Diary Series 10, DDE Diary April 1955 (1), DDEPL.

68 Telegram from Foreign Office to UK Embassy, Washington, October 22, 1958, The National Archives, Kew, PREM 11/3738.

Chiang had also agreed, with American assistance, to evacuate the Dachen Islands. Finally, the Formosa Resolution left it intentionally unclear which of the offshore islands the US government would choose to defend and which islands they would choose to evacuate. This ambiguity allowed tensions in the Taiwan Strait to die down, at least temporarily.

Chapter 4

THE EVACUATION OF THE DACHEN ISLANDS, 1955

The February 8–11, 1955, evacuation of the Dachens was a massive undertaking. The USN used a total of 132 ships and 400 aircraft to evacuate 14,500 civilians, 10,000 Nationalist troops, and approximately 4,000 guerrilla fighters, along with over 40,000 tons of military equipment and supplies. To protect the evacuation, the Seventh Fleet assembled a "backbone" of six aircraft carriers. China was warned not to interfere. USN forces "have instructions not to provoke incidents but they also have instructions not to accept any tactical disadvantages." Or, put another way, "American airmen were not to get 'altruistically shot down'."[1]

The international reaction to the Dachen evacuation was mixed. To the Australians, the loss of the Dachens was compared to the 1938 fall of Czechoslovakia, while the PRC threat to invade Taiwan was compared to the 1939 invasion of Poland. In a February 1955 Gallup poll, 66 percent of Australians "declared themselves in favour of Australia joining the United States in any war which might result from United States efforts to prevent Chinese Communists from invading Formosa." In a letter from April 1955, Australian Prime Minister Menzies advocated the "desirability of giving Formosa military and political strength to ensure the future will be decided peacefully and not as a result of Communist policies of force."[2]

What follows is a summary of the Army History entitled "Evacuation of the Tachen Islands." This final corrected copy dates to May 19, 1956. While protecting the Dachen evacuation was up to the USN, the US Army was put in charge of the actual evacuation of civilians, guerrillas, and military personnel, plus destroying anything of value. It was a mammoth undertaking, as reflected in the name of the operation "Operation King Kong."

---

1 UK Embassy, Washington, to Foreign Office, February 6, 1955, The National Archives, Kew, PREM 11/867.
2 Telegram from UK High Commissioner in Australia to Commonwealth Relations Office (Top Secret), April 16, 1955, The National Archives, Kew, DEFE 13/288.

Planning the evacuation of the Dachens

While it is true that the MAAG had sent an advisory team to the Dachens as early as 1953, it had normally consisted of but a single officer. Just prior to the Yichiang landing the total advisory effort on these islands consisted of Colonel Robert L. Walton and a three-man radio team. These personnel were serving a fixed tour on this offshore position after which they were scheduled for rotation to other duties on Taiwan proper. Since Colonel Walton's tour was to end in January, just prior to the Yichiang operation his replacement, Colonel Edward T. McConnell, reported to the Dachens for briefing and orientation prior to assuming command.[3]

During the intervals between bombings, these officers watched the Communists land on Yichiang on the 18th from observation posts on North Dachen. On the following day, Chief, MAAG ordered the withdrawal of these advisers to Taipei. Plans called for a departure from South Dachen on a motorized, guerrilla junk which was to proceed southwest for 10 miles to a rendezvous point where contact was to be made with a US destroyer. This vessel would then transport the team to Formosa.[4]

Plans miscarried and the pickup was not made, but Colonel Walton's orders covered such an eventuality. He was to turn due south and to proceed at a speed of seven knots until picked up. At approximately 0400 hours on the morning of January 20 the new course was laid. When, by 0700, there was still no contact with the destroyer, a conference was held to determine a new plan of action. The junk had begun to leak from the pounding that it was taking in the heavy seas; fuel supplies were far from adequate to carry the craft all the way to Keelung. Hence, it was decided to make for Nanchi which was Nationalist-held and which had good communications with Taipei. (The team's SCR 499, on order, had been destroyed prior to the withdrawal from the Dachens.) Without major incident the junk reached Nanchi and from there, at approximately 1700 hours on the 20th, Colonel Walton called Taipei by radio-telephone reporting the safe arrival of his team.[5] On the following day a Foshing Air Lines amphibian picked up the team and transported it to Taipei.[6]

---

3 Interview, May 8, 1956, Colonel Walton.
4 Cable, MG 5282, MAAG to Chief MAAG Advisor on Tachens, January 19, 1955, files of G3, MAAG (CS).
5 Interview, May 8, 1956, Colonel Walton.
6 Ibid.

Evacuation planning

Since the United States was pledged to assist Free China in the defense of Formosa and the Pescadores, and since she had long been using her good offices to prevent the spread of hostilities in the Formosa Strait area, it was only natural that she stood ready to assist should an evacuation of the Dachens be undertaken.

As early as January 18, the date of the Yichiang landings, Lieutenant General Yu Pak-chuan, Deputy Chief of the General Staff, MND, and Colonel Delmer P. Anderson, G3 MAAG, began a round of conferences that was almost continuous for the next few days. Each of these staff officers sought to evaluate the situation on Yichiang, and the effects of its loss, in order that appropriate recommendations might be made to their respective commanders. To various of their meetings came the MAAG Section Chiefs: General Macdonald (Army), Captain Robert Brodie, Jr. (Navy), and Colonel Reginald R. Vance (Air). From these commanders advice was sought, plus factual data as to what assistance their units could provide should an evacuation of the Dachens be ordered. By the 19th, both General Yu and Colonel Anderson were recommending to their superiors that such an operation be undertaken. Discussions then moved to the MND-Hq MAAG level (Minister Yu Ta-wei and General Chase) and a short time later from the military to the diplomatic stage (President Chiang and Ambassador Rankin).[7]

On January 21, 1955, the Nationalist Government of the Republic of China made its decision to withdraw from the Dachens. On the following day the Commander in Chief, CHQ Navy and the Commanding General, Dachen Defense Command (DDC) were instructed to prepare plans to cover such an eventuality; however, no orders for an evacuation were issued at this time.[8] Planning deadlines for these agencies were established by MND as noon on January 30, but it was not until the 31st of that month that formal directives to the C-in-C, GHQ and CG, DDC for this evacuation-planning were produced by the Ministry of National Defense. When issued, these labeled the overall operation "KING KONG" and informed the concerned commanders that

US amphibious forces will arrive at Dachen on D-day, and start to evacuate all personnel, equipment, material and weapons of Chinese Army, CAF and CSG from Dachen to Taiwan. At this time, CN

---

7 Interview, May 17, 1956, Lieutenant Colonel Robert V. Smart, G3 Section, MAAG, Taipei, Taiwan.

8 Rpt (translation), G3, MND, undated, "Review of Tachen Operation," files of G3, Army Section (File No. 109), hereafter cited as "G3, MND Review."

amphibious squadron will be placed under the operational control of the US Fleet.[9]

Evacuation of the Yushans and Pishan was to be areas of exclusive Chinese responsibilities.

Colonels Walton and McConnell arrived in Taipei on the same day that the decision to evacuate was made by the Chinese. Prior to their arrival, Chief, MAAG had been apprised of this decision, and Army Section had been informed that it would be responsible for the preparation of the ground force portion of an evacuation plan covering North and South Dachen. The project, as might logically be expected, was passed to Army Section's G3 Colonel Robert J. Hill, Jr., who in turn placed the requirement on his Plans and Operations Branch headed by Lieutenant Colonel Cud T. Baird, III. Within the P&O Branch, Major William L. Riles and Harold R. Aaron began work on this project late on the afternoon of January 21.[10]

Upon his return to Taipei, Colonel McConnell took over as Chief, DDCAT. At his disposal General Macdonald placed all of the facilities of Headquarters Army Section. For the remainder of the planning phase, Majors Riles and Aaron, in effect, became his personal staff.[11] Colonel Walton's new assignment was to the G3 Section, MAAG whose main mission became the coordination of MND's planning and that of the Dachen Defense Command with the work being done at Army Section.[12] Walton and McConnell from the Dachens was the Chief of Staff of DDC, Colonel Sun Chang-cheng. Already present in Taipei was the G4 of that organization.[13] Thus, by the end of the day on which the Nationalist Government made its decision to evacuate, there were present in Taipei all of the persons best qualified to plan and coordinate the ground force portion of the coming operation.

By the time that Colonel McConnell and Colonel Walton reached Taipei, they had already roughed-out a good deal of an operation plan for the evacuation of North and South Dachen. From this beginning, and from what had been accomplished by Majors Riles and Aaron, the Army Section's plan emerged. By the afternoon of Sunday, January 24, a draft was ready for presentation to Chief, MAAG. Meanwhile, work continued at Army Section to complete these annexes to the basic plan which were still missing. Liaison, in the days

---

9 MND Directive (44) Ying Miao 130 (translation), January 31, 1955, "Evacuation from Tachen," files of G3, Army Section (File No. 110).

10 Interview, April 19, 1956, Major Harold R. Aaron, G3 Section, Army Section, Taipei, Taiwan.

11 Ibid.

12 Interview, May 8, 1956, Colonel Walton.

13 Ibid.

that follow, between Army Section and G3, MAAG was close and constant; in turn, Colonel Anderson's section coordinated details with the Dachen Defense Command's planners who had established themselves at MND.[14]

From these efforts came "Operation Plan Evacuation of North and South Dachen." This document was prepared in English for the signature of Lieutenant General Liu Lien-chi, Commanding General, DDC. All that was required, before implementation became possible, was its translation into Chinese, minor adjustments, and the authentication of the appropriate authority. Thus, the tactical commander was relieved of practically all of his planning responsibilities in an effort to expedite an early execution of the operation.

"Operation Plan Evacuation North and South Dachen" was naturally an operation order. It defined Lieutenant General Liu's mission as follows: "Dachen Defense Command evacuates supplies, equipment, and personnel from North and South Dachen on order from the Commander, US Seventh Fleet."[15] Task organization for the operation was the Dachen Defense Command; the 46th Infantry Division, its principal subordinate unit; and the Zhejiang Provincial Government (ZPG) which had its seat in the Dachens. This document established the fact that "United States Forces will cover the evacuation and command all amphibious lift." It also appointed Chief, DDCAT as the "On-Shore Representative" of Commander, US Seventh Fleet.

The plan called for a four-phased evacuation. Phase I was to be devoted to the preparation and movement of heavy and bulky supplies, equipment and ammunition from depots to the loading beaches. Phase II would see the movement to the beaches of the islands' artillery and most of the Chinat vehicles; the evacuation of the civilian population; and the withdrawal of the Dachen Defense Command Headquarters, along with most of its attached units. In Phase III, the 46th Division, less its artillery and the covering forces, was to move to the beaches and load. Concluding phase of the operation, Phase IV, would be the withdrawal of the covering forces—a battalion each on North and South Dachen.

Chain of command during the operation was to be from the Commander, Seventh Fleet, to his On-Shore Representative (Colonel McConnell), to CG, Dachen Defense Command, with the latter responsible for the 46th Division, the ZPG, and those units belonging, or attached, to DDC. With the withdrawal of General Liu's headquarters, CO 46th Infantry Division would

---

14 Interviews: May 8, 1956, Colonel Walton; April 19, 1956, Major Aaron.
15 Operation Plan Evacuation of North and South Tachen, _____ January 1955, files of G3, Army Section (File No. 109).

assume command of all elements of the ZPG and those DDC units which were still ashore.

To the Provincial Government fell the task of determining the number of civilians to be evacuated and of providing for their security and control. ZPG, for the execution of these missions, was provided with detailed instructions in a separate annex to the operations plan entitled "Civilian Control and Evacuation." Each individual civilian was to be given free choice as to whether he or she elected to be evacuated or to remain on the Dachens. (The entire civilian population of these islands chose, with the permission of Lieutenant General Chiang Ching-Kuo, head of the Political Department, to migrate to Taiwan.) Persons desiring to leave with the Nationalists were to be organized by the civilian authorities into numbered units, each of which would contain 50 individuals. For each such civilian-platoon a leader was to be chosen. These individuals were required to carry "a two meter bamboo pole with distinctive banner or identification thereon." Companies were then to be formed, each of which would contain four civilian-platoons. Here again leaders were to be chosen and numerical designations assigned. Guidons to be carried by the company-leaders were to be three meters in length.

CG, DDC was made responsible for designating assembly areas for the evacuees and for ordering, at the appropriate time and through the Provincial Governor, their movement to the leading beaches. Food stocks were to be provided from military stores and each civilian was required to prepare three days rations (later changed to five) for use during the embarkation and movement portion of the evacuation. Total weight authorized for each evacuee in baggage was not to exceed 100 lbs. It was to consist of hand luggage only.

Other annexes to this plan provided an operations overlay, allocated transportation, detailed the procedures for beach loading, provided for the destruction of items that were not to be evacuated, detailed signal communication procedures, and provided an instruction sheet on "Conduct Aboard US Ships."

Among the annexes provided was one detailing the MAAG organization for the operation. In this, certain changes were required between the time that it was originally drafted and the plan's implementation. Most of the personnel involved were provided by Army Section though the now Dachen Defense Command Advisory Team had Navy, Marines, and Hq MAAG representatives in its ranks. Detailed below is the composition of this team as it finally evolved.

While these matters were developing in regard to the ground force portion of the forthcoming operation, both the Chinese Navy and the USN were far from idle. As soon as the decision had been made for US participation in the evacuation, Admiral Pride began the assembly of the necessary planning specialists. As a result, staff representatives of Commander, Amphibious

Group Western Pacific arrived at Keelung on the 24th for preliminary conferences with the Commander, US Seventh Fleet and his staff. American naval planning for the operation actually began on this date. The following day Commodore Franks, Commander, Amphibious Squadron No. 1 and elements of this staff arrived on Taiwan.[16]

At this time it was anticipated that the evacuation would begin momentarily, and the naval planners envisioned a two-phased operation. They looked for an evacuation of the civilian population of the Dachens on Chinese craft covered and protected by the combat elements of the Seventh Fleet and the Chinese Navy. For this phase of the operation one day was estimated as sufficient. Subsequently Chinese troops and supplies would be taken off the Dachens by US amphibious craft, which would likewise be protected by the combat elements of the two navies. American landing craft for the latter phase of the operation had to be gathered from points as far distant as Indochina.[17]

Meanwhile Seventh Fleet was working on its operation order (1–55) for the forthcoming evacuation. This was prepared well in advance of the time that it was ordered into execution. Opn O 1–55 established the fact that the USN was to be in command. Rear Admiral Lorenzo S. Sabin, Commander, Amphibious Group Western Pacific was designated Evacuation Force Commander and Commander, Combined Task Force 76. Immediately subordinate to him would be Commodore Franks of Amphibious Squadron No. 1, who had been designated as Embarkation Group Commander, Combined Tank Group 76.1, with the specific mission of preparing the Shore-to-Ship Embarkation Plan of Combined Tank Force 76, and then for executing the same.[18]

On the Chinese side, the Ministry of National Defense's deadline of January 30 for completion of naval and ground force planning was met: DDC's plans were submitted by the 28th: those of GHQ Navy arrived two days later. Commander in Chief, GHQ Navy had subdivided his plan (BOULEVARD) into three parts. BOULEVARD No. 1 concerned itself with the evacuation of civilians and guerrilla troops from North and South Dachen to Taiwan; BOULEVARD No. 2 directed the movement to Mazu of those guerrilla forces on the Yushans; BOULEVARD No. 3 laid down the procedures for evacuating to Nanchi the guerrilla forces holding the island of Pishan. For the execution of these tasks GHQ Navy brought into being Chinese Navy Task Force 85.[19]

---

16 Briefing, Commander, Amphibious Squadron No. 1, Amphibious Force, Pacific Fleet, undated, "Briefing Outline: Amphibious Operations—Embarkation Force," files of G3, Army Section (File No. 109) (CC), hereafter cited as "Briefings, CAS No. 1."

17 Interview, May 17, 1956, Lt. Col. Smart.

18 Ibid.

19 G3, MND Review.

Prior to the beginning of the operation it was necessary to dovetail the planning of all concerned Chinese and US agencies. This was accomplished by a series of conferences held during the last days of January and in the early part of the following month. As a consequence, the US portion of the undertaking was redesignated Operation KING KONG ABLE. BOULEVARD No. 1, the plan for Chinese operations on North and South Dachen, was rescinded and its provisions incorporated into Operation KING KONG CHARLIE; BOULEVARD No. 2 (the Yushans) and No. 3 (Pishan) were retitled, respectively, KING KONG B-1 and B-2. These were later combined as Operation KING KONG BAKER.[20] In addition to these changes in operation designation, these conferences brought about the following alterations in previously established basic concepts: loading would be accomplished on a 20-hour-a-day basis rather than just during daylight hours as had been the original MND idea; US forces would be responsible for the evacuation of all types of personnel from North and South Dachens (civilians, guerrillas, and regular troops); all guerrilla troops, regardless of the islands from which they lifted, would be evacuated to Taiwan.[21]

In the final analysis, all of Army Section's planning and adjustments thereto were completed by February 1; similar activities by the Chinese were concluded on the 5th of the month.[22] On the following day the Nationalist Government formally requested from the Government of the United States its aid and assistance in the redeployment of the troops holding the Dachens and in the evacuation of the civilian populations of these islands. Orders were immediately flashed to Commander US Seventh Fleet for the execution of previously prepared evacuation plans.[23] D-day was set for February 8.

On D-day CTF 76 was in the objective area by 0450 hours; at 1040 the first of the Dachen civilians started coming aboard.[24]

DDCAT becomes operational

From the point of view of the Dachen Defense Command Advisory Team, three major areas of responsibility existed: evacuation of the civilian

---

20 G3, MND Review; MND Directive (44) Ying Miao 129 (translation), January 31, 1955, "Supplementary Provisions and Revisions of Plan for Operation of King Kong," files of G3, Army Section (File No. 110).

21 G3, MND Review.

22 Rpt, DDCAT for Evac.

23 Rpt, Commander Seventh Fleet, April 10, 1955, "Report of the Evacuation of the Tachen Islands," copy in the files of G3, MAAG (CS).

24 Briefing, CAS No. 1.

population of North and South Dachen; destruction of existing military and civilian installations that might prove of value to the enemy, and of the military stores and equipment that could not be evacuated or were not worth being lifted from the Dachens; and lastly, evacuation of the military garrison along with its impedimenta.

Several days prior to the departure of the main body of the Dachen Defense Command Advisory Team from the port of Keelung, General Macdonald gathered the members of this team at Army Section for a final briefing. To them he stressed the importance of the mission that they were about to undertake, reminding them that they had been handpicked for this particular project. He impressed upon his advisors that they were to "go prepared for combat" and that capture was a distinct possibility. Should the latter occur, Chief, Army Section assured them that full legal protection would be afforded both to themselves and their families.[25]

Having stripped from their persons all documents and identifications not essential to the mission, the members of DDCAT departed for the Dachens on Sunday, February 6, 1955. For the moment, the team was broken into two echelons. While the main body departed by sea from Keelung at about 1500 hours aboard APD 124 (*Horace A. Bass*), an advance party moved by air to the objective area. The latter element consisted of Colonel McConnell, Lt. Col.[s] Sanford and Watkin, Lt. Comdr. Farwell, Major Riles, Captains Baade and Landrith. With this party went Major General Macdonald, who was to act as the Senior US Representative Ashore.[26] This air echelon left Shung shan about noon aboard a Foshing Air Lines amphibian piloted by Mr. Moon Chin. As planned, pursuit aircraft of the Seventh Fleet rendezvoused with the plane and escorted it part of the way to the Dachens[27] though, because of the heavy fog that blanketed Formosa Strait, the pilot and passengers never saw their fighter escort.

Finding the Dachens proved no small problem. Having missed these islands on the first approach, Moon Chin headed for the coast of the China mainland and then turned north through the fog guiding on the shoreline and flying practically "on the deck." This course was held until the pilot reached a point

25 Briefing notes in General Macdonald's handwriting, undated, "McConnell Command," files of G3, Army Section (File No. 109); Interview, April 27, 1956, Sfc Harold F. Swanson, PM Section, MAAG, Taipei, Taiwan.

26 Interview, May 1, 1956, Captain Thomas M. Constant, Secretary of the General Staff, Army Section, MAAG, Taipei, Taiwan.

27 For the entire Dachen operations US aircraft were responsible for operating from the 27th Parallel south to Taiwan, while Chinat air undertook all operations north of this line. Ibid.

south of Shanghai where the terrain was too familiar to be mistaken. With this
as a starting point, a new course, south along the shore, was flown until Moon
found the second landmark he sought: a peculiar ground formation which he
knew was situated exactly west of the Dachens. Here the amphibian turned
east, still only a dozen or so feet above the waves. Suddenly, out of the fog
loomed land. The plane was coming in between the two Dachens. Without
further incident a landing was made and the passengers were ferried ashore at
Beach Yellow 2 on the south shore of North Dachen.[28]

Evacuation of the civilians

Due to the thoroughness of the preparations that had been made by DDC and
the ZPG, evacuation of the civilian population of North and South Dachen
proceeded smoothly and without interruption. On D-Day, by 1800 hours on
North Dachen, and by 2100 hours on South Dachen, all of the refugees had
been embarked with the exception of some 190 loaders and sampan operators.
(These personnel were not lifted off the beaches until 0600 hours on the 10th
when their services in support of the military evacuation were no longer needed.)

At the Yushans and Pishan matters progressed equally satisfactory for the
Chinese Navy. By 1200 hours on D+1 the last of the civilians on those islands
had been removed.

In all, some 16,000 nonmilitary personnel were evacuated to Taiwan
from the Dachen Group.[29] At South Dachen, where the greatest number of
persons had to be loaded, operations were facilitated by the construction, by
the local inhabitants, of four improvised loading-causeways. Using sampans
as pontoons and planks and doors as flooring, these were projected as much
as 150 feet into the harbor. To no small extent these loading stages were
responsible for the speed with which the refugees were taken off the beaches.
They likewise contributed to the expeditious loading of military personnel
and lighter items of equipment in the succeeding phases of the operation.[30]

During the time that the civilians from North and South Dachen were
aboard US naval vessels, there was a total of two deaths among them, both

28 Interview, April 28, 1956, Lieutenant Colonel William W. Watkin, Jr., Engineer Section,
    MAAG, Taipei, Taiwan; Interview, May 1, 1956, Captain Thomas M. Constant,
    Secretary of the General Staff, Army Section, MAAG, Taipei, Taiwan.
29 Chief, DDCAT, in "Rpt, DDCAT for Evac," lists a total of 16,707 nonmilitary
    personnel evacuated; Commander, Amphibious Squadron No. 1, in "Briefing, CAS
    No. 1," lists a total of 15,627; Transportation Section, Army Section, in "Summary of
    Tachen Evacuation," February 14, 1955 (Files of said office), lists a total of 16, 105.
30 Rpt of DDCAT for Evac; Briefing, CAS No. 1.

attributable to natural causes. In addition, on February 8, there were three births. These babies "all were born healthy with no ill effects to the mother."[31]

The demolition program

Accompanied by Captain Landrith, the DDCAT engineer arrived on the Dachens with the advance party late on the afternoon of February 6. During what remained of the afternoon and that night, Lt. Col. Watkin and the naval and marine officers in the party conducted as detailed a reconnaissance as was possible of the beaches on North Dachen. This resulted in the decision to make the main evacuation effort over Beach Blue 1.[32] With Colonel Hu Sing, Commander of the 46th Division, arrangements were made to clear this beach of all mines and wire entanglements with the least possible delay; by noon the following day this had been accomplished. On this same afternoon, February 7, a US Marine Shore Party landed with organic, heavy engineer equipment. It assumed responsibility for all beaches that were to be used. Thus the DDCAT engineer and his assistants were left free to concentrate on the demolitions program for North and South Dachen.[33]

Upon investigation it developed that the engineer troops available for demolition work on North and South Dachen consisted of the 46th Division's Engineer Battalion, a guerrilla engineer company of some 100 officers and men, plus three NGRC officers and 27 enlisted demolition specialists that MND had dispatched to the Dachens. For this force Major Chi Co, 46th Engineer battalion, had prepared an excellent plan of operation. First, he had divided the islands of North and South Dachen into three sectors which exactly coincided with the regimental sectors of the 46th Division. In charge of each he placed one of his own officers. To each of these commanders he assigned one of the demolition experts from Taiwan as an advisor. Next, the available engineer personnel were apportioned among the three sectors; within each they were formed into demolition teams and to each a specified area of responsibility was given. Meanwhile, on a large-scale map, all known demolition targets had been plotted and numbered. From this map the assignment of demolition areas had been made to the individual teams.

Prior to the arrival of Lt. Col. Watkin, the charges required for each target had been computed and the available store of explosive material had been inventoried. The latter were found to be more than ample for the tasks at

---

31 Briefing, CAS No. 1.
32 Interview, April 28, 1956, Lt. Col. W. W. Watkin, Jr.
33 Rpt, DDCAT for Evac.

hand. In fact, sufficient reserve would remain after the demolition of those known targets to destroy any ammunition that was not to be evacuated.

Further inquiry revealed that the Division Engineer had arranged for the establishment of demolition supply points at strategic locations in each of the regimental sectors, for transportation, and for labor details sufficient to move these stocks into position.

Obviously Major Wang needed little in the way of advice. This being the case, the MAAG advisors concentrated on assisting the Division Engineer in the implementation of his plan in which they wholeheartedly concurred.

On February 8, the demolition forces available to the Division Engineer were reinforced considerably with the arrival of the USN's Underwater Demolition Team (UDT) No. 11. After conferences between the Chinese and American commanders, it was decided to give approximately one-third of the targets in each demolition sector to UDT No. 11, which was to be under the control of the DDCAT engineer. To his direct subordinates—the engineer advisors with him—Lt. Col. Watkin "assigned areas of advisory responsibility to supervise the work of the US demolition teams and coordinate their work with that of the Chinese engineers."[34] To avoid confusion and to circumvent the language problem, separate supply points were established for the UDT personnel in each sector.[35]

Due to the amount of demolition work facing Major Wang's forces, it was obviously impractical to attempt the performance of all scheduled destruction during the withdrawal of the covering force as originally planned. Therefore, authority was delegated to the Demolition Sector Commanders to begin "shooting" on February 9, commencing at 1400 hours. Twenty-nine hours later, or at 1900 hours on the 10th, all planned demolitions had been completed with the exception of the destruction scheduled for the Ta-Ao-Li area near Beach Blue 1. Here the safety factor prohibited work at this time; however, charges were set though not touched off until the 11th.

For this operation, the Chinese forces were under orders to evacuate all weapons and ammunition. With this Chief, DDCAT did not agree. On the Dachens were eighteen 120mm mortars for which DDC had some 200 tons of ammunition. These weapons were "worn and unstable"; their ammunition, which was years old, was known to have erratic muzzle velocities. Consequently, the American advisors recommended destruction rather than evacuation. To this the Chinese authorities did not accede. Consequently, valuable shipping space was wasted on this worthless materiel. In part this was responsible for

---

34 Rpt, DDCAT for Evac.
35 Interview, April 28, 1956, Lt. Col. Watkin.

the amount of other types of ammunition that had to be destroyed. Thus, on February 11, a five-man US team set charges under some 250 tons of ammunition of all calibers and that night, following the withdrawal of all other forces, executed this last demolition project.

DDCAT's Chief, Colonel McConnell, summarized the demolition phase of the operation as follows:

> The presence of an unusually competent Division Engineer and the availability of highly trained US demolition personnel enabled the execution of a very well conceived demolition plan. It was the most gratifying performance of Chinese engineering troops that MAAG advisors have witnessed. Approximately 30 tons of explosives were detonated in some 1400 separate shots on two busy and heavily populated islands without any serious injury resulting. All useful military installations were destroyed as well as all known unevacuated ammunition with the exception of 10 tons of small arms ammunition on the S. Dachen and 20 tons of 120mm mortar ammunition on N. Dachen, both so located as to preclude safe and complete destruction.[36]

The evacuation of the 46th Infantry Division

Colonel McConnell's plan for the employment of his advisory team called for the assignment of one infantry officer to accompany each of the regiments of the 46th Infantry Division and for the assignment of an American artillery advisor to the division's artillery. To the 137th Infantry Regiment he assigned Lieutenant Colonel Gail B. Lee; to the 138th, Major John O. Shoemaker; to the 250th, Captain Bill R. Blalock; and to the 46th Division Artillery, Captain Arthur T. Paul, Jr. These officers, along with the rest of the sea echelon of the Dachen Defense Command Advisory Team, had departed Taipei on Sunday, February 6, arriving off the Dachens at approximately 0600 hours the following morning. By 0830 they were ashore on Beach Blue 1. Meanwhile, the evacuation fleet (CTF 76) was still at sea and not scheduled to reach the Dachens until the following morning, February 8, 1955, which was D-day. *Bass* had made the run from Keelung accompanied by only one destroyer escort.[37]

The experiences of all three of the regimental advisers and of the division artillery adviser bore a marked resemblance. Upon joining their units these officers discovered that, while certain preparations were underway for the

---

36 Rpt, DDCAT for Evac.
37 Interview, May 1, 1956, Captain Constant; Interview, April 26, 1956, Major John O. Shoemaker, G3 Section, Army Section, MAAG, Taipei, Taiwan.

forthcoming operation, their commanders were in considerable doubt as to just what was expected of them. In the 138th Regiment, the CO protested that he was unaware that an evacuation was intended. He and his troops were prepared, and anxious, he claimed, to defend their positions. In no time at all it had been conclusively ascertained that the subordinate units of the 46th Division had received no orders to evacuate.[38]

Further inquiry proved, just as clearly, that the fault was not that of the Division Commander. He, too, was still awaiting orders.

Meanwhile, General Macdonald and Colonel McConnell, in their first conference with General Liu, were exploring the same startling subject. To his satisfaction, Chief, Army Section established the fact that, while General Liu had received the plans forwarded by MND for the evacuation of the civilian population, he was in receipt of no orders for the execution of this plan. In preparing a cable to Chief, MAAG in Taipei on this matter, General Macdonald wrote: "Gen Liu should receive order for total evacuation. Explained again (sic) Gen Liu has received plan to evacuate civilians only. He needs orders repeat orders to evacuate both civilian and military personnel and equipment to carry out recommended plan."[39]

Nevertheless, from the highest to the lowest Chinese echelon on the Dachens, wholehearted cooperation was given to the American advisors from the time that they stepped ashore. Even in the absence of specific orders from MND, the Chinese recognized, and accepted, the fact that there would be an evacuation and that the Americans were in charge. What was humanly possible for the Chinese units to do was done.[40]

Based on the plans that had been prepared by Army Section, copies of which DDCAT had carried to Dachen, the advisors, by their urgings, assistance, and sometimes by actually doing the job themselves, succeeded in producing within each unit the plans that were needed. It must of course be understood that changes and alterations to these plans were the norm rather than the exception. As loading progressed more rapidly than was expected, or was retarded by unforeseen difficulties, equipment and troops were diverted from congested to less occupied beaches. It was a situation that, particularly in the latter stages of the loading of equipment, was played "by ear" to a considerable extent.[41]

---

38 Ibid.
39 Interview, May 1, 1956 Captain Constant; Notes (in General Macdonald's handwriting), undated, text of cable to Chief, MAAG, document in personal possession of Capt. T. M. Constant.
40 Interview, April 26, 1956, Major Shoemaker.
41 Ibid.

Typical of the situation is the following comment from Colonel McConnell's final report on the operation:

> Decision NOT to use RED Beach at once affected planning and execution of ammunition evacuation tremendously. Ammunition had been carried to central points, many of which were adjacent to RED Beaches. Part of this ammunition was moved to BLUE Beach because of the priority of types. Then the decision to open RED Beach made it necessary to move by hand to RED Beach ammunition stacked for truck evacuation to BLUE Beach. This, of course, resulted in understandable confusion. Then after Chinese LCM boats had been promised for the evacuation of his ammunition from RED #2, all of our efforts not withstanding, over 40 tons were left and had to be destroyed due to inability of our control parties to obtain two Chinese LCM boats although many were tiedup (sic) at the causeway pontoon not being used through all MAAG combined efforts to obtain their use.[42]

Major Shoemaker, just prior to midnight on the 11th, found that he still had more than 18 tons of TDAP ammunition on Beach Red 2 on the west coast of North Dachen. At this beach there was no Naval Shore Party. The night was extremely foggy. Withdrawal of Combined Task Force 76 was scheduled for that very night. For Beach Red 2 there was only one more tide on which equipment could be evacuated. This was fast approaching. However, the Chinese landing craft scheduled for this lift had not made their appearance. They were, in fact, long overdue.

Having protested vigorously in the previous days against the evacuation of old Japanese ammunition over this beach, in preference to the newer and more critically needed MDAP supplies, the 138th's Regimental Advisor was determined that this material should not be abandoned.

By radio he learned that the Chinese landing craft had returned to their base off Blue 1 upon failing to find his beach in the fog. Requests for another attempt produced no results.

Having made arrangements with the 138th's beach party to build fires that would serve as beacons, Major Shoemaker took a jeep and made his way through the fog, over the ill-defined and muddy roads of North Dachen, to the southern end of the island where the landing craft were berthed. There he demanded that the crews be roused and that another attempt be made. When the coxswains protested that they could not find his beach in the fog, he volunteered to relieve them of their responsibility.

---

42 Rpt, DDCAT for Evac.

Assuring positions in one of the craft located in the center of the tiny armada, by hand and arm signals when they were visible, by shouts in English and pidgin Chinese, Major Shoemaker shepherded those craft to the waters off Red 2. Thanks to the improvised beacons, and to no small degree of luck, the landing craft were brought into position and beached two at a time since the beach could accommodate only this number. Loading began immediately. With little time to spare, these craft pulled off as the tide ebbed—aboard were all 18 tons of MDAP ammunition.[43]

While the morning tide on the 12th of February had been the target date originally planned for completion of the evacuation, on February 10, Commander, US Seventh Fleet issued orders for completion of the operation by the last tide of that night since the cost of keeping the entire Seventh Fleet "steaming" was mounting fast.

DDCAT, and General Macdonald in particular, received this change in plan with something akin to dismay. Obviously it would be impossible to get out everything of value. When, later that same morning, General Chase and Ambassador Rankin visited the Dachens, Chief, Army Section approached his superior on the possibility of securing additional time to complete the evacuation. Chief, MAAG, then gave permission for direct negotiations with Commander, Seventh Fleet, whereupon General Macdonald, accompanied by his aide, Captain Thomas M. Constant, proceeded to the U.S.S. Helena, Admiral Pride's flagship.

At lunch aboard the Helena the matter was discussed at length and DDCAT was given an additional 24 hours in which to complete operations ashore. Thus, the evening tide on the 11th became the new target deadline.

Despite this reprieve, deviation from the original plan caused considerable trouble ashore. By darkness on the 11th there were literally thousands of troops in the Ta-Ao-Li area of Beach Blue 1, the principal evacuation beach on North Dachen, and more were pouring into the area. In addition, there were still tons of equipment to be taken out.[44]

On Blue 1, heavy equipment moved from the beach to a steel, floating deck of Navy pontoon-cubes, and from this to landing craft. At approximately 2330 hours, on the night of the 11th, the two D-7 tractors that were supposed to be the last items of heavy equipment brought off began to move onto the causeway. Unbeknownst to the advisors, the Chinese had hooked two ¾ ton trucks, which were incapable of moving under their own power, to the last of these. Each of the trucks was loaded with all the miscellaneous gear they would hold. Under this concentrated weight, connections between two of the

43 Interview, April 26, 1956, Major Shoemaker.
44 Interview, April 28, 1956 Lt. Col. Watkin; Interview, May 1, 1956, Capt. Constant.

cubes broke. It resulted in a difference of some six feet of elevation between the levels of the broken causeway, with one of the tractors and the two trucks on the landward side of the break. Considerable time was lost in an attempt to remedy the predicament. When all else failed, the two trucks were pushed over the side and the sections of causeway brought to approximately the same level by skillful positioning of a D-7 on either side of the rupture. An improvised connection was then made and both tractors were finally moved to the end of the causeway and loaded.[45]

However, this was not the end of trouble on this hectic night. In the latter stages of the troop loading, a goodly portion of DDCAT wound up on the end of the steel causeway. Through the rain and the darkness, seemingly endless lines of troops staggered and slipped down the length of the floating pier. Bicycle carts, loaded with crew-served weapons and equipment, were frequent in the column. Having been engaged for days on end in man-handling cases of ammunition from the hills down to the loading beaches, the troops were bordering on absolute exhaustion. Weighted down as they were with individual weapons and equipment, many did not have the strength to clamber into the landing craft. In the final hours of the evacuation, much of the advisory effort was devoted to physically loading into the boats men to[o] weak and numb to take the last few steps. While the actions of the American personnel were far from gentle, and many a Chinese private and non-commissioned officer was heaved into his transport like a sack of meal, the end seemed to justify the means.[46]

Finally, at about 0200 hours on the morning of the 12th, the beach was clear of personnel and equipment. Beneath the last LST, the largest vessel of its class in the USN at that time, the tide was ebbing fast. Off the Dachens, all of CTF 76 waited for word that this final vessel had cleared and joined that movement to Taiwan could begin. She rode heavily laden as her skipper reversed his engines to pull off. The ship shuddered, groaned, and slowly began to move. Then, as he gathered momentum, she rammed fast on a mudbank. There the LST hung, some 400 yards offshore. All efforts of her master and crew proved fruitless. The tide slipped from beneath her: there was nothing to do but wait for morning and the next tide.[47]

From the point of view of the MAAG advisors, the accident was not without its benefits. Both Chief, Army Section and Colonel McConnell, from the very first, had been most anxious to have sufficient time to police thoroughly all of the area to ensure that nothing of value was left for the enemy. Hence,

45 Interview, April 28, 1956, Lt. Col. Watkin.
46 Ibid.
47 Ibid; Interview, April 30, 1956, Major Shoemaker.

with daylight, parties were put ashore to conduct final checks. As a result several generators that were still ashore were destroyed. Also, a large portion of the hillside above Beach Blue 1 was blasted away and dropped to the beach proper.[48]

About mid-morning, the tide being right, the LST began its next attempt to free itself. This time it succeeded, but in the process fouled its propeller in some unmarked, submerged cable on the harbor bottom. A diver had to be sent over the side. Finally, late on the afternoon of the 12th, the last element of CTF 76 struggled free of the Dachens.[49]

Conclusion of the evacuation

With the withdrawal of the covering forces on North and South Dachen, and the demolition of what stocks of ammunition had to be abandoned, the ground forces' portion of the operation drew to a close. Viewed objectively, the operation had been a complete success. That there had not been opposition from the Chinese Communists contributed most materially to what had been achieved, and to the speed with which it had been achieved. In summary, all of the civilian population had been evacuated. Well over 10,000 members of the Nationalist armed forces, along with their vehicles and artillery, had been embarked.[50] Nothing of military value was left standing on the islands of North and South Dachen. Also, between 8,000 and 10,000 tons of ammunition and supplies had been moved to the ports of Taiwan.[51]

Time had proven the accuracy of General Chase's 1951 estimates of the basic qualities of the Chinese soldier for Colonel McConnell was lavish in his praise:

> The Chinese soldier was magnificent. His morale was high, he worked long hours under very adverse conditions. They reported to a United States linguist that they had not been informed that they were being evacuated to Formosa, but when they saw the US ships, they knew that the evacuation was in progress. The absence of enemy air and artillery harassment increased their morale. Their cooperation was to the extent

---

48 Interview, April 28, 1956, Lt. Col. Watkin.

49 Ibid.

50 Chief, DDCAT reported a total of 13,701 army personnel evacuated (Rpt, DDCAT for Evac); Commander, Amphibious Squadron No. 1 set the number of military evacuees at 11,120 (Briefing, CAS No. 1); Rpt, Transportation Section, Army Section, February 14, 1955 "Summary of Tachen Evacuation" (Files of Transportation Section), lists 14,216 military.

51 G3, MND Review.

of each man's physical and mental ability. Nothing more could have been desired.[52]

Unfortunately, this operation revealed that many of the early criticisms of the first Chief, MAAG still applied. Control was still overcentralized: commanders were still being given grave responsibilities without the authority to exercise initiative and freedom of action in the execution of same. Strict compliance with the very letter of the order was still the norm. This factor was pointed up repeatedly when Colonel Hu of the 46th Division had to defer to DDC before making what were obviously logical deviations from the wording of the instruction. Absence of decentralization actually jeopardized the operation by the delays that it occasioned. Had the evacuation been opposed by the Communists, failure might well have been the result.

The advisors found Headquarters, Taiwan Defense Command a stumbling block rather than an asset throughout the operation. Certainly, it should have been phased out with the evacuation of the civil population as called for in KING KONG ABLE. However, it remained in being. From this point onward it exerted a detrimental influence on the operation: "There was (sic) perhaps 150 persons standing around observing members of the 46th Division working on Blue beach. These were mostly DDC Headquarters personnel who would not work, did not supervise and provided excuse and cover for 46th Division personnel who desired to shirk work."[53]

Within the 46th Division criticisms were somewhat similar. Here the principal complaints were against the failure of commanders to decentralize to their staffs functions that rightly belonged in the hands of such officers. In this regard the division reflected the headquarters to which it was subordinated. The division commander, and his regimental commanders, proved repeatedly that they could control their units and that they possessed the ability to react quickly to constant fluctuations in the plan.

The attachment of one unit to another caused considerable trouble on South Dachen where the 336th Field Artillery Battalion was subordinated to the 137th Infantry Regiment for the evacuation. Neither of the concerned commanders could initially bring himself to believe that the artillery battalion commander was no longer under the control of 46th Division Artillery. In all sincerity, the CO of the infantry regiment assured the Artillery Adviser that he had no responsibility for providing for the transportation or the movement of this attached battalion. On the other hand, "The artillery battalion commander, confronted with a confusing situation, showed no initiative in

---

52 Rpt, DDCAT for Evac.
53 Rpt, DDCAT for Evac.

seeking clarification."[54] It took the concerned advisors to straighten out the situation.

Lack of adequate preventive maintenance on vehicles, as in the early days of MAAG, came in for considerable comment by DDCAT. Evacuation plans were predicated on using all available vehicles to the maximum extent up to the time scheduled for their evacuation. The fact that breakdowns were frequent resulted in a great reduction in the amount of transportation actually dispatched to the regiments when compared with what they had been allocated. Apropos of this situation, the 138th Infantry throughout the operation "never received more than 50% of the trucks allocated and the last day [...] it received none."[55] Obviously little progress had been made in this area of the endeavor over the previous three and one-half years of MAAG's existence.

Akin to the problem of vehicle maintenance was that of traffic control. Here, too, much was left to be desired. Colonel McConnell pronounced traffic control on the Dachens "ineffective." On at least one occasion General Macdonald spent better than an hour in the vicinity of Ta-Ao-Li personally unsnarling a traffic jam and acting as an MP.[56]

Nevertheless, and despite the deficiencies that were uncovered, the operation was a success. The mission of evacuating Nationalist personnel, supplies and equipment from the Dachens had been accomplished.

Conclusions

Operation King Kong was carried out almost without a hiccup. Although a huge operational success, the 1955 decision to evacuate the Dachens had a serious psychological impact on the Nationalists, since it gravely undermined Nationalist morale. During US–British talks in February 1955, the importance of Nationalist morale was emphasized by Admiral Stump and Dulles to their British colleagues:

> Admiral Stump explained to Eden defense relationship between offshore islands and Taiwan. They block launching attack on Taiwan, provide advance warning and are closer to hostile area in case of fighting. Field Marshal Harding interjected to differ with Stump. Comparing situation to Allied assault in Operation Overlord, Harding expressed opinion

---

54 Rpt, DDCAT for Evac.
55 Ibid..
56 Interview, May 1, 1956, Captain Constant.

critical question is not launching or lodging initial attack across water but in being able afterwards sustain assault forces. He thought Chinese Communists military leaders would advise against attack on Taiwan as long as Seventh Fleet commanded sea and air. Hence he did not (repeat not) believe possession offshore islands would have much to do with whether Chinese Communists would or would not attack Taiwan.[57]

Later, during a July 17 meeting between Eisenhower and Eden, Ike emphasized the symbolic value of the offshore islands to Chiang. He warned that "another single backward step in the region would have the gravest effects on all of our Chinese friends," and then was able to report of the meeting that Eden "had no trouble understanding the importance of morale in Chiang's army on Formosa."[58]

After the evacuation, the Flag of the Republic of China in the Dachen Islands was lowered by Chiang Ching-kuo, Chiang Kai-shek's son. The Zhejiang provincial government was also abolished in the Republic of China. This meant that Nationalist forces now held disputed mainland territory only in Fujian province. Rather than pushing the United States and Taiwan further apart, however, as Beijing had undoubtedly hoped would happen, cooperation during the evacuation of the Dachens unexpectedly led to closer relations between Washington and Taipei. The possible use of force to protect the other offshore islands was detailed in the Formosa Resolution. After the successful evacuation, Vice Admiral A. M. Pride was awarded the Distinguished Service Medal.

---

57 Telegrams from Dulles to Eisenhower, TOP SECRET, February 25, 1955, DH 4, Dulles, J.F., February 1955 (1).
58 Notes dictated by the President regarding his conversation with Sir Anthony Eden, held Sunday, July 17, in the afternoon, July 19, 1955, DDE Diary Series 11, DDE Diary July 1955 (1).

Chapter 5

THE SECOND TAIWAN STRAIT CRISIS, 1958

Tensions between the PRC and Taiwan remained high after the first Taiwan Strait crisis in 1954–55. The Nationalist blockade of the PRC continued, albeit at a reduced level, after the Dachens were evacuated. The blockade halted a lower percentage of international shipping with the PRC, since its range was more strictly limited to southeast China. However, the combined effects of the blockade plus the US-sponsored strategic embargo, which lasted until 1971, had a significant impact. To make up for the loss of international seaborne commerce, the PRC was forced to turn to the Soviet Union, conducting an ever larger share of trade via the trans-Siberian railway.

During the late 1950s, the PRC sought to break away from its overreliance on the USSR. China's debts to the USSR were equal to well over a billion US dollars, with one estimate of China's total debt equaling $1.5 billion rubles (almost $2 billion in 1962 dollars).[1] In 1957, there was increasing opposition by the British, Japanese, Germans, Canadians, and French to the Chinese sanctions. In early May 1957, the British argued that the "China differential should be completely abolished."[2] Dulles wrote to Foreign Minister Selwyn Lloyd, offering to try to meet Britain halfway, but that: "In our opinion, this differential has a real significance in retarding the buildup of Communist China's vast military potential."[3]

A similar message from Eisenhower to Prime Minister Macmillan warned "that many of the items which you would take off the China list will in fact appreciably help the Chinese Communists to build up the military potential which threatens us in this area and which we have the primary responsibility to

---

1 Frank Dikötter, *Mao's Great Famine: The History of China's Most Devastating Catastrophe, 1958–1962* (New York: Walker, 2010), 105.
2 Staff Notes No. 107, SECRET, May 4, 1957, DDE Diary 24, May 1957 Diary, Staff Memos, DDEPL.
3 Draft of Suggested Message from the Secretary of State to Foreign Minister Selwyn Lloyd, SECRET, May 17, 1957, JFD Papers, W.H. Memo, Box 6, Meeting Press 1957 (5), DDEPL.

resist."[4] Occurring as it did in the midst of the Nationalist retightening of the blockade, the second Taiwan Strait crisis during 1958 was linked to the PRC goal of halting the blockade once and for all, and thereby diversify its international trade away from the USSR. To try to catch up with the West, Mao Zedong even adopted unsound economic policies like the 1958 "Great Leap Forward," which eventually produced a nationwide famine that killed millions of average Chinese. Beijing's renewed attacks during 1958 on Jinmen—the Nationalists' main blockade base—put extreme pressure on Taiwan.

The gradual decline of the Nationalist blockade

During the early 1950s, the US government supported the Nationalist blockade, in particular when its enforcement helped to strengthen the US-led strategic embargo of the PRC. During the year-and-a-half between 1954 and mid-1955, there were 35 reported incidents against British shipping; the number of serious attacks from the sea (9), land (2), and air (3) dropped to a total of 14, however, with no reported deaths or casualties.[5] The British government opposed the blockade with its own Formosa patrol, and in 1957 even announced that it was planning to increase trade with China. The British Formosa Strait Patrol, unlike its American counterpart, operated more sporadically during the mid-1950s. Usually one Royal Navy ship was engaged on a patrol, and each patrol only lasted two to three days. During a five-month period in late 1954, for example, only seven ships patrolled the Taiwan Strait, each for two to three days, which meant that ships were only present during 24 out of about 150 days, or about 16 percent of the period.[6]

Unlike the complex duties carried out by USN vessels, which included patrolling, training, and morale-building, the Royal Navy sought to protect British shipping from interference by the Nationalists and their guerrilla allies. One sure sign of the British patrol's impact appeared on September 8, 1955, when the Nationalist government's Department of Defence ordered that "attacks on shipping off the coast of China must in future be confined to Communist vessels, and that no (repeat no) neutral ships are to be molested unless this is 'unavoidable in the inherent right of self-defence'." This sole exception citing "self-defence" would appear to be covering a hypothetical

4 Draft of Suggested Message from the President to Prime Minister Macmillan, Secret, May 17, 1957, JFD Papers, W.H. Memo, Box 6, Meeting Press 1957 (5), DDEPL.
5 "Incidents involving British merchant Ships off the China Coast," July 18, 1955, The National Archives, Kew, ADM 116/6245.
6 Letter from A. H. E. Allingham to P. Wilkinson, Far Eastern Department, Foreign Office, March 24, 1955, The National Archives, Kew, ADM 1/26157.

situation where a neutral vessel "happened to be in the way of a *bona fide* attack on a Communist vessel."[7]

During spring 1956, the US government tried its best to deescalate tensions. As Dulles told Eisenhower after a March visit to Taiwan, he did not find "any feeling that an all-out Chicom assault was likely in the early future." As a result of the lower threat level, he concluded: "From my talks with the US Country Team I think there is a somewhat excessive tendency on the part of the Chinats to aggravate the situation by minor plane and artillery initiatives, and I think we should try to bring this under closer control."[8] Although British-flagged vessels continued to be stopped and searched from time to time, during July 1956 the British consulate in Taiwan reported that so far that year no British ship had "sustained damage or casualties as a result of Nationalist air and naval action or by shore batteries from coastal islands."[9] Almost a year after that, in May 1957, it was further reported that since December 1955: "No British ships have been damaged and there have been no casualties."[10]

After numerous US–UK talks, covering several years, there was no agreement on how to adjust the trade restriction regime with China. On May 24, 1957, Eisenhower wrote one final plea to Prime Minister Harold Macmillan not to change the Chinese trade differential:

> As an individual I agree with you that there is very little of profit in the matter either for your country or for any other. Commercially, it affects this nation not at all, for the simple reason that we have a total embargo on Chinese trade. However, many of our people think that the free nations could make a terrific psychological blunder in this matter and possibly even lose all the areas of the Southeast [Asia] that have strong Chinese minorities.
>
> We understand your predicament and even though we may be compelled, in the final result, to differ sharply in our official positions, I think that each of our Governments should strive to prevent the possible popular

---

7 Telegram from the United States to the UK informing them of the Nationalist order to halt attacks on neutral shipping, September 8, 1955, The National Archives, Kew, ADM 116/6245.

8 Telegram from Seoul, Korea, from Secretary of State Dulles to President Eisenhower, SECRET, March 19, 1956, Dulles-Herter 6, JFD March 1956, DDEPL.

9 Telegram from Tamsui, Formosa, to Foreign Office, July 6, 1956, The National Archives, Kew, ADM 116/6245.

10 Telegram from Tamsui, Formosa, to Foreign Office, May 31, 1957, The National Archives, Kew, ADM 116/6245.

conclusion in its own country that we are committed to going "separate ways."[11]

Macmillan ignored this plea and the British announced that they would diversify its trade with China. The British government broke with the US embargo policy by shipping a wider range of goods to the PRC. In response, the Nationalist government increased its blockade efforts. On June 7, 1957, the Nationalist Minister for Foreign Affairs pledged that the Taiwan "Government would stand firm on its mainland port closure order whether or not Britain used warships to escort merchant ships sailing into Communist ports."[12] On June 15, 1957, the US government cautioned Taiwan:

> We are advising the GRC [Government of the Republic of China] that while we recognize the importance to them of preventing the shipment of strategic materials to Communist China, their own interest calls for caution in intercepting foreign commercial shipping, particularly British, in the Taiwan Strait. We shall point out that a serious incident involving a free world ship could seriously hurt the Nationalists.[13]

By 1958, the Nationalist blockade of the PRC had been underway for almost 10 years. A combination of British protests, plus the presence of the Royal Navy, gradually limited the usefulness of the Nationalist blockade against British shipping. The US government was also less willing to support the Nationalist effort. During June 1957, after years of internal debate and discussion, the British government finally decided to eliminate its support for the US-led embargo. Beginning in early 1958, the total size of the Sino-British trade, plus the total number of items traded, began to increase dramatically. This prompted the US Embassy in Taipei to warn during summer 1957 that "the Chinese Communists may wish to neutralize it [Jinmen] in order to facilitate a greater use of the harbor following the British action on trade controls."[14] PRC attempts to "neutralize" Jinmen resulted in the second Taiwan Strait crisis.

---

11 Letter from President Eisenhower to Prime Minister Macmillan, TOP SECRET, May 24, 1957, DDE Diary 24, May 1957 Misc. (2), DDEPL.

12 Telegram from Tamsui, Formosa, to Foreign Office, June 9, 1957, The National Archives, Kew, ADM 116/6245.

13 The White House, Staff Notes No. 131, Secret, June 15, 1957, DDE Diary 25, June 1957 Diary Staff Memos, DDEPL.

14 John Foster Dulles Papers, Princeton University, Reel 217/218, June 26, 1957, 97827.

The second Taiwan Strait crisis, 1958

As the US Embassy had predicted, one of the PRC's top priorities in 1958 was to increase its trade with Britain. The key to making this new policy work was to undermine the effectiveness of the Nationalist base on Jinmen. Since the mid-1950s, an estimated 750,000 PLA troops had been permanently stationed along the mainland coast opposite the offshore islands. This deployment was a constant drain and "definitely slowed down military probing that Communists might otherwise have been inclined to do."[15] The PRC's "first objective" during the second Taiwan Strait crisis "was to deter the Nationalists from using the offshore islands for harassment of the mainland, or as a base for a future invasion of the mainland."[16]

On August 23, 1958, Communist forces began shelling Jinmen, using an estimated 40,000 shells during the first attack. Dulles told Eisenhower that even an early estimate of 25,000 rounds seemed "exaggerated," but even "if it was only half that it would still be serious."[17] The British decision to liberalize trade with China was an important contributing factor. For example, during August 1958, Prince Norodom Sihanouk, the president of the Council of Ministers of Cambodia, visited China to mediate with Mao Zedong and Zhou Enlai, and in mid-September he explained to Walter S. Robertson, Assistant Secretary to the US Mission to the UN, that the PRC leaders were "concerned by the fact that the offshore islands are being used to mount Commando attacks on the mainland and to impose a blockade."[18]

Immediately after the shelling began, the Nationalists requested full US military support. But Eisenhower rejected the notion that the United States had no choice but to defend the offshore islands:

> The President said there is no military reason for the Chinese Nationalists to hold the offshore islands, just as there is no military advantage that the Chinese Communists would gain from them from an attack on Taiwan. However, we have to take our decision not on the basis of our military evaluation, but on an evaluation of the moral[e] factor.[19]

---

15 UK Consulate, Tamsui, to Foreign Office, January 27, 1958, The National Archives, Kew, FO 371/33522.

16 Joseph F. Bouchard, *Command in Crisis: Four Case Studies* (New York: Columbia University Press, 1991), 59.

17 Telephone Calls, August 23, 1958, DDE Herter, CAH Tel Calls, Box 11, CAH Tel Calls 7/1/58-9/30/58 (1), DDEPL.

18 "Memorandum of Conversation," September 16, 1958, *China; 1958–1960*, vol. XIX, *FRUS* (Washington, DC: Government Printing Office, 1996), 201–3.

19 Memorandum of Conference with the President, TOP SECRET, August 14, 1958, DDE Diary 35, August 1958, Staff Notes (2), 1–3, DDEPL.

Dulles agreed with this view, stating that if "Quemoy and Matsu were lost, the Chinese Nationalists do not consider that they could hold Formosa. Morale would crumble and Chiang's control would be lost. [...] The loss of Formosa would in his opinion be a mortal blow to our position in the Far East."[20] There was great fear that the Soviets would become involved: "The President said we should not be drawn into spreading out the area of conflict, and thereby probably bringing the USSR in to render support to its principal ally, thus leading to general war. We must try to define fixed limits to the action."[21]

On August 27, 1958, Chiang Kai-shek sent Eisenhower a long letter describing the PRC attack on Jinmen, including shelling, strafing by Communist MiG planes, and the "sinking and damaging of two vessels" involved in evacuating the wounded. He specifically asked for three actions: a US declaration invoking the Formosa Resolution, assigning the USN to convoy vessels from Taiwan to Jinmen and Mazu, plus giving the local MAAG officer "appropriate authority to make decisions when the United States and Chinese Governments hold consultations on military operation in pursuance of the exchange of notes following the signing of the mutual defense treaty." He also reminded the president that he had upheld his part of the 1954 secret exchange of notes: "I am sure that Your Excellency is aware of the fact that we have never once made any provocative move against the Communists in the Taiwan straits during the past three years because of the Sino-American mutual defense treaty relationship."[22]

But Eisenhower was determined not to escalate the incident. In response to Chiang's claims the Nationalists were too weak, it was "suggested that Chiang may be using this line to gain leverage on us."[23] As for invoking the Formosa Resolution, on August 29, 1958, President Eisenhower told Governor Herter: "The President said he did not wish to put ourselves on the line with a full commitment. The Orientals can be very devious; they would then call the tune."[24] Vice Admiral Roland N. Smoot, the Commander of the United States Taiwan Defense Command from 1958 to 1962, had no choice, therefore, but

---

20 Memorandum of Conference with the President, TOP SECRET, August 12, 1958, DDE Diary 35, August 1958, Staff Notes (2), 1–2, DDEPL.

21 Memorandum of Conference with the President, TOP SECRET, August 14, 1958, DDE Diary 35, August 1958, Staff Notes (2), 1–3, DDEPL.

22 Telegraphed letter from Chiang Kai-shek to President Eisenhower, August 27, 1958, DDE AWF, Int. Series 11, Formosa (China), 1958–61 (3), DDEPL.

23 Memorandum of Conference with the President, August 29, 1958, DDE AWF Int. Series 11, Formosa (3), 1–2, DDEPL.

24 Memorandum of Conference with the President, August 25, 1958, DDE Diary 35, August 1958, Staff Notes (1), 2, DDEPL.

to tell Chiang that according to the US–ROC defense treaty "we would not be directly involved in this affair."[25]

The PRC attack on Jinmen eventually drew in the Seventh Fleet, but only in a supporting role. A USIA foreign public opinion poll determined that "Nationalist China would greatly increase its world stature if it were able to handle the [PRC] threat itself."[26] General Taylor and Admiral Burke reported to Eisenhower that Chiang had already allocated "one-third of the effective Chinese Nationalist forces" to his defense of the offshore islands, and that the Nationalists "given the will [...] could hold out against interdiction." Artillery alone could not push the Nationalist troops off the islands: "No amount of artillery fire nor of bombing would by themselves occupy the Islands for the Communists; therefore a major element in the defensibility of the Islands is the ability and especially the willingness of the 80,000-odd Chinese Nationalist forces on them to continue their defense." The USN could support the Nationalists, but its "authority did not include operations inside the three mile limit off the China coast."[27]

From the Nationalist point of view, this left a sizable area of China's littorals unprotected. The United States and China disagreed on how far out sovereignty reached from shore. This difference impacted how close US ships could steam along the Chinese coast. The United States supported a three-mile limit, but the Communists declared a 12-mile limit. Admiral Felt wanted to make "occasional, purposeful intrusions so as to indicate our nonacceptance of this limit." Secretary Dulles and General Twining, however, disagreed and "pointed out that our position in the Warsaw conference makes our attitude clear and there is no need to demonstrate our attitude by overt acts at this time."[28] This was the same policy being carried out with regard to the Soviet Union. The only exception was a "certain discretion given to Admiral Smoot to meet unpredictable emergencies." However, General Twining assured the president that "he did not conceive an emergency that could occur that would not, in fact, permit prior consultation with Washington, but he still thought some discretion was appropriate."[29]

---

25 Bouchard, *Command in Crisis*, 76–77.

26 Staff Notes, September 3, 1958, DDE Diary 36, Toner Notes September 1958, DDEPL.

27 Taiwan Straits: Issues Developed in Discussion with JCS, TOP SECRET, September 2, 1958, DDE AWF, Int. Series 11, Formosa (2), 1–6, DDEPL.

28 Memorandum of Conference with the President, TOP SECRET, October 1958, DDE Diary 36, Staff Notes October 1958, 1–2, DDEPL.

29 Memorandum of Conversation with the President, TOP SECRET, October 30, 1958, JFDP, WH M7, WH Meetings J-December 1958 (3), 1–2, DDEPL.

Indirect American support for Taiwan

Washington helped Taiwan, even though US Naval forces were ordered not to operate within three miles of the Chinese coast. However, the US military did assist Taiwan in other ways, for example, with naval demonstrations. Naval demonstrations could also be costly in terms of aircraft and pilots. In demonstrations carried out in September 1958, for example, the aircraft carrier "group commanders were a little too enthusiastic," and the "Navy paid a price for the show of force put on by the combat air patrol over the Taiwan Strait, losing four planes and three pilots in accidents."[30] In addition: "We could and did take over military defense of Taiwan itself, thus releasing his [Chiang's] military forces to defend and resupply the offshore islands."[31]

The Secretary of State's September 4, 1958, assessment was that the PRC attack on the offshore islands was just the first step of a larger military program, which the PRC had been preparing "for over the past 3 years [...] with Soviet backing":

> The program has been begun by intense pressure on the weakest and most vulnerable of such positions, namely, the Chinat-held offshore islands of Quemoy and Matsu. It seems that the operation is designed to produce a cumulating rollback effect, first on the offshore islands, and then on Taiwan, the "liberation" of which is the announced purpose of the present phase. The "liberation," if it occurred, would have serious repercussions on the Philippines, Japan, and other friendly countries of the Far East and Southeast Asia.

The offensive against the offshore islands was "primarily military," but the follow-up "might be primarily subversive," although "armed Chicom attack against Taiwan is not to be excluded."[32]

To make sure the PRC could not successfully attack Taiwan militarily, by mid-September 1958, the USN had positioned five carriers and their accompanying escort ships near Taiwan, and another two were on their way. A clear message was sent to the PRC when it was revealed on October 1 that a number of eight-inch howitzers, capable of firing nuclear shells, had been delivered to Jinmen Island.[33]

30 Bouchard, *Command in Crisis*, 76–77.
31 Vice Admiral Roland N. Smoot, "As I Recall [...] The U.S. Taiwan Defense Command," *Proceedings*, September 1984, vol. 110/9/979, 56–59.
32 Summary, Estimate of Factors Involved in the Taiwan Straits Situation, TOP SECRET, September 4, 1958, DDE 36, Staff Notes September 1958, 1–2, DDEPL.
33 Chang-Kwoun Park, "Consequences of U.S. Naval Shows of Force, 1946–1989" (University of Missouri-Columbia, PhD Diss., August 1995), 257–60.

A top US priority was "concentrating on getting the F-86s on the islands into operational status quickly."[34] Another example was providing Taiwan with high-tech equipment by means of cargo planes. On September 8, 1958, the first of 12 F-104s left Hamilton air force base on a C-124 cargo plane. According to Admiral Felt, it was the "first time it had ever been done, I guess. They took the little old stub wings off of them and flew them out to Taiwan, unloaded them, stuck the wings on, and there we had an F-104 squadron!"[35]

The F-104 held world records for both altitude (over 90,000 feet) and speed (1,404 MPH), and it was noted that "This deployment will be a real test of its combat capability."[36] Eventually Taiwan acquired 247 of them, mainly from the United States but also purchasing them second-hand from Belgium, Canada, Denmark, Germany, and Japan. One of their primary missions was to patrol the Taiwan Strait. On September 30, 1958, a USN situation report estimated that the PRC's MiG losses since August 14 totaled 25 destroyed, 5 probable, and then 11 either damaged or "possibly destroyed." Meanwhile, the Nationalists had only lost one F-86, and that was "due to mechanical difficulty while returning to home base."[37]

While the USN conducted shipboard training, Nationalist pilots were trained at the Naval Ordnance Test Station at China Lake on how to use the Sidewinder missile in combat. The US Air Force also assigned experts to train Nationalist pilots. According to Admiral Felt:

We had an Air Force section of the MAAG down there, the Military Assistance Group, which trained our Chinese friends and they were well trained, every bit as good tactically as the U.S. Air Force or Naval Air fighters. They'd go out on these patrols, out over the straits, and just loiter at their best fighting altitude, more or less presenting themselves as bait. The Chinese would come out at higher altitudes and finally couldn't resist the temptation to come down, and when they came down they got took. Also it was the first combat introduction of the Sidewinder, which had been given to the Chinese. I can't remember the numbers, but I think it was something like 21 of the Communist planes shot down and success for the Sidewinders, not 100 percent but a very fine performance.

---

34 Memorandum of Conference with the President, SECRET, August 11, 1958, DDE Diary 35, August 1958, Staff Notes (2), DDEPL.
35 Philip A. Beshany, *The Reminiscences of Vice Admiral Philip A. Beshany*, Oral History 45, 395.
36 "F-104s to Taiwan," Staff Notes 423, September 15, 1958, DDE Diary 36, Toner Notes September 1958, DDEPL.
37 Memorandum for the Chief of Naval Operations, SECRET, September 30, 1958, DDE AWF Int. Series 11, Formosa (3), DDEPL.

In one air battle on September 24, 1958, the Nationalist F-86s shot down an impressive 10 MiGs, with two other "probable" hits, without sustaining a single loss.[38] These were the first ever "kills" by these air-to-air missiles.[39] As such, they were "the first use of any American air-to-air guided missile in actual armed engagement." A total of 360 Sidewinders were allocated for the Chinese National Air Force.[40] As a result of superior US equipment and training, the Nationalist pilots could exert air control and the "Red Chinese weren't much interested in challenging in the air."[41] Very soon, American assistance also gave the Nationalists equally potent sea control.

Keeping the sea-lanes open

Getting supplies to Jinmen was the top priority. Most importantly, the USN helped protect the sea-lanes. The Nationalists were expected to take the supplies all the way to the island. Through late August, they had done a poor job. For example, if fired on by the Communists many Nationalist resupply ships turned around and headed back to Taiwan, rather than "waiting over horizon awhile and then trying again." Ordered by Washington not to assume responsibility for delivering supplies, the USN needed to convince the Nationalists that they "should understand that U.S. is willing to help them but cannot be expected to assume further responsibility for getting supplies all the way ashore on the islands unless GRC has first demonstrated that they themselves have the real determination to see the action through to the finish, despite the hazards involved, including artillery fire at the beaches."[42] The head of the MAAG even told Chiang: "That to date the Chinese Navy has made no effort to even try" to break the Communist blockade of Jinmen, and that if Chiang could just "give me one Chinese admiral with a can do spirit then let *us* use a little imagination and a little guts and some tenacity" they could "stabilize this situation and thumb our noses at the Communists."[43]

38 Robert Keng, "Republic of China F-86's in Battle," at http://www.aircraftresourcecenter.com/Stories1/001-100/021_TaiwanF-86_Keng/story021.htm (accessed on March 22, 2011).
39 Edward J. Marolda, "Confrontation in the Taiwan Straits," in M. Hill Goodspeed, *U.S. Navy: A Complete History* (Washington, DC: Naval Historical Foundation, 2003).
40 Staff Notes No. 432, SECRET, September 30, 1958, DDE Diary 36, Toner Notes September 1958, DDEPL.
41 Harry Donald Felt, *Reminiscences of Admiral Harry Donald Felt*, Oral History 138, 391.
42 JCS WASH DC to ADM Felt, TOP SECRET, September 2, 1958, DDE AWF Int. Series 11, Formosa (1), 1, DDEPL.
43 Telegram from COMTAIWANDEFCOM (US)/MAAG TAIWAN to CINCPAC, TOP SECRET, September 2, 1958, DDE AWF, Int. Series 11, Formosa (1), 2, DDEPL.

The Nationalist behavior led to speculation that they were trying to pull US forces deeper into the conflict: "There is a possibility that GRC is being deliberately inept in order to draw U.S. inextricably into conflict with CHICOMs."[44] To ensure that the United States was not drawn unwillingly into Chiang's fight, when the Joint Chiefs requested authority to "approve U.S. air support" in support of the Nationalists, Eisenhower is recorded as replying: "The President recalled that the Chiefs had estimated such U.S. air support would not be required unless Chicom air forces attack en masse in support of land operations, and that there would be time for his decision in such cases. Accordingly, he prescribed that U.S. air attack against mainland targets could be ordered only upon his approval."[45]

In early September 1958, the Taiwan Patrol Force was ordered to assist the Nationalist effort to resupply Jinmen by providing Landing Ships plus escort and support forces to protect the Nationalist convoy vessels. They were warned to stay in international waters, that is, "beyond the three-mile limit." Additional equipment was being rushed to the scene, including 8 LCMs and 28 LCVPs, a squadron of Sidewinder-equipped F-100 aircraft, plus 12 eight-inch howitzers plus ammunition.[46] On September 6, the first US-escorted Nationalist convoy, code-named "Lightning," reached Jinmen with crucial supplies. By September 19, nine convoys had been conducted, with the final four landing an average 151 tons of supplies apiece. With USN assistance, Nationalist supply ships began to reach Jinmen in sufficiently large numbers that by mid-September they successfully broke what was being called a PRC artillery blockade of the island. By the end of September 1958, it was estimated that Jinmen had a minimum of 31 days of food and 32 days of Ammo on hand, while other categories—such as spare parts—was twice that; the average had increased from 50 days to 55 days during the past two weeks alone.[47] General Twining told the president that the JCS believed the supply crisis on the offshore islands was now "broken."[48]

Of particular importance was safeguarding the supply ships' arrival and withdrawal from the area. To assist this effort, aircraft were provided for ASW and surface reconnaissance within 25 miles of Jinmen. While US aircraft

44 JCS WASH DC to ADM Felt, TOP SECRET, September 2, 1958, DDE AWF Int. Series 11, Formosa (1), 1, DDEPL.

45 Memorandum of Conference with the President, TOP SECRET, September 8, 1958, DDE Diary 36, Staff Notes September 1958, 1–2, DDEPL.

46 JCS WASH DC to CINCPAC, TOP SECRET, August 29, 1958, DDE AWF, Int. Series 11, Formosa (3), 1–3, DDEPL.

47 Memorandum for the Chief of Naval Operations, SECRET, September 30, 1958, DDE AWF Int. Series 11, Formosa (3), DDEPL.

48 Memorandum of Conference with the President, SECRET, September 30, 1958, DDE Diary 36, Staff Notes September 1958, DDEPL.

were told to stay at least 20 miles off the Chinese coastline, USN vessels were ordered to remain at least three miles from shore. USN ships were particularly warned not to "shoot at the mainland."[49] However, a special ROE was reissued, stating: "US Commanders are authorized to engage hostile surface vessels in territorial or international waters if they are attacking the RCN [Republic of China Navy] forces."[50] Meanwhile, intensive training was undertaken by USN personnel to ensure that the Nationalists could carry out a successful convoy operation. A map from September 15, 1958, showed how USN ships—stationed in the dotted boxes well outside China's sovereign waters—were prepared to protect the Nationalist ships resupplying Jinmen (see Map 2).

Although committed to the defense of Taiwan, Washington's support for the Nationalists with regard to the offshore islands was not unconditional. About four months before the crisis broke out, in May 1958, the NSC wrote a lengthy report on Taiwan stating: "Loss of Taiwan and the Penghus would out-flank the United States base on Okinawa and would seriously breach the Free World's defense line in the West Pacific, which stretches from South Korea and Japan to the Philippines." This same study, however, hypothesized that when attacked by the PRC, the Nationalist forces would evacuate Jinmen and Mazu but that Chiang would agree "only after strongest U.S. representations" and that during the evacuation there might be "some casualties and ship damage due to mines."[51]

Washington did not give Taipei a blank check. For example, when Chiang Kai-shek told Admiral Smoot that he wanted to use Taiwanese planes to bomb the mainland, Washington expressed its concern that this might escalate the conflict and draw US forces into the fight. According to Admiral Smoot, a USN study proved that for every gun they destroyed through bombing they might lose a squadron of planes: "This, of course was too big a price to pay, and they were convinced of the proposal's infeasibility."[52] Chiang was not pleased by America's decision not to conduct "retaliatory air attacks against Communist air fields, et cetera," calling the US attitude "inhuman" and "unfair" to his soldiers on the offshore islands, and generally "destructive of public morale." According to Drumright in Taipei, Chiang's "reaction was the

---

49 Smoot, "As I Recall [...] The U.S. Taiwan Defense Command," 56–59.
50 U.S. Navy Operation Order, CTF 72 No. 325–58, September 15, 1950, NHHC Archives, Post-1946 Operation Plans, Task Force 72.
51 U.S. and Allied Capabilities for Limited Military Operations to July 1, 1961, TOP SECRET, May 29, 1959, WH Office, OSANSA, Records 1952–61, NSC Series, Policy Paper Subseries, Box 22, A6 NSC 5724-Gaither Report (1), B2, B5, DDEPL.
52 Smoot, "As I Recall [...] The U.S. Taiwan Defense Command," 56–59.

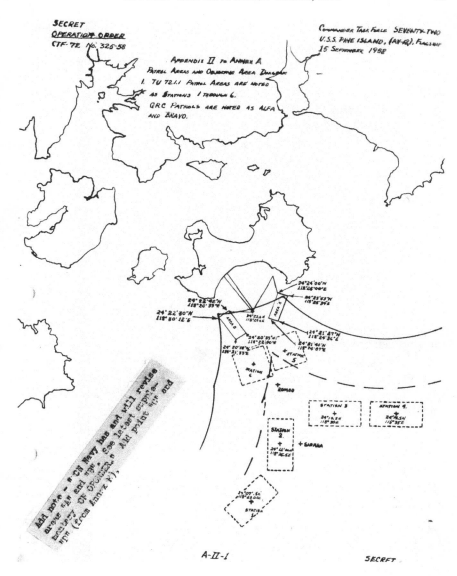

Map 2 USN's Jinmen Convoy Operations.

most violent I have seen him exhibit and at one point he called our policy 'not that of an allied nation'."[53]

---

53 Telegram from Drumright in Taipei to Secretary of State, August 31, 1958, DDE AWF, Int. Series 11, Formosa (3), 1, DDEPL.

In early September 1958, feelers on behalf of the US government from the New Zealand embassy appealed to Soviet official Menshikov "to restrain" Beijing.[54] During late September 1958, the PRC sent a message through Indian intermediaries that if the Nationalists withdrew from the islands they would not be attacked, and that Beijing was "not concerned to press immediately their claims to Taiwan."[55] The Chinese leaders were clearly concerned about further US intervention, and they warned the artillery units not to aim at American ships. However, Mao Zedong refused to accept US demands that a ceasefire precede Sino-US talks to resolve the crisis. For this reason, a negotiated settlement appeared unlikely.

By the end of October 1958, the convoying situation had been largely resolved. The Communists allowed the Nationalists to send convoys in on even-numbered days. As a result, the new tasking for the Navy was: "U.S. Commanders are instructed to convoy only in case of military necessity, which would be limited to situations where the Communists attack supply convoys on even numbered days." So long as the Nationalist supply ships were not attacked, the US ships did not need to convoy at all. Admiral Smoot agreed to the even-numbered day plan, but Admiral Felt disagreed, and "in light of political considerations, Secretary Dulles sides with Admiral Felt." But the president decided that "pending further instructions, [the U.S. Navy] would not engage in convoying operations unless the Chinese Communists attempted by sea and/or air to interfere with the re-supply on even days in what we regard as international waters."[56] However, the United States did not want to force the Nationalists to "jump through a hoop" at the PRC's bidding, so would support them if "they might feel a political reason to attempt some resupply on the days when the Chicoms had announced they would fire."[57]

Dulles convinces Chiang to withdraw troops from the offshore islands

One way to deescalate the crisis was to withdraw Nationalist troops from the offshore islands. The US government and the British government were

54 Note from New Zealand Embassy, SECRET, September 3, 1958, JFDP WHM 7 WH Meet J-D 1958 (7), DDEPL.
55 "Secret" Telegram from Peking to Foreign Office, September 25, 1958, The National Archives, Kew, PREM 11/3738; this offer appears to have been offered by Zhou Enlai to Parthasarathi during a meeting held Sunday, September 21, 1958.
56 Memorandum of Conference with the President, TOP SECRET, October 30, 1958, DDE Diary 36, Staff Notes October 1958, 1–2, DDEPL.
57 Memorandum of Conversation with the President, TOP SECRET, October 30, 1958, JFDP, WH M7, WH Meetings J-December 1958 (3), 1–2, DDEPL.

in constant consultation during the offshore island crisis. On September 9, 1958, the British charge in Beijing warned that to obtain "great power status," the PRC was willing to foment foreign crises. In conducting these crises, the "Chinese Government seems thoroughly arrogant and overconfident in their diplomacy." Their staying power was almost limitless, since they "are ready, if necessary, to sacrifice enormous numbers of men in limited military operations," and they would rather deliberately "extend" a limited war rather than look like they were defeated. According to the British charge, in consultation with his "Dutch, Norwegian, Danish and Pakistan colleagues," to resolve the ongoing crisis the PRC must "have at least a diplomatic victory to show their people" in order to give them an excuse to "back down."[58]

Washington was concerned that fighting in the Taiwan Strait might escalate into all-out war. Dulles even told Eisenhower in August 1958 that Jinmen and Mazu were now so integrated with Taiwan and the Penghus that "I doubted whether there could be an amputation without fatal consequences to Formosa itself."[59] On October 13, 1958, General Twining reported to Eisenhower that the Joint Chiefs plus Dulles had just met and decided that once the PRC artillery fire "quiets" then they would need to "withdraw at least two-thirds of the Chinese Nationalist Troops." Eisenhower cautioned that the next step was to convince Chiang Kai-shek of this, and "We must accomplish our end through persuasion rather than pressure, since otherwise we will be charged with reversing the stand we have taken." In response, Twining told the president that Chiang could be offered US assistance, including to "modernize his Army; we could partially modernize his Air Force, although this would be very expensive; we could give him shipping and amphibious lift to enlarge his capabilities for flexible action; perhaps we could even give him additional economic aid."[60]

In a conversation with Ambassador Lodge on September 19, 1958, Dulles explained his goals with regard to Chiang Kai-shek:

I said that we had tried repeatedly to get the [Taiwanese] government to withdraw or at least greatly reduce its forces on Quemoy and Matsu and to treat them as lightly held forward positions to be retired from if necessary but that we had constantly come up against the fact

58 Excerpt of Personal Assessment by British Charge, Peiping, CONFIDENTIAL, September 9, 1958, DDE AWF, Int. Series 11, Formosa (1), DDEPL.
59 Memorandum of Conversation with the President, TOP SECRET, August 12, 1958, JFD P, WHM 7, WH Meet J-D, 1958 (8), DDEPL.
60 Memorandum of Conference with the President, SECRET, October 15, 1958, DDE 36, Staff Notes, October 1958, 1–2, DDEPL.

that Chiang Kai-shek was adamant in rejecting such a viewpoint as incompatible with the entire basis for his government and that if we attempted to coerce through a cut-off of military assistance and financial aid, that itself would be as destructive of a friendly position on Formosa as though it was taken over overtly by the Communists.

A second issue was to stop the Nationalist attacks against the mainland. To deescalate tensions, the PRC was told that the US government was working to end these attacks. Dulles told Lodge, however, that "I was not confident that we could get the Chinese Nationalists to accept the plan to end 'provocations' from the Offshore Islands as we had proposed to the Communists."[61]

During a telephone call between Dulles and Vice President Richard Nixon, Dulles explained that they had repeatedly tried to get Chiang to give up the offshore islands, even sending Radford and Robertson to talk with him, but that Chiang had firmly said no. The dilemma was that: "We can break them if we cut off aid but if you break them, you lose Formosa." They could not afford to do that:

> The broad challenge is are we going to keep the Western shores of the Pacific in friendly hands or not? We can fall back initially by giving up Q[uemoy] and M[atsu] which will carry with it the loss of Formosa and then we lose the Philippines, Japan will make terms with Communist China and we will have suffered an overall setback even worse than when we lost the Mainland.[62]

On September 21, 1958, the president met with Selwyn Lloyd, Foreign Minister of the UK, and told him that "he would be very happy indeed if the United States could make some arrangement with Chiang Kai-shek which would not lose face for him but which would get his troops off the islands of Quemoy and Matsu."[63] In a separate conversation with Dulles, the president "expressed regret that there seemed to be no way to persuade Chiang to re-direct the focus of his leadership, in a way which would enable him to

---

61 Memorandum of Conversation with Ambassador Lodge, TOP SECRET, September 19, 1958, Dulles, J.F., Gen Cor Box 1, Memos L-M (1), 1–2, DDEPL.
62 Telephone Call from the Vice President, September 25, 1958, Dulles, J.F. Tel Conv. Box 9 August–October 1958 (3), 1, DDEPL.
63 Memorandum of Conversation between the President, Selwyn Lloyd, Foreign Minister of the United Kingdom, and Sir Harold Caccia, British Ambassador to the United States, TOP SECRET, September 21, 1958, DDE Diary 36, Staff Notes September 1958, 1–6, DDEPL.

re-group his military forces into more sensible positions."[64] However, Eisenhower clarified that "it was essential that the free world keep control of the island of Formosa and that if Formosa were lost, then a hole would result in the very middle of the island chain of defense. Should the Reds eventually control Formosa, that, in the President's opinion, would be a real Munich." If, in the worst case scenario, "Chiang Kai-shek were to quit and Formosa went to the Reds, then the overseas Chinese would have no place to go except to the Communist camp."[65] To convince Chiang to cooperate Dulles decided to sign a second secret agreement.

Signing a second secret agreement

Reducing forces on the offshore islands would also necessarily end the blockade. During late October 1958, Dulles's task was to try to persuade Chiang Kai-shek to reduce the number of Nationalist forces on the islands so as to halt Nationalist "commando raids and blockades."[66] Eisenhower repeatedly wrote "strong" letters to Dulles suggesting that Chiang "be offered an amphibious lift in exchange for getting his troops out of Quemoy and Matsu."[67] Dulles flew to Taiwan to convince Chiang to withdraw from the offshore islands.[68] During private talks, Chiang refused to withdraw, rejecting "any proposal that seems to him to imply retreat from his position as head of the only legitimate Chinese Government."[69] Dulles instead urged him "to renounce the use of force in an attempt to reunify China."[70] Included in this plan would be "a substantial reduction of forces" on Jinmen and Mazu.[71]

---

64 Memorandum of Conversation with the President, SECRET, September 23, 1958, JFD P WHM 7, WH Meet J-D 1958 (6), 1–2, DDEPL.

65 Memorandum of Conversation between the President, Selwyn Lloyd, Foreign Minister of the United Kingdom, and Sir Harold Caccia, British Ambassador to the United States, TOP SECRET, September 21, 1958, DDE Diary 36, Staff Notes September 1958, 1–6, DDEPL.

66 Foreign Office to Washington (Secret), October 22, 1958, The National Archives, Kew, PREM 11/3738.

67 Diary, October 7, 1958, DDE Papers 10, ACW Diary, October 1958, DDEPL.

68 Telegram from the UK Embassy, Washington, to Foreign Office (Secret), October 17, 1958, The National Archives, Kew, PREM 11/3738.

69 Letter from President Eisenhower to Prime Minister Macmillan (Top Secret), September 6, 1958, The National Archives, Kew, CAB 21/3272.

70 Letter from John Foster Dulles to British Ambassador (Secret), October 25, 1958, The National Archives, Kew, FO 371/133543.

71 Letter from John Foster Dulles to Selwyn Lloyd (Secret), October 25, 1958, The National Archives, Kew, PREM 11/3738.

On October 23, 1958, Dulles reported to the president in an "Eyes Only" telegram from Taipei that Chiang had "accepted the principle of an appreciable reduction of forces on Quemoy to be effected whenever there was a suspension of the fighting."[72] In return for Chiang agreeing to reduce forces on Jinmen by "not less than 15,000 men," including "1 infantry division plus additional units and/or individuals," Dulles agreed to greater arms shipments, including "a minimum of 12 240mm howitzers," a "minimum of 12 155mm guns," for Jinmen and four or more 240mm howitzers plus one battalion of 155mm gun "when available" for Mazu. The possibility was also raised of "Lacrosse missiles to be considered at a later date," a "minimum of 1 tank battalion," plus if changes to the M-8 assault gun "proves feasible, provide sufficient converted vehicles to motorized [sic] 2 battalions of infantry." The Nationalists had eight months to reduce forces on the offshore islands, and: "The target date for completion of the implementation of the above agreement is 30 June 1959." That this agreement was more of a "face-saving" measure for Chiang than a true necessity was suggested by the comment by O. M. Gale, Special Assistant: "The materiel and equipment outlined in this agreement had already been earmarked for GRC and do not actually represent an increase in previously planned assistance."[73]

Although left unstated, any decision to cut forces from the offshore islands would also necessarily terminate the Nationalists' decade-long blockade of China. Certainly, this was one of the US goals that Dulles outlined to the British Foreign Office immediately before he left for Taiwan to meet with Chiang Kai-shek.[74] The blockade was no longer considered as important as before, since the PRC was already beginning to experience an economic implosion due to the Great Leap Forward. Meanwhile, it was well-known in Washington that Sino-Soviet diplomatic relations were already in decline. As Gordan Chang has pointed out, Eisenhower was careful not to comment on the Sino-Soviet relationship, for fear of strengthening it. For example, the Eisenhower memoir barely mentions Sino-Soviet tensions so as "to avoid saying anything that could hinder the emergence of the Sino-Soviet split."[75]

72 Eyes only Acting Secretary for President from Secretary, October 23, 1958, DH 10, Dulles October 1958, DDEPL.

73 Memorandum for Major John S. Eisenhower, SECRET, December 11, 1958, DDE Papers, White House Office, Office of the Staff Secretary, Records, 1952–61, Int. Series, Box 3, File "China (Republic of)" (1), September 1958–April 1960, 1–3, DDEPL.

74 Telegram from Foreign Office to UK Embassy, Washington, October 22, 1958, The National Archives, Kew, PREM 11/3738.

75 Gordan H. Chang, *Friends and Enemies: The United States, China, and the Soviet Union, 1948–1972* (Stanford: Stanford University Press, 1990), 331n24.

Dulles clearly wanted to put even more pressure on the Sino-Soviet alliance, telling newspapermen in Newport, RI, that he did not think the PRC or USSR acted in "accordance with treaty obligations," and that there "have been plenty of treaty obligations which they have evaded or broken."[76] According to a Bonn intelligence report, Khrushchev had warned Mao about the risks of attacking the offshore islands, but Mao was convinced that it would force a retreat, such as had happened in the Dachen Islands three years before, and that "liberating" these Nationalist-held islands "was necessary for internal and external prestige reasons and that Nationalist loss of the islands would undermine their position, increase their large rate of military defections, and facilitate Communist subservice activity."[77]

After 44 days, on October 6, 1958, the PRC halted the shelling of Jinmen. Civilian casualties were 138 dead and 324 injured, while the number of dead and wounded soldiers numbered close to 3,000. In addition, an estimated 7,000 buildings on Jinmen were either damaged or destroyed.[78] Sporadic artillery fire from the PRC side continued for the next 20 years, ending for good only in January 1979 after President Jimmy Carter and the Chairman Deng Xiaoping recognized each other's government. This barrage took place on alternate days of the week and the shells mainly contained propaganda leaflets. An estimated one million steel shell casings were fired at Jinmen during this period, making it "the longest sustained artillery warfare in world military history."[79]

It was no "coincidence that the Nationalist naval blockade also ended during 1958, right at the time the first signs of what would soon be called the Sino-Soviet 'split' began to appear."[80] The USSR's failure to support China in the offshore islands crisis undoubtedly helped Washington obtain the US objective of undermining the Sino-Soviet alliance. However, all US attempts to resolve PRC–Taiwan differences peacefully failed. On October 27, 1958, British Foreign Secretary Selwyn Lloyd even wrote to Dulles that the Chinese "seem to be in no hurry" to make peace with Taiwan and would "pursue their aims by whatever political means offer themselves from time to time. They do not want mediation and their ultimate goal appears to be some direct

76 News Conference, U.S. Naval Base, Newport, RI, September 4, 1958, JFDP, WHM 7, WH Meet J-D 1958 (8), 5.
77 Staff Notes No. 415, SECRET, DDE Diary 36, Toner Notes, September 1958, DDEPL.
78 Michael Szonyi, *Cold War Island: Quemoy on the Front Line* (New York: Cambridge University Press, 2008), 76–77.
79 Mark A. Ryan, David Finkelstein, and Michael Devitt, *Chinese Warfighting* (Armonk, NY: M.E. Sharpe, 2003), 167.
80 Elleman, "The Nationalists' Blockade of the PRC," 142.

arrangement with the Nationalists." Lloyd concluded by predicting, with great accuracy from the viewpoint of half-a-century later, that: "We are, therefore, likely to be in for a fairly long period of such tactics."[81]

Conclusions

A second secret agreement signed by Dulles and Chiang ended the second Taiwan Strait crisis. This agreement also had the subsidiary effect of ending the Nationalist blockade of the PRC. This blockade had already lasted 10 years and, in combination with the ongoing US strategic embargo, had exerted extreme economic pressure on the PRC. Sino-Soviet economic tensions eventually forced a major realignment in the PRC's foreign trade. But the military standoff over the offshore islands remained unresolved. During this crisis the Taiwan Patrol Force "accomplished one of the most important missions of her career by playing a major role in aiding the Chinese Nationalists."[82]

According to Dulles, the real dispute was not geography but "human wills." If the United States "seems afraid, and loses 'face' in any way, the consequences will be far-reaching, extending from Viet Nam in the south, to Japan and Korea in the north."[83] Periodic PLA attacks against Jinmen were intended to make it a "whipping boy" for Taiwan itself.[84] Since the PRC leaders were pursuing mainly a political, not a military, strategy, "they intend to play a 'cat and mouse' game with the offshore islands." To Dulles, therefore, the PRC announcement that shelling of Jinmen might switch from even-numbered days to odd-numbered days seemed to substantiate this assessment: "This rather fantastic statement seems to confirm our analysis of the Chinese Communist attitude as being essentially political and propaganda rather than military."[85]

Meanwhile, the US government's public statements remained intentionally vague about Washington's decision to use or not to use military force to support the Nationalist bases on Jinmen and Mazu. However, a "secret" December 26, 1959, Operation Order, while admitting that the offshore

---

81 "Secret" Letter from Foreign Secretary Selwyn Lloyd to Secretary-of-State John Foster Dulles, October 27, 1958, PREM 11/3738, DDEPL.

82 "Post 1946, Command File, Taiwan Patrol Force," NHHC Archives, Box 784, 7–8.

83 Telegram from John Foster Dulles to Harold Macmillan (Top Secret), September 13, 1958, The National Archives, Kew, CAB 21/3272.

84 Telegram from UK Embassy in Washington to Foreign Office, October 25, 1958, The National Archives, Kew, PREM 11/3738.

85 Letter from John Foster Dulles to Selwyn Lloyd (Secret), October 25, 1958, The National Archives, Kew, PREM 11/3738.

islands "are not covered by this agreement," did acknowledge that the United States had committed itself to the defense of Taiwan, the Pescadores, and— most importantly—to the offshore islands of Jinmen and Mazu, "insofar as a threat to them is considered to be a threat against Taiwan and the Penghus."[86] The US government decision to defend any offshore island that posed a direct threat to Taiwan arguably included the use of atomic bombs, a hotly debated topic during both the Truman and Eisenhower administrations.

---

86 US Navy Operation Order, CTF 72 No. 201–60, December 26, 1959, NHHC Archives, Post-1946 Operation Plans, Task Force 72.

Chapter 6

THE US THREAT TO USE ATOMIC WEAPONS

To most outside observers, the opposing forces facing each other across the Taiwan Strait during the early 1950s may have seemed unevenly matched on the side of the United States and its allies. However, asymmetric warfare can give advantages to both sides. For example, China's enormous manpower allowed it to send "human waves" in the Korean War against its United Nation's opponent. Therefore, the possibility of being forced to use atomic weapons was seriously discussed, in particular against an approaching surface and subsurface invasion force aimed at Taiwan.

During the early 1950s, atomic bombs were often thought of much like regular bombs. The use of the A-bomb was considered in Korea, and later in Vietnam during the Dien Bien Phu crisis. With regard to Taiwan, during July 1950 Truman authorized the movement of B-29 bombers to Guam. These planes were capable of carrying atomic bombs. Meanwhile, an air unit in Guam was given control of non-radioactive atomic bomb components, with the nuclear core to be provided only during an emergency. This information was leaked to the *New York Times* so as to give the PRC pause before they decided to attack Taiwan.[1]

During times of crisis, planning sessions often included discussion on using atomic bombs. For example, on September 12, 1954, the NSC submitted a Top Secret paper discussing the ongoing Taiwan Strait crisis. It warned that a war with China over the offshore islands would necessarily include a sharp rise in tensions that could "probably lead to our initiating the use of atomic weapons."[2] Clearly, the use of atomic weapons was considered to be an important element in the defense of Taiwan.

---

1 Edward J. Marolda, "The U.S. Navy and the Chinese Civil War, 1945–1952," PhD Diss., The George Washington University, 1990, 180.
2 NSC Talking Paper, TOP SECRET, September 12, 1954, JFD Papers, WHM 8, Gen For Pol (4), DDEPL; all underlining in original.

Consideration of the nuclear option

It is still unclear whether the US government would have actually used A-bombs in Korea or to halt a PRC invasion of Taiwan. In 1950, MacArthur evidently told Harriman during their talks on August 6–8 that if there were a PRC attack against Taiwan then Seventh Fleet ships, fighter jets from the Philippines and Okinawa, B-29s, and other aircraft could destroy any invasion attempt that might be made. He further stated that it would be a one-sided battle: "Should the Communists be so foolhardy as to make such an attempt, it would be the bloodiest victory in Far East history."[3]

Although use of the A-bomb may not have been specifically discussed during these meetings, the fact that the A-bomb-equipped B-29s were mentioned by MacArthur suggests that he had their use in mind. Even if MacArthur was not referring to using the A-bomb in 1950, the use of atomic weapons was certainly considered later during the 1950s. On December 1, 1950, for example, at a meeting of the US Chief of the JCS, General J. Lawton Collins stated that if the Russians actively intervened in the Korean conflict then "we would have to consider the threat of the use of the A-bomb."[4] On December 27, 1950, Acheson was asked what would happen if Russia also intervened in Korea and was told that the only retaliation against Port Arthur, a Russian-held port in Manchuria, and Vladivostok would be "by using the atom bomb."[5]

On September 12, 1954, during the first Taiwan Strait crisis, the JCS similarly recommended considering the use of nuclear weapons against China. However, when the decision to evacuate the Dachen Islands was made during January 1955, it was determined that "atomic weapons will not be used."[6] A special annex to this OP-PLAN, entitled Atomic Operations, specified that if the enemy attacked the evacuation forces, then one assumption would be that the "use of atomic weapons will be authorized." Although subsection 9 listed possible PRC locations for atomic strikes, the city names were blackened out prior to declassification on December 29, 2011. However, this document does state: "Other targets suspected as source of enemy attacks may be nominated by COMSEVENTHFLT for atomic strikes."[7]

---

3 Marolda, "The U.S. Navy and the Chinese Civil War, 1945–1952," 189–90.
4 Memorandum of Conversation, Notes on Meeting in JCS Conference Room, TOP SECRET, December 1, 1950, Dean G. Acheson papers, Box 68, HSTPL.
5 Memorandum of Conversation, TOP SECRET, December 27, 1950, Dean G. Acheson papers, Box 68, HSTPL.
6 CINCPACFLT OP-PLAN 51-Z-55, TOP SECRET, January 1955, DDE AWF, Int. Series. 10, Formosa Area, U.S. Mil. Ops. (3), DDEPL.
7 CINCPACFLT OP-PLAN 51-Z-55, TOP SECRET, January 1955, DDE AWF, Int. Series. 10, Formosa Area, U.S. Mil. Ops. (3); ANNEX ABLE, TOP SECRET, "Atomic Operations," DDEPL; underlining in original.

On February 21, 1955, Dulles warned Eisenhower that a Communist buildup across from Jinmen and Mazu meant these islands might soon be indefensible "in the absence of massive U.S. intervention, perhaps with atomic weapons."[8] On March 7, 1955, Dulles reported on his recent trip to Taiwan, telling Eisenhower that to support Chiang Kai-shek's position on the offshore islands might "require the use of atomic missiles," to which the president replied "he thoroughly agreed with this," but clarified that this did not mean "weapons of mass destruction," which would include larger atomic bombs or nuclear devices. But Eisenhower stated that "with the number of planes that we had available in the Asian area, it would be quite impractical to accomplish the necessary results in the way of putting out airfields and gun emplacements without using atomic missiles."[9]

On March 10, 1955, Dulles stated at a NSC meeting that the United States might use atomic weapons against China. If a Communist attack occurred, the use of atomic weapons had to be considered:

Determination must soon be made whether in such defense atomic weapons will be tactically used. The need for such use, to make up for deficiency in conventional forces, outweighs the repercussive effect of such use upon free world nations in Europe and the Far East (especially Japan, where attempt may be made to immobilize US forces). US and world public opinion must be prepared.[10]

During a meeting the next day, which included both of the Dulles brothers, Radford, Twining, Carney, Goodpaster, and the president, Eisenhower summarized the situation as follows:

The U.S. should do every practical thing that could be done to help the Chinats to defend themselves; that if it was necessary later for the U.S. to intervene, it should do so with conventional weapons; that the U.S. should improve the air defense of the Formosa air fields, but should avoid greatly augmenting U.S. troops on Formosa; that we should give the best possible advice and training to the Chinats about how to take

8 Dulles Telegram to Eisenhower, TOP SECRET, February 21, 1955, DH 4, Dulles, J.F., February 1955 (1), DDEPL.

9 Memorandum of Conversation with the President, TOP SECRET, March 7, 1955, Dulles, J.F. W.H. Memo, Box 3, Meet Press 1955 (7), DDEPL.

10 Memorandum for the Record, TOP SECRET, March 11, 1955, DDE WH Office, Office Spec. Assist. for National Security Affairs, NSC Series, Briefing Notes Subseries, Box 17, Taiwan and the Offshore Islands, U.S. Policy Toward (1955–58), DDEPL.

care of themselves; that he recognized that if we had to intervene with conventional weapons, such intervention might not be decisive; that the time might come when the U.S. might have to intervene with atomic weapons, but that should come only at the end, and we would have to advise our allies first.[11]

On March 15, Admiral Stump told the president that at the current levels, the Communist air force could be held off by "U.S. conventional operations," but that if the PRC moved "air forces in strength into the area, the U.S. would have to be prepared to employ atomic weapons."[12] Stump later clarified that if airfields deep in Fujian province were being used to attack the offshore islands or Formosa, then the potential "danger it would pose to the U.S. fleet units would require that it [airfields] be destroyed" through the use of "special weapons," that is, atomic weapons.[13]

At this point, atomic weapons were considered as just one weapon in a large arsenal of possible weapons. Eisenhower publicly confirmed that "A-bombs can be used [...] as you would use a bullet." About ten days later, on March 25, 1955, the CNO, Admiral Robert B. Carney, stated that the president was planning to destroy Red China's "military potential," which certainly implied possible use of the atomic bomb.[14] But considerations of how the public would react to the use of atomic bombs were an important factor. Admiral Radford later reflected that to defend the offshore islands against a determined PRC attack, "it would undoubtedly be necessary to use atomic weapons," and that when contemplating using atomic bombs Eisenhower had to "consider feeling generated throughout the world and in China too, particularly if many civilians were killed."[15] Because of the potential negatives of using atomic weapons, they were often thought of as deterrent weapons.

---

11 Memorandum for the Record: Meeting in President's Office, TOP SECRET-EYES ONLY, March 11, 1955, DDE Ann Whitman, Int. Series 9, Formosa Visit to Cincpac 1955 (1), DDEPL.

12 Memorandum for the President, TOP SECRET, March 15, 1955, DDE AWF, Int. Series 9, Formosa Visit 1955 (1) DDEP; underlining in original.

13 Memorandum for the Record, TOP SECRET, March 18, 1955, DDE AWF, Int. Series 9, Formosa Visit 1955 (2), 3, DDEPL.

14 *First Taiwan Strait Crisis: Quemoy and Matsu Islands*, http://www.globalsecurity.org/military/ops/quemoy_matsu.htm (accessed on December 14, 2010).

15 Telegram to Secretary of State Dulles from Asstsecstate Roberson, TOP SECRET, April 25, 1955, DDE AWF, Int. Series 10, Formosa (China) 1952–57 (4), Sec. 1, 3, Sec. 2, 2, DDEPL.

Atomic bombs as deterrents

Atomic bombs were thought to be perfect deterrent weapons. When speculating on how best to deter a PRC attack on the offshore islands, one idea was to: "Let it be known that the presently deployed U.S. fighter unit on Formosa has an atomic capability—as do the carrier task forces in the area—and that they will use them to repel attack." A second suggestion was to redeploy a fighter-bomber wing with "atomic capability to Korea and, perhaps, another to Formosa." If these were not sufficient, then "even more conclusive actions by the U.S." could include: "Practice bombings-up of bomber units in the Far East with tactical atomic weapons." Or even: "Test of a penetration A-Bomb on some stand-by airfield, possibly in the Marianas' or other islands under U.S. control in the Eastern Pacific."[16]

There was always the possibility that the PLA would take one or more of the offshore islands by force. One adviser suggested to Dulles that if the Communists took the offshore islands from the Nationalists, the United States could "from time to time, drop an A-bomb on them to neutralize them and give the CHINCOMS no advantage by their capture." But Dulles thought that this would be a "considerable waste of armament" that would "accomplish nothing but the killing of a number of harmless fishermen."[17] He was also concerned about using too many bombs, commenting that "we cannot splurge our limited supply of atomic weapons without serious danger to the entire international balance of power; and therefore any use which is made of them must be very carefully planned and thought out."[18]

In addition, the use of large numbers of atomic bombs to defend the islands could backfire, since it might involve the "wholesale use of atomic weapons against the densely populated mainland where land bursts would be required which would have a fall-out which might involve heavy casualties."[19] There would also "be risk of large civilian casualties through after-effects, and indeed the inhabitants of Quemoy, and even of Taiwan, might not be immune under certain atmospheric and wind conditions." Such a strategy would not be in

---

16 Immediate Actions Re the Formosa Situation, TOP SECRET, March 19, 1955, Dulles, J.F., W.H. Memo, Box 2, W.H. Memo 1955, Formosa Straits (2), 6–7, DDEPL.

17 Memorandum of Meeting Held in the Secretary's Office, TOP SECRET, March 28, 1955, Dulles, J.F., W.H. Memo, Box 2, W.H. Memo 1955, Formosa Straits (1), 11, DDEPL.

18 Memorandum of Meeting Held in the Secretary's Office, TOP SECRET, March 28, 1955, Dulles, J.F., W.H. Memo, Box 2, W.H. Memo 1955, Formosa Straits (1), 7, DDEPL.

19 Memorandum of Meeting with the Senators, April 27, 1955, TOP SECRET, April 28, 1955, Dulles, J.F., Gen Cor Box 1, Memos J-K (2), DDEPL.

the "long-range interest of the Republic of China," since the use of atomic weapons might "destroy any hope of good will and future favorable reception of the Republic of China by the [PRC] Chinese people."[20] Furthermore, it "might alienate Asian opinion and ruin Chiang Kai-shek's hopes of ultimate welcome back to the mainland."[21]

Chinese leaders responded quickly to these US announcements of the possible use of atomic weapons. In February 1955, Mao Zedong warned the Finnish Ambassador to China that "if the Americans atomic-bombed Shanghai or Peking, 'they' [meaning the Soviets] would retaliate by wiping out American cities, which would cause the replacement of the present leaders of the United States." When the Finnish Ambassador double-checked with the Soviet Ambassador to China, he was assured that "if the Americans bombed the Chinese mainland, the Soviet Government would give the Chinese all possible support under the Sino-Soviet Agreement."[22]

There was enormous concern in Washington that Moscow would use atomic bombs to support China. The use of the phrase "all possible support" certainly implied that the USSR might resort to nuclear weapons to back China. However, at the same time Eden warned Dulles that Russia's goal might be quite different: "Involving US in these islands will put US on weakest ground with its allies and public opinion generally [...] [and the] Russians would probably find this situation to their advantage."[23] In other words, embroiling the PRC and the United States in a no-win conflict over the offshore islands would potentially give the USSR increased leverage over both.

Tactical nuclear bombs and missiles

As weapons development progressed, smaller atomic bombs were created that could be used in tactical warfare. In April 1955, General M. B. Ridgway notified the Chairman of the JCS that if requested as many as seven of the Army's eight batteries of "Honest John" rockets could be transferred to Taiwan; one of these batteries would be diverted from Japan to Taiwan in June

20 Preliminary Draft of Possible Statement of Position for Communication to the Republic of China, SECRET, April 7, 1955, Dulles, J.F. W.H. Memo, Box 2, Offshore April–May 1955 (4), 10–11, DDEPL.
21 Memorandum of Meeting with the Senators, April 27, 1955, TOP SECRET, April 28, 1955, Dulles, J.F., Gen Cor Box 1, Memos J-K (2), DDEPL.
22 From UK Embassy in Peking to Foreign Office (Secret), February 5, 1955, The National Archives, Kew, PREM 11/867.
23 Telegrams from Dulles to Eisenhower, TOP SECRET, February 25, 1955, DH 4, Dulles, J.F., February 1955 (1), DDEPL.

1955, while six batteries in Europe could be deployed to Taiwan. According to an appendix dated April 4, 1955, this would allow 161 nuclear missiles to be allocated to Taiwan. While the Honest John missile could be used with conventional warheads, it could be converted to use the Mark 7 bomb's nuclear components. According to Ridgway: "Honest John batteries would provide a significant contribution to the defense of the island of Formosa. Their most effective use would be with atomic warheads."[24] As Eisenhower reminded the Joint Chiefs during July 1955, however, the "principle of having a considerable amount of dispersal" was intended to "limit the effects of surprise attack."[25]

Because of the threat that any American use of atomic weapons might spur the USSR into responding, the United States began to develop tactical nuclear weapons. As CinCPac Admiral Harry Felt later recounted, by the end of the 1950s new breakthroughs meant that there were many more military options available and "at that time we had plans for use of tactical nuclear weapons."[26] During June 1957, President Eisenhower met with Drs. Earnest O. Lawrence, Mark M. Mills, and Edward Teller to talk about the development of "clean" nuclear weapons and "tactical" fusion weapons. According to Teller, such weapons could be "easily packaged" and their effects would be limited to "only in the damage sought, i.e., only in the area of initial effects, free of fall-out outside this area." Lawrence emphasized that the development of "clean" nuclear weapons, versus "dirty" bombs, would be necessary to make such weapons more useful on the battlefield, and "our failure could truly be a 'crime against humanity'." While clean nuclear weapons were considered more useful, at the end of the meeting it was pointed out that "after clean weapons have been developed, it is possible to put 'additive materials' with them to produce radioactive fall-out if desired."[27]

In May 1958, the NSC submitted a report examining the use of nuclear weapons in a conflict with China. While making the assumption that the president would give permission for their use, this report cautioned: "Nuclear weapons will be employed with the greatest selectivity, initially against the invading forces and supporting facilities, then against other airfield complexes, ports, staging bases, communications networks and similar military targets." While it was assumed that the USSR would come to China's assistance, "Soviet

24 General M. B. Ridgway Memorandum to Chairman, Joint Chiefs of Staff, TOP SECRET, April 4, 1955, DDE AWF, Int Series 10, Formosa Area U.S. Mil. Ops. (1), DDEPL.

25 Memorandum of Conference with the President, TOP SECRET, July 7, 1955, DDE Papers 6, ACW Diary July 1955 (5), DDEPL.

26 Harry Donald Felt, *Reminiscences of Admiral Harry Donald Felt*, Oral History 138, 396.

27 Memorandum of Conference with the President, Restricted Data, June 24, 1957, DDE Diary 25, June 57 Diary Staff Memos, DDEPL.

support would not be expected to include provision of nuclear weapons, at least not at the commencement of hostilities."[28]

Unlike using larger A-bombs, many military officers during this period did not believe that tactical nuclear weapons would lead to a larger war. On August 14, 1958, General Twining told Eisenhower that if the Chinese Communists attacked the offshore islands the US response might include "small atomic weapons." When questioned, Twining said that the JCS "did not expect atomic retaliation if we attacked the two or three airfields nearest the coast with atomic weapons."[29] On August 29, 1958, the Draft Operational Plan was sent to the Pacific Fleet, which stated that: "It is probable that initially only conventional weapons will be authorized, but prepare to use atomic weapons. Prepare, if the use of atomic weapons is authorized, to extending bombing of ChiCom targets deeper into China as required."[30]

On August 29, 1958, the president met with Acting Secretary of State Herter, Allen Dulles, General Cabell, Secretary Quarles, General Twining, and Admiral Burke, among others. Three possible enemy scenarios were outlined, including (a) simple harassment and interdiction by the Communists, (b) an attack on one or more offshore islands, or (c) an attack "extending operations against Taiwan." It was decided:

With regard to phase a, Mr. Quarles suggested that our action broadly should be to support the Chinese Nationalists but try to stay out of the battle ourselves. In case phase b develops, we should authorize our commander to join the battle, but not to use atomic weapons nor to extend the area of combat beyond the immediate tactical area, including air fields. In case phase c develops, we would expect our commander to seek further instructions for more extended action. The President said he retains some question as to whether we should not authorize tactical atomic weapons in case of phase b. However, we cannot be sure this would be necessary, and since we do not want to outrage world opinion, perhaps we had better reserve this.

28 U.S. and Allied Capabilities for Limited Military Operations to July 1, 1961, TOP SECRET, May 29, 1959, WH Office, OSANSA, Records 1952–61, NSC Series, Policy Paper Subseries, Box 22, A6 NSC 5724-Gaither Report (1), B11, B12, DDEPL.
29 Memorandum of Conference with the President, TOP SECRET, August 14, 1958, DDE Diary 35, August 1958, Staff Notes (2), 1–3, DDEPL.
30 Draft Message to CINCPAC, August 29, 1958, DDE AWF, Int. Series 11, Formosa (3), 1, DDEPL.

It was decided, however, that even in phase *a* operations, the Chinese Nationalists could undertake "hot pursuit" against the enemy, and that it was agreed that with regard to USN "escort and protection operations could be authorized to the extent deemed militarily necessary and beyond Chinat capabilities, but confined to international waters."[31]

Control over use of atomic bombs rested with the president. When the final message was sent, a note was added at the end: "It was emphasized that during all three phases, atomic weapons could not be used until after specific authority has been obtained from the President."[32] When asked by a reporter whether local commanders would really ask Washington "for permission to use such weapons which are available," and then whether they would wait to "receive a reply or approval," Dulles responded: "I certainly can. The orders are very, very strict with regard to that."[33]

On August 29, 1958, advance copies of a draft message to CINCPAC were produced and circulated. It clearly stated the US government's intent:

The United States Government will not permit the loss of the offshore islands to Chinese Communist aggression. In case of major air or amphibious attacks, which in the opinion of the United States seriously endanger the islands, the United States will concur in the ChiNat attack of ChiCom close-in mainland bases. In such an event, the United States will reinforce the ChiNats to the extent necessary to assure the security of these islands. This action may include joining in the attack of ChiCom bases, with atomic weapons used if needed to gain the military objective.[34]

Anglo-American discussions about the use of atomic bombs

US military leaders treated atomic bombs like any other weapon. Many civilian leaders in Washington were not as optimistic as their military counterparts about using atomic bombs as if they were conventional weapons. But, as Dulles told Prime Minister Macmillan during September 1958: "It seems that the Sino-Soviet strategy is designed to put strains upon us at many separate

---

31 Memorandum of Conference with the President, August 29, 1958, DDE AWF Int. Series 11, Formosa (30), 1–2, DDEPL.
32 JCS WASH DC to CINCPAC, TOP SECRET, August 29, 1958, DDE AWF, Int. Series 11, Formosa (3), 1–3, DDEPL.
33 News Conference, U.S. Naval Base, Newport, RI, September 4, 1958, JFDP, WHM 7, WH Meet J-D 1958 (8), 5, DDEPL.
34 Draft Message to CINCPAC, August 29, 1958, DDE AWF, Int. Series 11, Formosa (3), 3, DDEPL.

places and our various commitments to N.A.T.O., in Korea, to individual allies, are spreading our forces too thin for comfort—certainly unless atomic weapons are to be used."[35] Later that month, however, Eisenhower assured UK Foreign Minister Selwyn Lloyd that nuclear weapons should be used for an "all-out effort rather than a local effort," and he concluded: "He said that he did not plan to use nuclear weapons in any local situation at the present time."[36] Due to fears that first use of atomic weapons could lead to reprisals, however, Admiral Felt was eventually directed to draw up a plan for use of only conventional weapons, which took some doing.[37]

Ongoing US–British talks on the use of nuclear weapons were particularly important. Eisenhower thought a bit differently from his advisers, who were against using these weapons, informing Churchill one day at a meeting in Bermuda in 1953 that if the Communists orchestrated a major attack again in Korea, then "we intended to use every weapon in the bag, including our atomic types." Later, they discussed "use of atomic bomb in Korea in the event hostilities are initiated by the Reds." Eisenhower stated his belief that the "atom bomb has to be treated just as another weapon in the arsenal," in particular since "anyone who held up too long in the use of his assets in atomic weapons might suddenly find himself subjected to such wide-spread and devastating attack that retaliation would be next to impossible."[38]

On September 2, 1958, General Twining, Chairman of the JCS, explained to Dulles that a 7–10 kiloton airburst bomb would have a lethal range of three to four miles, but there would be "virtually no fall out." If tensions over the Taiwan Strait got out of hand, it might be necessary to use tactical weapons against the PRC: "The initial attack would be only on five coast airfields (with one bomb being used per airfield)."[39] However, a different report from the same day envisioned using 10–80 kiloton weapons "for air burst, not ground burst," which suggested higher levels of fallout. The use of atomic weapons against the mainland was a necessity, since "conventional

35 Letter from John Foster Dulles to Harold Macmillan (Top Secret), September 5, 1958, The National Archives, Kew, CAB 21/3272.
36 Memorandum of Conversation between the President, Selwyn Lloyd, Foreign Minister of the United Kingdom, and Sir Harold Caccia, British Ambassador to the United States, TOP SECRET, September 21, 1958, DDE Diary 36, Staff Notes September 1958, 1–6, DDEPL.
37 Felt, *Reminiscences of Admiral Harry Donald Felt.*
38 Discussion in Bermuda between Eisenhower and Churchill, December 4, 1953, DDE Diary Series 9, Diary: Copies of DDE Personal 1953–54 (1), DDEPL.
39 "Memorandum of Conversation," September 2, 1958, *China; 1958–1960*, vol. XIX, *FRUS* (Washington, DC: Government Printing Office, 1996), 120.

weapons would not be adequate to accomplish the elimination of the [PRC] installations."[40]

When assessing all of the factors involved with the PRC attack on the offshore islands, the Secretary of State emphasized the importance of a determined resistance: "If the Chicoms believe the US would actively intervene to throw back an assault, perhaps using nuclear weapons, it is probable there would be no attempt to take Quemoy by assault and the situation might quiet down, as in 1955." While there would be "strong popular revulsion against the US in most of the world," and particularly intense in Asia and "particularly harmful to us in Japan," it was hoped that if "relatively small detonations were used with only air bursts, so that there would be no appreciable fallout or large civilian casualties, and if the matter were quickly closed, the revulsion might not be long-lived."[41]

During January 1958, Vice Admiral Austin K. Doyle, Commander United States Taiwan Defense Command, also reported that Matador missiles had been stationed in Taiwan and are "now set up ready for action if trouble should start." Although Doyle refused to say whether any atomic weapons were in Taiwan, it was public knowledge by this time that the Matador missiles were capable of delivering nuclear payloads in the 40–50 kiloton range. During 1958, the USN also began to deploy the Mk-101 (code named *Lulu*) Nuclear Depth Bomb (NDB), with an 11 kiloton payload, which was intended to destroy deeply submerged submarines.[42]

Conclusions

The American views of atomic warfare changed during the 1950s from the use of the A-bomb immediately, to deterrence, to selected use of tactical weapons. The USN operations were being conducted in a highly sensitive part of Asia, and special strategic concerns included the possible use of nuclear weapons by China's ally, the USSR, and—after the PRC exploded its own atomic bomb in 1964—by the PRC. USN vessels conducting patrols had to always be aware of the PRC's hostile intentions. The possibility of a small clash growing into a nuclear exchange was an ever-present danger.

---

40 Taiwan Straits: Issues Developed in Discussion with JCS, TOP SECRET, September 2, 1958, DDE AWF, Int. Series 11, Formosa (2), 2, DDEPL.

41 Summary, Estimate of Factors Involved in the Taiwan Straits Situation, TOP SECRET, September 4, 1958, DDE 36, Staff Notes September 1958, 2–5, DDEPL.

42 The Nuclear Information Project, "USS Randolph and the Nuclear Diplomatic Incident," http://www.nukestrat.com/dk/randolph.htm (accessed on May 14, 2021).

Without a doubt, the US nuclear policy had a direct impact on Taiwan. For example, during the mid-1960s, the Nationalists began their own nuclear weapons program. According to some declassified reports, the US military stored numerous atomic bombs in Taiwan, and these weapons were not removed until the early 1970s.[43] In 1976, under pressure from the US government, Taiwan agreed to dismantle its nuclear program but following the 1995–96 Taiwan Strait crisis, President Lee Teng-hui proposed reactivating Taiwan's nuclear program.

Although the nuclear aspect of US policy toward the Taiwan Strait was always kept highly secret, it was clear from 1950 onward that atomic weapons were kept available in the region should they be needed to prevent a PRC invasion of Taiwan. These included both larger bombs and smaller tactical A-bombs. Over time, however, conventional weapons like the Sidewinder missile were perceived as being more useful than tactical nukes and so began the replacement of atomic bombs. Also, as the Sino-Soviet "monolith" began to crumble during the late 1950s, it became less likely that the Soviet Union would come to China's rescue.

---

43 In 1974, all nuclear weapons were moved from Taiwan to Clark Air Base in the Philippines "CINCPAC Command History, 1974." http://oldsite.nautilus.org/archives/library/security/foia/Japan/CINCPAC74Ip263.PDF at http://oldsite.nautilus.org/archives/library/security/foia/japanindex.html (accessed on May 14, 2021).

Chapter 7

USING TAIWAN TO UNDERMINE THE SINO-SOVIET ALLIANCE

Rather than resort to force in the Taiwan Strait, the US government hoped to defuse military tensions and to focus instead on longer term goals, like breaking up the Sino-Soviet alliance. As early as November 3, 1948, the CIA hypothesized that "when the issue of subservience to Moscow has become more immediate than that of 'US imperialism', Chinese nationalism will prove stronger than international Communism."[1] A National Intelligence Estimate from September 10, 1952, identified three specific issues that might at some point undermine this alliance: (1) "the Chinese Communists might make demands upon the USSR, or even take action, incompatible with long-range Soviet global interests"; (2) "frictions might arise because of Soviet inability or disinclination to supply capital equipment"; and (3) resistance to "a Communist world dominated from Moscow."[2]

China was portrayed as the weak link in the Sino-Soviet alliance, since the Russians had surrounded themselves with friendly governments in the Baltic and Eastern Europe, while "in the Far East there was a more direct confrontation between the Communist and non-Communist world."[3] This was exemplified in the PRC–ROC standoff over the offshore islands, and in the determination of both Chinese governments to reunify all of China under their authority. In December 1954, for example, Taiwan's Foreign Minister Yeh had vehemently opposed any promotion of a "two-China" theory.[4] But during a February 10, 1955, conversation with Yeh, Dulles stated that he

---

1 Central Intelligence Agency, Possible Developments in China, SECRET, November 3, 1948, PHST, President's Secretary's File, Box 178, P.S.F. Subject File, HSTPL.
2 National Intelligence Estimate, Relations between the Chinese Communist Regime and the USSR: Their Present Character and Probable Future Courses, SECRET, September 10, 1952, PHST, President's Secretary's File, Box 215, P.S.F. Intelligence File, HSTPL.
3 Summary of Remarks of the Honorable John Foster Dulles at Cabinet Meeting Ottawa, TOP SECRET, March 18, 1955, DH 5, Dulles, J.F., March 1955, 1, DDEPL.
4 Memorandum of Conference with the President, December 20, 1954, DDE Papers 3, ACW Diary, December 1954 (2), DDEPL.

believed the solution to the communist threat would take time. Instead of trying to "force Chinese unification by military means" the United States and Taiwan should instead focus on "the vulnerability of Communist regimes to economic and other pressures."[5]

Rather than resorting to war, the US government hoped to use economic tools to undermine the Sino-Soviet alliance. As early as January 17, 1951, the NSC had pointed out that making China more economically dependent on Russia "might strain their relations."[6] On May 4, 1951, a revised version of this report recommended "continue United States economic restrictions against China" and "persuade other nations to adopt similar positions" so as to "stimulate differences between the Peiping and Moscow regimes."[7] Dulles's goal was to "strain the Sino-Soviet alliance by compelling the Chinese to increase economic and military demands for Soviet support to the point where Moscow would be forced to drop Beijing."[8] The primary tool for carrying out this ambitious policy was the multilateral export controls, which "continued or enhanced stresses and strains on the ties between Communist China and its Soviet partners."[9]

Weakening the Sino-Soviet alliance

Washington's goal was to weaken the Sino-Soviet alliance. On September 15, 1947, the CIA assessed that Soviet removal of industrial machinery from Manchuria was to make China a "de-industrialized source of food and raw materials for the Soviet Far East," which, of course, also helped make China a "minimum military threat to the USSR."[10] The NSC noted in 1949 that while wanting to avoid the "appearance of intervention" in China, the US government "should be alert to exploit through political and economic means any rifts between the Chinese Communists and the

---

5 John Foster Dulles Papers, Princeton University, Reel 210/211, February 21, 1955, 92802.
6 NSC, Statement of the Problem, TOP SECRET, January 17, 1951, PHST, President's Secretary's File, Box 182, P.S.F. Subject File, HSTPL.
7 NSC, United States Objectives, Policies and Courses of Action in Asia, TOP SECRET, May 4, 1951, PHST, President's Secretary's File, Box 183, P.S.F. Subject File, HSTPL.
8 Lorenz M. Lüthi, *The Sino-Soviet Split: Cold War in the Communist World* (Princeton, NJ: Princeton University Press, 2008), 247.
9 Multilateral Trade Controls against Communist China: U.S. Position Supporting No Reduction, Draft, Secret, January 7, 1956, DDE White House Office, OSANA Records, NSC Series Policy Paper Subseries, Box 12, NSC 5429/5 Policy Toward the Far East (1), 3, DDEPL.
10 Central Intelligence Agency, Implementation of Soviet Objectives in China, SECRET, September 15, 1947, PHST, President's Secretary's File, Box 216, P.S.F. Intelligence Reports, ORE 45, HSTPL.

USSR."[11] Two years later, the NSC stated that the ultimate goal was to "detach China as an effective ally of the USSR and support the development of an independent China which has renounced aggression."[12]

On October 13, 1948, the NSC submitted a highly prescient report entitled "United States Policy toward China." While acknowledging that the USSR desired to exploit China's natural resources, it was the political situation that was most important:

> But it is the political situation in China which must arouse the aggressive interest of the Kremlin. In the struggle for world domination—a struggle which the Kremlin pursues essentially through political action (even in civil war)—the allegiance of China's millions is worth striving for. That allegiance is worth struggling for if only to deny it to the free world. In positive terms, China is worth having because capture of it would represent an impressive political victory and, more practically, acquisition of a broad human glacis from which to mount a political offensive against the rest of East Asia.

The CIA wisely concluded that Stalin would want only part of China, so he did not want the Chinese Communists to dominate all of China: "China is too big, too populous."[13]

Stalin's desire for control, of course, completely ignored Mao Zedong's desire to unify all of China under the Chinese Communist Party, which meant that the Soviet government had to oppose Mao: "Even Mao and his colleagues cannot be permitted eventually to acquire all of it [Mainland China]—the temptation might be too great for them, especially as they would have, in part, risen to power on the heady wine of nationalism. The Kremlin prefers, where possible, not to take chances in such matters."[14] The USSR was particularly concerned about the growth of Chinese nationalism because of its own predatory actions against China, including "obvious Kremlin cupidity in northern Manchuria, its extraterritorial activities in Sinkiang and the dispatch

11 NSC, Policies of the Government of the United States of America Relating to the National Security, Volume II, TOP SECRET, 1949, PHST, President's Secretary's File, Box 171, P.S.F. Subject File, HSTPL.

12 NSC, Policies of the Government of the United States of America Relating to the National Security, Volume IV, TOP SECRET, 1951, PHST, President's Secretary's File, Box 171, P.S.F. Subject File, HSTPL.

13 NSC, United States Policy toward China, SECRET, October 13, 1948, PHST, President's Secretary's File, Box 178, P.S.F. Subject File, HSTPL.

14 NSC, United States Policy toward China, SECRET, October 13, 1948, PHST, President's Secretary's File, Box 178, P.S.F. Subject File, HSTPL.

of the Soviet Ambassador with the Nationalist Foreign Office to Canton" in the far south. Thus, "the full force of nationalism remains to be released in Communist China."[15]

On January 5, 1950, Truman told Senators Knowland and Smith that he "felt the Soviets were going to encounter increasing difficulties by way of their program of subjugation" of China.[16] The obvious policy to pick would be one that was the opposite of whatever the USSR wanted. Thus, a Sino-Soviet split could be accomplished in a number of ways, including using "all feasible overt and covert means, consistent with a policy of not being provocative of war, to create discontent and internal divisions within each of the Communist-dominated areas of the Far East, and to impair their relations with the Soviet Union and with each other, particularly by stimulating Sino-Soviet estrangement."[17] Dean Acheson told Truman on November 17, 1949, that the best policy was to try to "detach" China from its "subservience to Moscow and over a period of time encourage those vigorous influences which might modify it." In response, Truman said that he thought that "this was the correct analysis."[18]

Soviet eyes are bigger than their stomach

Arguably the most important US government policy, however, was the most counterintuitive: to let the Chinese Communists dominate all of mainland China. The reasoning was actually quite simple: "there appears to be no chance of a split within the Party or between the Party and the USSR until the time of Communist domination of China."[19] Once the Communists took all of the mainland, it was necessary to make China as dependent as possible on the USSR. For example, prior to Mao Zedong's visit to Moscow in early 1950, the US government refused to recognize Beijing, which meant "the Chinese Communists cannot now play off one

---

15 NSC, U.S. Policy toward China, TOP SECRET, February 28, 1949, PHST, President's Secretary's File, Box 179, P.S.F. Subject File, HSTPL
16 Memorandum of Conversation, Formosa Problem, CONFIDENTIAL, January 5, 1950, Dean G. Acheson Papers, Box 66, HSTPL.
17 NSC 5429/5, Policy toward the Far East, TOP SECRET, December 22, 1954, DDE WH Office, OSANSA, NSC Series, Policy Paper Subseries, Box 12, 13, DDEPL.
18 Conversation with the President, China and the Far East, November 17, 1949, Dean G. Acheson Papers, Memorandum of Conversation File, Box 66, HSTPL.
19 Central Intelligence Agency, Chinese Communist Capabilities for Control of all China, SECRET, December 10, 1948, PHST, President's Secretary's File, Box 217, P.S.F. Intelligence Reports, ORE 77–48, HSTPL.

great power against another, since they have no non-Soviet allies at the moment."[20]

Truman did this on purpose. Learning as a boy the classic Ozark saying "one's eyes are bigger than one's stomach," Truman's goal was to push the USSR and China closer together, with the ultimate goal of breaking them apart. According to one June 1950 CIA report, this is exactly what the Soviet government tried to do: "In China, Soviet policy is currently directed toward creating a situation that will preclude any possibility of the Chinese Communists asserting their independence from the Soviet bloc. The USSR undoubtedly assumes that, since the Chinese Communist program depends on Soviet aid, the Peiping regime will not resist Soviet penetration."[21] China's foreign trade was particularly important, and the USSR was interested in the "realignment of China's foreign trade with the Soviet area instead of China's traditional trading partners among the Western nations."[22]

By early 1950 the United States was considering using Taiwan's strategic position to exert economic pressure on the PRC. On January 5, 1950, Edward C. Spowart, Major US Army Reserve, told Truman that they could "turn the table" on Russia:

If we sent Generalissimo Chiang Kai Shek the necessary military equipment such as radar, tanks (preferably M-5a) light bombers, fighter craft, and small arms and ammunition with which he can defend Formosa and continue his attacks on the mainland from Formosa and place a blockade around China proper, Communist China's only sources of supply would be from Russia; and when Russia failed to keep the civilian and military personnel supplied with food, clothing and other essential materials, Communism will have failed in China.[23]

On May 17, 1951, the NSC announced that its top goal was to "detach China as an effective ally of the USSR and [...] Deny Formosa to any Chinese regime aligned with or dominated by the USSR."[24] According to

20 Summary of Telegrams, TOP SECRET, November 27, 1949, PHST, SMOF-Naval Aide, Box 23, State Department Briefs File, HSTPL.
21 Central Intelligence Agency, Review of the World Situation, SECRET, June 14, 1950, PHST, President's Secretary's File, Box 181, P.S.F. Subject File, CIA 6–50, HSTPL.
22 Central Intelligence Agency, Review of the World Situation, SECRET, June 14, 1950, PHST, President's Secretary's File, Box 181, P.S.F. Subject File, CIA 6–50, HSTPL.
23 Letter from Edward C. Spowart to Harry S. Truman, January 5, 1950, PHST, Official File, OF 150-G, Box 761, Formosa, HSTPL.
24 NSC, United States Objectives, Policies and Courses of Action in Asia, TOP SECRET, May 17, 1951, PHST, President's Secretary's File, Box 183, P.S.F. Subject File, HSTPL.

Consul General McConaughy in Hong Kong, the Korean War made the PRC "so thoroughly dependent on the USSR for weapons and ammunition for the Korean war [...] the point has now been reached where additional dependence on the Soviets may hasten the day when the Chinese become disillusioned with Russian aid."[25] The NSC directed the Psychological Strategy Board to "place maximum strain on the Soviet structure of power, including the relationships between the USSR, its satellites, and Communist China."[26] The top goal was to promote "conflict between Chinese national interest and Soviet imperialism."[27] On December 22, 1954, Dulles told Eisenhower that he was depending on "the traditional Chinese dislike of foreigners which was bound in the long run to impair relations with Russia."[28] Or as William R. Gruber had put it more succinctly, "Every nation that has ever tried to control China has mired down in the attempt."[29]

Economic and "other pressures" adopted by the US government were all designed to increase Sino-Soviet frictions. A major focus was on cutting necessary imports to China. The top Western imports China needed to feed its most modernized factories included raw cotton ($75 million in 1951 dollars imported from outside the Soviet bloc), chemicals, dyes, and drugs ($30 million), crude rubber ($25 million), iron and steel products ($25 million), machinery and vehicles, cereals ($14 million), petroleum products ($12 million), jute products ($10 million), and nonferrous metals and manufactures ($10 million). By forcing China to buy these goods from the Soviet bloc, it would require the use of "long and costly transport routes" that would "likely involve losses on the part of one or the other of the trading partners."[30] The result of such a program of economic warfare "would make Communist China more dependent on the very limited Chinese rail facilities connecting with the USSR," which in turn would "hamper current industrial production, retard

---

25 Summary of Telegrams, TOP SECRET, September 18, 1951, PHST, SMOF-Naval Aide, Box 24, State Department Briefs File, HSTPL.

26 NSC, Scope and Pace of Covert Operations, TOP SECRET EYES ONLY, August 22, 1951, PHST, President's Secretary's File, Box 169, P.S.F. Subject File, HSTPL.

27 Central Intelligence Agency, Memorandum for the Senior NSC Staff, SECRET, January 11, 1951, PHST, President's Secretary's File, Box 173, P.S.F. Subject File, HSTPL.

28 Memorandum of Conversation with the President, TOP SECRET, December 22, 1954, Dulles, J.F., W.H. Memo, Box 1, Meetings with the President, 1954 (1), DDEPL.

29 Letter from William R. Gruber to Major General Harry H. Vaughan, November 14, 1948, PHST, Official File, OF 150, Box 759, File O.F. 150 Misc. (1947–48) [2 of 2], HSTPL.

30 Department of State Office of Intelligence Research, Vulnerability of the Soviet Bloc to Existing and Tightened Western Economic Controls, SECRET, January 26, 1951, PHST, President's Secretary's File, Box 183, P.S.F. Subject File, HSTPL.

industrial development and might seriously limit China's ability to sustain large-scale military operations."[31]

When Dulles was talking with the Canadian Cabinet in Ottawa, he explained that the PRC's goal was to expand their power throughout all of East Asia: "I felt that the Chinese Communists felt that they were strong enough to make a worthwhile try at driving US influence away from the entire offshore island chain from the Aleutians to New Zealand and becoming themselves dominant in that part of the world."[32] One method of diverting or even stopping the PRC was to make use of "both Sino-Soviet present weaknesses," and in particular those that might undermine China's alliance with the USSR. Considering that the Soviet Union was facing many severe challenges of its own, including "unreadiness to wage general war, conflicts over its foreign policy, trouble in its leadership and agricultural crisis," how might these factors be used to impact "Soviet willingness adequately to support indirectly or to become directly involved in Chinese Communist military operations against the off-shore islands or Formosa?"[33]

With Chinese coastal shipping blocked by the Nationalists, much of the PRC's domestic North–South trade was diverted inland by train, and China's international trade had to be conducted over the Trans-Siberian railway. Forcing all trade onto the railway resulted in four additional costs: "(a) excessive transport costs, (b) adverse terms of trade for China, (c) significant delays in the delivery of industrial goods and consequent difficulties in procurement and planning, and (d) restrictions on Communist China's ability to earn foreign exchange and to obtain credit." When calculating just the added transport costs alone, it was estimated that China spent $32,000,000 in 1955 while the USSR spent from $53,000,000 to $76,000,000, so a total added transport cost of approximately $100,000,000. When higher prices for imported goods were also factored in, it was estimated that China had to spend $172,000,000 in 1955 just to offset the trade controls. Although, admittedly, the sum total of these costs was "small," the total effect was huge: "They have an important immediate impact on military-industrial expansion which increases internal economic pressures and restricts Communist China's ability to embark on new military ventures in the Far East."[34] When Anthony Eden tried to argue

---

31 Central Intelligence Agency, Vulnerability of the Soviet Bloc to Economic Warfare, SECRET, February 19, 1951, PHST, President's Secretary's File, Box 183, P.S.F. Subject File, HSTPL.

32 Summary of Remarks of the Honorable John Foster Dulles at Cabinet Meeting Ottawa, TOP SECRET, March 18, 1955, DH 5, Dulles, J.F., March 1955, 1, DDEPL.

33 Immediate Actions Re the Formosa Situation, TOP SECRET, March 19, 1955, Dulles, J.F., W.H. Memo, Box 2, W.H. Memo 1955, Formosa Straits (2), 3–4, DDEPL.

34 Multilateral Trade Controls Against Communist China: U.S. Position Supporting No Reduction, Draft, Secret, January 7, 1956, DDE White House Office, OSANA

that trade restrictions for China should be the same as those for Russia, the US side explained that "even though the Soviets might try to ship considerable quantities of supplies to China, a much longer route and higher expense was involved for the Communists, and consequently we did not see any advantage in relaxing controls in the East."[35]

Meanwhile, China's international maritime trade was largely conducted by either foreign-registered or Hong Kong ships, which—in theory at least—were neutral vessels. In response to these US-imposed trade restrictions, the bulk of China's foreign trade now had to be conducted overland either with the Soviet Union directly or via the USSR with a number of friendly Eastern European countries. This put enormous strains on China's own railway system, not to mention the Trans-Siberian railway. This was on purpose, and a 1954 Top Secret study admitted that China could offset the embargo through "importations via the Soviet Union," but that "at the moment transportation facilities limit this possibility."[36] As a result, by 1957, fully "50 percent of China's foreign trade was with the USSR."[37]

The impact of Sino-Soviet relations on a Taiwan Strait resolution

The impact of Sino-Soviet diplomatic relations on resolving the first Taiwan Strait crisis is all too rarely considered. Following Stalin's death in 1953, the leadership of the USSR was in turmoil. The last thing Soviet leaders wanted was for tensions in the Taiwan Strait to drag them into a new World War, especially one that might escalate into the use of nuclear weapons. The same time that the US government was attempting to restrain Chiang Kai-shek, the USSR was actively reducing its military support for China. In fact, right as the first Taiwan Strait crisis reached its peak in early 1955, Moscow decided to withdraw important defensive installations from its former naval base at Lüshun. This action made Manchuria vulnerable to attack from the sea, which—by making possible a USN attack against the north—put pressure on Beijing to deescalate its military operations in the Taiwan Strait.

Records, NSC Series Policy Paper Subseries, Box 12, NSC 5429/5 Policy Toward the Far East (1), 3, 7, DDEPL.

35 Eisenhower Diary, The Eden Talks, February 8, 1956, DDE Diary Series 9, Diary Copies of DDE Personal 1955–56 (2), DDEPL.

36 Report on U.S. Government Policies in Relation to China, TOP SECRET, undated, Dulles, J.F., W.H. Memo, Box 2, 1954, Formosa Straits (1), 7, DDEPL.

37 Bruce A. Elleman and Stephen Kotkin, eds., *Manchurian Railways and the Opening of China: An International History* (Armonk, NY: M.E. Sharpe, 2010), 199.

On February 1, 1955, Eisenhower wrote a long letter to General Alfred Gruenther, Supreme Commander of the Allied Powers in Europe. The president made it clear that while US policy included breaking up the Sino-Soviet alliance, it should not be done through war:

> I do not believe that Russia wants war at this time—in fact, I do not believe that if we became engaged in rather a bitter fight along the coast of China, Russia would want to intervene with her own forces. She would, of course, pour supplies into China in an effort to exhaust us and certainly would exploit the opportunity to separate us from our major allies. But I am convinced that Russia does not want, at this moment, to experiment with means of defense against the [atomic] bombing that we <u>could</u> conduct against her mainland. At the same time, I assume that Russia's treaty with Red China comprehends a true military alliance, which she would either have to repudiate or take the plunge. As a consequence of this kind of thinking, she would probably be in a considerable dilemma if we got into a real shooting war with China. It would not be an easy decision for the men in the Kremlin, in my opinion.

Eisenhower's goal, therefore, was to "do what we believe to be right" and by showing firmness they could undermine the enemy's constant attempts "to disrupt the solidarity of the free world's intentions to oppose their aggressive practices."[38]

Changes in Sino-Soviet relations were an important backdrop to the peaceful resolution of the first Taiwan Strait crisis. An intense leadership struggle erupted in Moscow during March 1953. Political infighting continued through until the February 20, 1956, Twentieth Party Congress, when the First Secretary of the Communist Party of the Soviet Union, Nikita Khrushchev, delivered his "secret speech" denouncing Stalin. During this three-year period, Mao Zedong attempted to renegotiate some of the more onerous aspects of the 1950 Sino-Soviet Treaty, plus he began to assert his own leadership over the international communist movement.

Even before Stalin's death in 1953, important alterations in the 1950 Sino-Soviet Treaty had been made, especially concerning the status of the Manchurian port cities of Lüshun and Dalian. According to a 1952 agreement, all Soviet military forces were scheduled to withdraw from these Manchurian ports by May 31, 1955. Moscow also agreed to transfer "the installations in the area of the Port Arthur [Lüshun] naval base to the Government of the

---

38 Eisenhower letter to Gruenther, TOP SECRET, DDE Ad Series 16, Gruenther, General Alfred 1955 (4), DDEPL; all underlining in original.

People's Republic of China." When Moscow agreed to return the various Manchurian railways and the Lüshun naval base to China without charge, Mao evidently thought that the USSR would also leave the large-caliber guns that were protecting the port. But at the last minute the First Secretary of the Communist Party of the USSR, Nikita Khrushchev, refused to transfer the artillery protecting this strategic base from attack by sea. Instead, Khrushchev demanded that China must pay for these guns: "These are very expensive weapons, we would be selling them at reduced prices."[39]

Moscow's decision during spring 1955 to strip the Port Arthur naval base of its main defensive weapons left China highly vulnerable in Manchuria, since the history of the Sino-Japanese War of 1894–95 and the Russo-Japanese War of 1904–5 had shown that naval invasions could easily reduce these bases from the sea. This Russian decision to not give the Chinese these weapons was perhaps intentional. During May 1955, Dulles even told Molotov during meetings in Vienna that "we had obtained from the Chinese Nationalists arrangements which we thought would enable us to influence the situation for peace from our side and he suggested that the Soviet Union could do the same with the Chinese Communists," in particular since "the Chinese Communists were dependent upon Russia for various strategic supplies and planes and could not develop their plans without Russian support."[40] Khrushchev's decision not to leave the port defenses intact was a clear sign that the USSR was unwilling to back Mao's offensive to retake the offshore islands. He further hinted that the USSR's nuclear umbrella might not cover the Taiwan Strait.

With its northern ports now defenseless, the PRC had little choice but to back down from its aggressive stance far to the south. The Eisenhower administration realized immediately that Beijing's policies had changed. Prior to February 1955, the PRC attacks on the offshore islands were clearly intended as the "first phase of an attack against Taiwan [...] by force." However, after the enactment of the Formosa Resolution on January 29 and the Senate's approval of the Mutual Defense Treaty on February 9, 1955, "Communist propaganda on this subject has fallen to its lowest point for the past year," in part due to the sobering effect of the "display of U.S. sea and air power in the area."[41] The immediate crisis appeared to be over. On April 23, 1955, Beijing

39 Nikita Sergeevich Khrushchev, Sergei Khrushchev, *Memoirs of Nikita Khrushchev: Statesman, 1953–1964* (College Park, PA: Penn State Press, 2007), 434.

40 Conversation at Ambassador's Resident, Vienna on May 14, 1955, TOP SECRET, May 17, 1955, DDE Subject Series Box 70, State, Dept. of (May 1955), 2, DDEPL.

41 Edgar Eisenhower's (?) copy of "Formosa" sent to Maxwell M. Rabb, SECRET, April 7, 1955, Dulles, J.F., W.H. Memo, Box 2, Offshore April–May 1955 (5), 6, DDEPL; this copy includes paragraph 14, which was cut from the draft.

even stated that it was willing to negotiate the status of Taiwan, and on May 1, 1955, the PRC halted the shelling of Jinmen Island. Three months later, on August 1, 1955, as a sign of goodwill China even released 11 captured US airmen previously sentenced to lengthy jail terms.[42]

One can only speculate on the impact of Sino-Soviet relations on Beijing's decision to halt the southern offensive against Taiwan. Certainly, the firm linkages between north and south had been shown before, in particular by the impact of Eisenhower's "unleasing Chiang" policy on the successful negotiation of the Korean armistice, which had then freed up the PLA to redeploy troops to the south. Lacking firm Soviet support in the north, Beijing called off the attack against the offshore islands. Given the correlation of forces arranged against it, the PRC leadership clearly felt that they had little choice but to back down in the first Taiwan Strait crisis. Ultimately, China's coercive tactics against Taiwan did not succeed, in large part because the USSR "failed to come to the PRC's rescue when it was intimidated by the United States."[43]

Growing Sino-Soviet economic tensions

Behind the scenes, there were several important Sino-Soviet diplomatic factors contributing to the second cross-strait crisis. The PRC was determined to break the Nationalist blockade. This decision was in turn linked to growing Sino-Soviet tensions over the PRC's recently adopted economic plan, called the "Great Leap Forward." Mao's decision to shell Jinmen in 1958 without first seeking Soviet approval has even been portrayed as "a challenge not just to Taipei and Washington but to Moscow's domination of the international Communist movement as well."[44]

Due to the US-led economic embargo of China, the PRC's economic dependency on the USSR grew rapidly throughout the 1950s. In 1950, the PRC had borrowed three hundred million US dollars from the USSR, a sum that was clearly insufficient to solve China's economic problems. The PRC's fall 1950 intervention in the Korean War not only led to huge military losses but to even greater debts to the USSR, since to "add insult to injury, Stalin

42 http://www.globalsecurity.org/military/ops/quemoy_matsu.htm   (accessed   on December 14, 2010).

43 John F. Copper, "The Origins of Conflict Across the Taiwan Strait: The Problem of Differences in Perceptions," in Suisheng Zhao, ed., *Across the Taiwan Strait: Mainland China, Taiwan, and the 1995–1996 Crisis* (New York: Routledge, 1999), 49; citing Weiqun Gu, *Conflicts of Divided Nations: The Case of China and Korea* (Westport, CN: Praeger, 1995), 26–28.

44 Ibid., 179.

also demanded payment from China for the Soviet military equipment he had sent to Korea."[45]

During August 1958, Mao initiated a new phase of the "Great Leap Forward." Due to the combined effects of the Nationalist blockade and the US embargo, Mao was initially forced to rely mainly on imports from the USSR to support the Great Leap Forward: "Imports from the Soviet Union rose by an astounding 70 per cent in 1958 and 1959."[46] But Beijing's constant demands on Moscow entailed a financial cost. During summer 1958, for example, when Mao requested that Khrushchev provide Soviet-made nuclear submarines, Khrushchev asked Mao how China could pay for them. Mao responded that "China had unlimited supplies of food." Beginning in 1959, the PRC exported millions of tons of grain, worth an estimated US $935 million, largely to fund its purchases from the USSR.[47]

To increase foreign grain sales to pay for the "Great Leap Forward," the PRC needed to increase its maritime trade. PRC officials attempted to exploit Anglo-American differences in trade policy to achieve this goal. Mao also put pressure on Taiwan to give up its last offshore island bases, which were the "only part of the mainland" the Nationalists still controlled.[48] Not only would this undermine Chiang's goal of returning to the mainland, but the PRC could finally claim to have reunified all of mainland China. All of these foreign policy, economic, and political factors contributed to Mao's decision during August 1958 to attack Jinmen. According to secret reports given to President Eisenhower, morale in the PRC was poor, in fact "so bad that the regime has just cancelled the visas of all foreign newspapermen and ordered them out of the country, apparently to prevent reports of how bad the situation is."[49]

Archival documents prove that Truman's and Eisenhower's common goal was to break apart Russia and China. On November 18, 1958, Ike even talked to Dulles about "our policy of holding firm until changes would occur within the Sino-Soviet bloc." It was neither a quick nor easy goal to achieve: "He felt that these [changes] were inevitable but realized that the policy we were following might not be popular. There were some who wanted to give in;

---

45 Frank Dikötter, *Mao's Great Famine: The History of China's Most Devastating Catastrophe, 1958–1962* (New York: Walker, 2010), 5.

46 Ibid., 73–83.

47 Jung Chang and Jon Halliday, *Mao: The Unknown Story* (New York: Alfred A. Knopf, 2005), 428.

48 Telegram from Washington to Foreign Office (Top Secret), September 5, 1958, The National Archives, Kew, CAB 21/3272.

49 Memorandum of Conversations with the President, TOP SECRET, September 11, 1958, JFDP, WHM 7, WH Meet J-D 1958 (6), 1–3, DDEPL.

others who wanted to attack. The policy that required patience was rarely popular."[50]

Conclusions

Rather than "losing" China, American policy was to let the Russians have it. As early as January 2, 1950, Truman was told that the Chinese would never follow the "Moscow line" because the "Chinese are not built that way." Furthermore, due to the potency of the "Asia for the Asiatics" movement, the Russians were "not accepted by Orientals as Asiatics."[51] Pushing the two countries into working together tore them apart. This political outcome largely achieved one of Dulles's prime strategic goals of forcing the USSR and the PRC closer, on the theory "intimacy breeds contempt." In 1957, Former French Premier Edgar Faure visited Beijing. While he thought the US policy of isolating China was a mistake, he agreed that it "will increase China's extreme dependency on the USSR."[52]

In the immediate aftermath of the Sino-Soviet split, which occurred right after the 1958 Taiwan Strait crisis, the PRC's trade with the USSR began to decline, just as its trade with the West began to grow. Chinese grain trade with Canada and Australia helped offset the effects of the Great Famine. According to one view of the US embargo's impact:

> China's dependence on Soviet assistance inevitably created heavy economic burdens on Moscow and could slow down Soviet development, thus making the Moscow-Beijing alliance quite costly. On the other hand, Sino-Soviet economic leverage placed the Kremlin in a politically favorable position from which to dictate relations within the alliance and influence the CCP's domestic and foreign policies. This paradoxical situation turned out to be a major contributor to the collapse of the Soviet economic cooperation and the eventual deterioration of the alliance between the two Communist powers.[53]

---

50 Memorandum of Conversation with the President, SECRET, November 18, 1958, JFD Papers, W.H. Memo, Box 7, Meetings July–December (3), 1–23, DDEPL.

51 Letter from H. T. Goodier to Harry S. Truman, January 2, 1950, PHST, Official File, OF 150-G, Box 761, Formosa, HSTPL; underlining in the original.

52 Faure Views on Red China, Confidential, July 16, 1957, DDE Diary 25, July 1957, Staff Memos (1), DDEPL.

53 Shu Guang Zhang, *Economic Cold War: America's Embargo against China and the Sino-Soviet Alliance, 1949–1963* (Stanford: Stanford University Press, 2001), 268–69.

The US government carried out a highly secretive and complex policy, using a wide variety of military, economic, and political means, of pushing China and the USSR together so as to heighten their bilateral tensions. In the end, the "indirect and long-term effect" of US policies like the strategic embargo produced sufficiently high tensions in Beijing's economic relations with Moscow that by 1960 it "led to the disintegration of the Sino-Soviet alliance."[54] Control over the offshore islands was crucial to the ultimate success of these policies. During the rest of the Cold War, Taiwan continued to control these offshore islands.

---

54 Zhang, *Economic Cold War*, 268–69.

Chapter 8

TAIWAN DURING THE COLD WAR AND AFTERWARD

The Taiwan Strait was ignored through the 1960s, especially after the USSR and PRC went to war in 1969. In 1972, President Nixon visited Beijing, and in 1979 President Carter recognized the PRC. From 1979 through 1989 the United States and the PRC actively cooperated against the USSR, with Washington authorizing sales of high-tech naval equipment to China.[1] This helped to limit tension in the Taiwan Strait. In fact, after 1979 the need for the Taiwan Patrol Force itself seemed to be long past. However, the US government maintained a strong interest in Taiwan's defense and continued to sell it weapons.[2] With the end of the Cold War in 1989, followed soon afterward by the 1991 collapse of the USSR, the unsteady balance of power in the Taiwan Strait began to shift once again.

These events gave China an unforeseen opportunity to expand its influence in Asia. It rapidly began to build up its naval forces, in part to fill the military vacuum left by the Soviet Union's retreat. With the help of the new Russian Federation—mainly sales of advanced naval equipment, including *Sovremennyy* destroyers and Kilo submarines—the PLAN began a long period of growth.[3] The PRC also developed a large missile force, deployed mainly against Taiwan. Arguably, it has been this rapid military growth that has in recent years upset the PRC–Taiwan military balance.

The growth of the PLAN has, in turn, created a strategic shift that has produced in a sense an unofficial reinstitution of the Taiwan Patrol Force. During 1995–96, as a result of PRC missile testing off Taiwan, the USN responded by sending aircraft carriers and destroyers into the region. This

---

1 James Bussert and Bruce A. Elleman, *People's Liberation Army Navy (PLAN) Combat Systems Technology, 1949–2010* (Annapolis, MD: Naval Institute Press, 2011), 2, 12.
2 Michael S. Chase, "U.S.-Taiwan Security Cooperation: Enhancing an Unofficial Relationship," in Nancy Bernkopf Tucker, ed., *Dangerous Strait: The U.S.-Taiwan-China Crisis* (New York: Columbia University Press, 2005), 164.
3 Bussert and Elleman, *People's Liberation Army Navy (PLAN) Combat Systems Technology, 1949–2010*, 14–15, 101, 175.

naval demonstration was similar to the USN's response to the Taiwan Strait crises of the 1950s and early 1960s. In fact, these events represented yet another Taiwan Strait crisis.[4]

The 1995–96 Taiwan Strait crisis

After 37 years of relative peace in the Taiwan Strait, tensions broke out again in 1995. The July 1995 missile tests by the PRC are often portrayed as a response to the granting of an American visa to Taiwan's President Lee Teng-hui for an unofficial visit to Cornell University in early June. However, the real issue was the PRC's concern over Taiwan's rapid democratization and the growing separatist claims by large numbers of Taiwanese. On July 18, 1995, China announced that ballistic missile tests would take place between July 21 and 28. These dates corresponded to the 50th anniversary of the 1945 Potsdam Treaty, by which China was to regain all territories it had lost to Japan, including Taiwan, after World War II.

In connection with the tests the PRC declared an exclusion zone, a 10-nautical-mile circle, in which ships and planes could not safely enter. This zone was about 85 miles north of Taiwan, outside ROC sovereign waters but in a location that actively interfered with flight paths and shipping lanes. Beijing's announcement warned other states "against entering the said sea area and air space" during the firing period. Six DF-15 (CSS-6/M-9) short-range ballistic missiles (SRBMs) were fired, two each on July 21, 22, and 23. Unlike similar tests by Taiwan itself during the mid-1960s, which were generally ignored, this one diverted hundreds of commercial flights heading for Taipei.[5]

The following month, from August 15 to 25, the PRC held military exercises involving about 20 warships and 40 aircraft in a large area to the northwest of the SRBM splash zone; both antiship and antiaircraft missiles were fired. In November 1995, just prior to Taiwan's December parliamentary elections, the PLA staged further naval, amphibious, and air-assault operations, near Dongshan Island. The scenario included blockade tactics, which made it appear that the PRC was planning to mount a naval blockade against Taiwan.

The PRC's use of a missile firing as an occasion to create an exclusion zone around Taiwan was not new, in that it essentially copied Taiwan's own Nike and Hawk tests in April 1965. Those tests had elicited no public protest, but

---

4   Overlooking a 1962 episode, Wikipedia incorrectly refers to these events as the "Third Taiwan Strait Crisis"; *Wikipedia*, wikipedia .org/, s.v. "Third Taiwan Strait Crisis."

5   Richard D. Fisher, "China's Missiles over the Taiwan Strait: A Political and Military Assessment," in James R. Lilley and Chuck Downs, eds., *Crisis in the Taiwan Strait* (Washington, DC: American Enterprise Institute, 1997), 170–71.

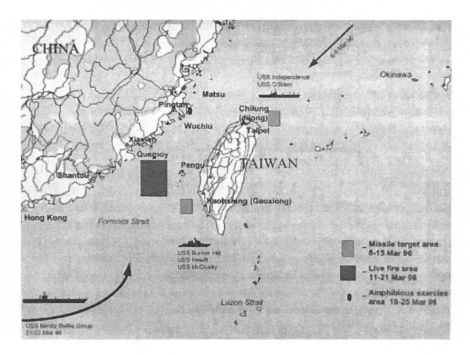

Map 3 1995–96 Missile Blockade Incident.

due to the higher number of airplanes now overflying these waters, the PRC's 1995 exclusion zone put intense pressure on Taipei. It has accordingly been referred to as representing a new form of "missile blockade"[6] (see Map 3).

In response, the USN sent USS *Nimitz* (CVN 68) near the Taiwan Strait on December 19, 1995, on its way to the Indian Ocean. The reported reason for transiting the strait rather than going east of Taiwan was poor weather, and the PRC did not seem to know about, or at least did not acknowledge, the transit. But on January 27, 1996, the *United Daily News* and *New York Times* reported it. If true, this was the first time an American aircraft carrier had transited the Taiwan Strait since the late 1970s. Whether intentionally or not, it sent a sharp signal to Beijing not to interfere in Taiwan's domestic politics. In many ways, the December 1995 transit by a US aircraft carrier of the Taiwan Strait paralleled the June 29, 1950, visit by *Valley Forge*, which had signaled the establishment of the Taiwan Patrol Force. The *Nimitz* transit,

---

6 Chris Rahman, "Ballistic Missiles in China's Anti-Taiwan Blockade," in Bruce A. Elleman and S. C. M. Paine, ed., *Naval Blockades and Seapower: Strategies and Counter-Strategies, 1805–2005* (London: Routledge, 2006), 215–24.

even if serendipitously, sent a similar hands-off message and in fact has been described as "a carefully controlled and minimally provocative use of military power which allowed the United States to reemphasize the 'ambiguous' policy of previous U.S. presidents designed to maintain a balance in U.S. relations with both sides of the strait."[7]

In response to what it now perceived as an American show of force, Beijing warned the US Assistant Secretary of Defense, Charles W. "Chas" Freeman, Jr., that the PRC would launch a missile per day against Taiwan for a period of 30 days if Taipei continued on its path toward formal independence. A Chinese official, in an almost exact repeat of Mao's February 5, 1955, meeting with the Finnish ambassador in which he had threatened the United States with Soviet nuclear retaliation, even warned Freeman that Washington should not intervene in a cross-strait crisis, because American leaders "care more about Los Angeles than they do about Taiwan."[8] China's missile-a-day strategy and implied nuclear threat against the United States were also reminiscent of similar PRC pressure tactics during the 1950s in connection with Jinmen.

Sino-US tension was now high. On March 5, 1996, the 43rd anniversary of the death of Stalin—one of the three world leaders at Potsdam—Beijing announced that it would conduct a new series of ballistic missile exercises during March 8–15, which corresponded with the run-up to Taiwan's first presidential elections under universal suffrage. This time there were two missile splash zones. One was a square just 30 miles from Keelung, close to air and sea-lanes serving Japan and Korea. The other, also square, lay about 47 miles west of Kaohsiung, close to air and sea-lanes to Hong Kong.

The tests were clearly intended to cut trade routes from Keelung in the north and Kaohsiung in the south. These two ports accounted for about 70 percent of Taiwan's commerce. Between March 8 and 13 four dummy missiles landed in the target areas. On March 9 the PRC warned ships and aircraft to avoid a live-fire exercise from March 12 to 20 in the southern part of the Taiwan Strait. The rectangular zone declared for these exercises was just south of Jinmen Island. A further exercise was announced on March 15, to be carried out from March 18 to 25, continuing the military pressure until after the presidential election. Although this new zone was smaller, it was strategically located between Mazu and Wuchiu.[9] The PRC tests were timed

---

7 Rick M. Gallagher, *The Taiwan Strait Crisis*, Research Report 10–97 (Newport, RI: Naval War College, Strategic Research Department, October 1997), 2–3.
8 Patrick E. Tyler, "As China Threatens Taiwan, It Makes Sure U.S. Listens," *New York Times*, January 24, 1996.
9 Tyler, "China Warns U.S. to Keep Away from Taiwan Strait.".

to influence Taiwan's presidential election, scheduled for March 23, in such a way that the proindependence candidates would not win.

In response, the USN dispatched the USS *Independence* (CV 62) aircraft carrier battle group to the area. Its aircraft patrolled about a hundred miles off Taiwan. The USS *Nimitz* group was ordered to return to the strait from the Persian Gulf at high speed. Other naval assets included two Aegis guided-missile cruisers and Rivet Joint electronic surveillance aircraft.[10]

CinCPac, Adm. Joseph Prueher, decided to put *Independence* east of Taiwan and to assign the Aegis cruisers north and south of Taiwan: "Got them there fast. Got them there quietly. But nobody knew that they were there, so we had to tell the media in Okinawa and Japan. Media switch is not vernier switch but on/off switch. Pictures in the press began to appear." Apparently as a result of the presence of *Independence* and the recall of *Nimitz* from the Persian Gulf, the Chinese fired only five missiles, three in the north and two in the south, instead of the much larger number originally planned.[11] As noted by Adm. Lyle Bien, Commander, Carrier Group 7, "ordering *Nimitz* to sail all the way from the Gulf at flank speed was an unmistakable signal to the PRC that we were serious and it was noted by all onboard *Nimitz* that the missile firings stopped only when we approached on-station."[12]

The United States also sent official protests to the Chinese government, Secretary of State Warren Christopher calling the PRC's actions "reckless" and a White House spokesman stating that Washington was "deeply disturbed by this provocative act."[13] Congress resolved that in the face of overt threats by the PRC against the ROC and consistent with its commitment under the Taiwan Relations Act, the United States would continue to supply defensive weapons systems, including "naval vessels, aircraft, and air defense, all of which are crucial to the security of Taiwan." Congress further resolved that the "United States is committed to the military stability of the Taiwan Straits and United States military forces should defend Taiwan in the event of invasion, missile attack, or blockade by the People's Republic of China."[14] Not only did this closely parallel congressional resolutions during the first Taiwan

---

10 Michael Richardson, "Asia Looks to U.S. to Protect Trade Routes around Taiwan," *International Herald Tribune*, March 14, 1996.

11 Bruce A. Elleman, "The Right Skill Set: Joseph Wilson Prueher (1941–)," in John B. Hattendorf and Bruce A. Elleman, ed., *Nineteen-Gun Salute: Case Studies of Operational, Strategic, and Diplomatic Naval Leadership during the 20th and Early 21st Centuries* (Newport, RI: Naval War College Press/Washington, DC: GPO, 2010), 237.

12 Vice Adm. Lyle Bien, USN (Ret.), e-mail to author, March 23, 2011.

13 Tyler, "China Signaling U.S. That It Will Not Invade Taiwan."

14 "104th Congress, 2d Session, H.Con.Res. 148," March 7, 1996, available at ftp.resource .org/gpo.gov/bills/104/hc148ih.txt.

Strait crisis, of 1954–55, but its wording matched almost exactly the stated goals of the long-gone Taiwan Patrol Force.

The USN's intervention gave the PRC pause. Washington's decision to send not one but two aircraft carriers—plus the two Aegis cruisers and other naval assets—to the Taiwan Strait constituted the largest demonstration of American naval diplomacy against China since the first two strait crises in the 1950s.[15] The strategic rationale was much the same as in 1950: to neutralize this region so as to not allow a cross-strait invasion. While not officially part of a new Taiwan Patrol Force, therefore, *Independence* and *Nimitz* carried out a similar function. Seen in this larger historical context, Washington's decision to send in the USN was a direct continuation in spirit of that earlier operation. That spirit continues to the present day.

The April 1, 2001, EP-3 incident

USN patrols in the Taiwan Strait have played a continuing and important role since the turn of the twenty-first century. After remaining fairly quiet since the 1995–96 events, US–Chinese relations became extremely tense following a collision on April 1, 2001, between Chinese and American planes and the resulting unauthorized landing of the damaged US aircraft, an EP-3 surveillance aircraft, on Hainan Island. The subsequent standoff over the return of the EP-3 crew led to discussion in Washington about whether to send yet another aircraft carrier to China. While USN vessels were not sent into the area, the suggestion shows that the same calculations that had led to the creation of the Taiwan Patrol Force still existed in 2001.

To resolve the standoff, Joseph Prueher, now the US ambassador to China, worked closely with two Annapolis classmates, Richard Armitage, who was Secretary of State Colin L. Powell's deputy at the State Department, and Adm. Dennis C. Blair, CinCPac. At one crucial stage Admiral Blair offered to send an aircraft carrier to the waters off China. This would normally have been Prueher's favored solution, as shown by his own actions in 1995–96, but the ambassador declined this suggestion, fearing that too strong a signal might backfire and lead to the prolongation of the incident.[16]

Rather than turning to the USN, then, Prueher urged the administration to ease tension and instead negotiate a way out.[17] Early in the talks the

---

15 Fisher, "China's Missiles over the Taiwan Strait," 178.
16 David E. Sanger and Steven Lee Myers, "How Bush Had to Calm Hawks in Devising a Response to China," *New York Times*, April 13, 2001.
17 Steven Mufson and Dana Milbank, "Diplomats Resurgent in Bush's 1st Test," *Washington Post*, April 13, 2001.

Chinese tried to get the United States to say it had invaded China's airspace, but Powell refused: "We're not going to take that charge to the President, and we're not going to accept it." Prueher, however, having originally offered to express the "regret" of the United States for the unauthorized landing, shifted significantly to saying that his government was "sorry" for it, then "very sorry."[18] This language made it seem to the Chinese public that the United States was taking responsibility for the collision. After 10 days of tense negotiation, this ambiguous apology helped break the diplomatic impasse. After the "two sorrys" letter was signed and delivered by Prueher, the EP-3's 24 crew members were released.

Resolving the EP-3 crisis peacefully was largely possible thanks to Prueher's qualifications as an aircraft carrier pilot with actual combat experience in the region, as a test pilot familiar with the capabilities of the airframes involved, and as a recent CinCPac with experience dealing with China. As he later explained, the dispute was not about an airplane but about "face," and China needed a "signal that it is taken seriously."[19] Prueher wanted to find a graceful way for Beijing to back down from its untenable position. His solution was the "two sorrys" letter, which the Chinese could interpret as a "formal apology" but the US government could portray as "merely a polite expression of regret."[20]

Ultimately no aircraft carrier was sent into the region during 2001, but the fact that it was seriously considered emphasizes the flexibility inherent in having USN forces within easy reach of the Taiwan Strait. During the following eight years, Sino-US naval relations remained outwardly calm, and there were few publicly acknowledged maritime disputes. This situation changed in March 2009, when two survey ships were accosted while conducting operations in international waters near China.

The 2009 *Impeccable* and *Victorious* incidents

For almost a decade after the EP-3 incident, Sino-US military-to-military relations seemed friendly. This situation suddenly changed during March 2009, however, when PRC ships confronted the civilian-manned US ocean surveillance vessel USNS *Impeccable* (T-AGOS 23) while it was conducting maritime research in international waters in the South China Sea. Two months

---

18 Johanna McGeary, "Safe Landing: A Carefully Engineered Game Plan Helped Bush Bring the U.S. Flight Crew Home," *Time*, April 23, 2001.
19 Elisabeth Rosenthal, "China Gets White House's Attention, and Some Respect," *New York Times*, April 12, 2001.
20 Elleman, "The Right Skill Set," 242.

later, in May 2009, American defense officials announced that Chinese vessels had surrounded a second surveillance ship, USNS *Victorious* (T-AGOS 19), in the Yellow Sea. These two incidents prompted a strong USN response.

On March 8, 2009, five PRC ships harassed *Impeccable* in international waters about 75 miles south of Hainan Island. Two of the Chinese vessels came within 50 feet, and its sailors were observed "waving Chinese flags and telling the U.S. ship to leave the area." The State Department lodged a protest with Chinese officials, and spokesman Robert Wood later told reporters, "We felt that our vessel was inappropriately harassed."[21]

The USN's reaction to these Chinese provocations was rapid. Within days a guided-missile destroyer, USS *Chung-Hoon* (DDG 93), "armed with torpedoes and missiles," was sent to protect USNS *Impeccable*.[22] The Chinese government condemned this USN action as provocative. One Chinese scholar declared, "The '*Impeccable* Incident' constitutes the most serious friction between China and the United States since the collision of their military aircraft near Hainan Island in April 2001."[23]

At about the same time as the *Impeccable* incident, another surveillance ship, *Victorious*, operating 120 miles off China's coast in the Yellow Sea, was harassed several times on March 4–5, 2009, by Chinese patrol ships and aircraft. On May 1 American defense officials announced the confrontation.[24] Pentagon officials claimed that two Chinese ships had come within 30 yards of *Victorious*, which had been forced to use water hoses to warn them off. Once again protesting, the US government reiterated that it would not "end its surveillance activities in the region."[25]

Both incidents took place in international waters. As part of the US government's long-time support for freedom of the seas, USN officials emphasized that it should not be necessary to send armed ships to protect USNS survey ships.[26] The fact that the *Impeccable* incident took place in the

21 Tony Capaccio, "Chinese Vessels Harass U.S. Navy Ship, Pentagon Says," *Bloomberg*, March 9, 2009, www.bloomberg.com/.

22 Ann Scott Tyson, "Destroyer to Protect Ship near China," *Washington Post*, March 13, 2009.

23 Ji Guoxing, "The Legality of the '*Impeccable* Incident,'" *China Security* 5, no. 2 (Spring 2009).

24 Jane Macartney, "Chinese and American Ships Clash Again in the Yellow Sea," *Times/Sunday Times*, May 6, 2009, www.timesonline .co.uk/.

25 "Pentagon Reports Naval Incident in Yellow Sea," VOANews.com, May 5, 2009.

26 Barbara Starr, "Chinese Boats Harassed U.S. Ships, Officials Say," *CNN World*, 5 May 2009, articles.cnn.com/. For an examination of the issues from both perspectives, see Peter Dutton, ed., *Military Activities in the EEZ: A U.S.-China Dialogue on Security and International Law in the Maritime Commons*, China Maritime Study 7 (Newport, RI: Naval

South China Sea, south of Taiwan, and the *Victorious* incident in the Yellow Sea far to the north gives an impression of testing the USN's readiness and resolve at the geographic extremes of the Taiwan Strait. The USN's rapid responses to these PRC provocations were largely in line with operational procedures first adopted by the Taiwan Patrol Force, beginning in late June 1950.

Conclusions

Although the Taiwan Patrol Force officially ended on January 1, 1979, the American reaction to the 1995–96 PRC missile tests proved remarkably similar to those to the earlier Taiwan Strait crises. In 2009 there was even a "touch of irony" in assigning *Chung-Hoon* to guard *Impeccable*, since that vessel was "named for a Chinese-American naval officer awarded the Navy Cross, the nation's second-highest combat decoration, for heroic action against Japanese kamikaze pilots during World War II."[27] Assigning this particular ship to patrol duty could not help but remind the PRC that the two countries had been close allies in World War II against Japan. It also showed American resolve not to cede freedom of the seas.

Even today the lingering effects of the Taiwan Patrol Force can be felt. While fixed patrols have not been carried out in the strait since 1979, the USN's presence in the region remains strong. There is a compelling argument to be made, therefore, that the Taiwan Patrol Force never really ended. In fact, the 1995–96 decision to send in aircraft carriers was part and parcel of the same 1950s buffer operation mounted to ensure that PRC–ROC tension did not escalate into a larger war.

The 1995–96 "missile blockade," the 2001 EP-3 incident, the US–Chinese naval incident during spring 2009 in the South China Sea, and the similar incident in the Yellow Sea, all occurred either in or at the ends of the Taiwan Strait. The similarity of the USN's reactions to all of them highlights not only the continuing strategic value of this region but also the importance of the USN's maritime presence to peace in the Taiwan Strait. In this sense, all these recent USN deployments to international waters near China have carried on the historical legacy of the Taiwan Patrol Force.

War College Press, December 2010), available at www.usnwc.edu/Publications/ Publications.aspx.

27 Richard Halloran, "US-Chinese Contacts Are Imperative for Military," *Taipei Times*, March 17, 2009.

CONCLUSIONS

THE TAIWAN STRAIT'S STRATEGIC SIGNIFICANCE TODAY

Tensions during the 1950s between the PRC and Taiwan were focused mainly on offshore islands in or near the Taiwan Strait. The US government was concerned that a spark in this critical theater might erupt into war, perhaps even a global war between the United States and the Sino-Soviet "monolith." Washington usually sought to deescalate tensions over the offshore islands through its diplomatic relations with Taiwan. But at other times the US government actively sought to exert military pressure—by means of "unleashing Chiang"—in order to force the PRC to reallocate military units away from north and move them to the south. As Senator Alexander Smith told Secretary of State Dulles during April 1955, if Korea and Indochina were the two flanks then Taiwan was the center, and that "we should keep open a threat to the center in order to protect the two flanks."[1] In this regard, the Taiwan Patrol Force acted much like a Vernier light switch, allowing the USN to "dial" up or down cross-strait tensions to suit US larger policy objectives throughout East Asia.[2]

Truman's refusal to become involved in China's civil war saved the United States from becoming bogged down in a quagmire. On January 11, 1949, the NSC explained that while the "objective of the U.S. with respect to China is the eventual development by the Chinese themselves of a unified, stable and independent China friendly to the U.S.," this goal was "not likely to be accomplished by any apparent Chinese group or groups within the foreseeable future."[3] On September 26, 1952, Truman received a fan letter quoting

---

1 Memorandum of Meeting with the Senators, April 27, 1955, TOP SECRET, April 28, 1955, Dulles, J.F., Gen Cor Box 1, Memos J-K (2), DDEPL.
2 Bruce A. Elleman, *High Sea's Buffer: The Taiwan Patrol Force, 1950–1979* (Newport, RI: NWC Press, 2012).
3 NSC, United States Policy Toward China, TOP SECRET, January 11, 1949, PHST, President's Secretary's File, Box 178, P.S.F. Subject File, HSTPL.

Republican Senator Lehman from a speech the previous day as admitting that China "could have been saved, if at all, [only] by all-out military intervention on our part." Not only would the United States have "become bogged down in the immense expanse of China, in a war to keep Chiang-Kai-Shek in power, [but it] […] would have cost us millions of men and billions of dollars."[4]

US diplomacy with Chiang Kai-shek proved to be one of the greatest challenges. As the Department of State warned on January 19, 1949, when working with Taiwan the "choice is not between satisfactory and unsatisfactory courses of action but rather of the least of several evils or an amalgam of the lesser of them."[5] Two U.S.-Taiwanese secret agreements, one signed in December 1954 and the other in October 1958, allowed Washington to exert crucial leverage over Chiang in order to minimize the chances that a small conflict in the Taiwan Strait might accidentally escalate into an all-out war between the PRC and ROC, or even a larger global conflict between the USSR and the United States. By keeping both agreements a secret, however, Chiang could retain "face" even while ceding actual authority to Washington over whether his forces would go to war with the PRC.

While the positive side of keeping all agreements secret is that it allowed Washington to call the shots, there was also a highly negative side to keeping these arrangements secret. Because the specific terms of these agreements were unknown to the public, Washington often received the lion's share of global blame for rising tensions in the Taiwan Strait, even though it was, in fact, often working behind the scenes to quell these tensions. Meanwhile, this self-same secrecy provided Chiang with greater public leverage to obtain his goals. In the end, however, this was a price that Eisenhower and Dulles decided they would willingly pay to keep the peace in East Asia.

The US military policy in the Taiwan Straits was critical to supporting stability throughout East Asia. On October 12, 1950, the CIA released a Top Secret study that determined: "Without direct Soviet participation and given strong naval and air assistance by the US armed forces, the Chinese Nationalist defense forces are capable of holding Formosa against a determined Chinese Communist invasion."[6] During March 1956, the British intelligence services

---

4 Letter from Guy Carolin to Harry S. Truman, September 26, 1952, PHST, Official File, OF 150, Box 760, File O.F. 150 Misc. (1951–53) [1 of 2], HSTPL.
5 The Department of State, The Position of the United States with Respect to Formosa, TOP SECRET, January 19, 1949, PHST, President's Secretary's File, Box 178, P.S.F. Subject File, HSTPL.
6 CIA Report "Background on Possible Items for Discussion on Wake Island," TOP SECRET, October 12, 1950, PHST, President's Secretary's File, Box 208, P.S.F. Korean War File, Wake Island Talks [1 of 2], HSTPL.

concluded that although the Communists were capable of launching a full-scale attack on the offshore islands, it is "highly improbable that they will conduct military operations of this magnitude as long as the Seventh Fleet remains in the area." Instead of trying to stage an invasion, therefore, the PRC falsely assumed that time was on its side, and that "it would be pointless to fight for areas which they hope to acquire in due course through subversion and propaganda."[7]

The most important US military goal was to protect Taiwan from being invaded by the PRC. An equally important political goal, however, was reassuring America's East Asian allies, including Japan, South Korea, the Philippines, and Australia, that the PRC could not expand onto the first island chain. As early as June 10, 1949, Chennault warned: "A Communist Asia Means the Loss of the Pacific Islands," and that "the loss of China sets off a chain reaction that may take months or even several years to accomplish."[8] This was an early description of the dreaded "domino effect," with this theory stating that the fall of even a small East Asian nation to communism would set off a chain reaction leading to the fall of the rest.

The Japanese were especially impacted by Russian and Chinese expansionism. In early 1950, Hollington K. Tong argued: "As long as the National Government survives at Formosa, with its constant threat of invasion of the mainland, Russia will go slow in its aggressive action against Japan. It is important to American security in Japan thus to keep Russia off-base in China."[9] During 1955, a Japanese official in Taipei clarified that it was "the strategic value of the island itself," dominating the sea-lanes from Japan to the south and "keeping it from the Chinese Communists," that mattered most to Tokyo.[10] Eisenhower privately told his friend Lew Douglas: "It is true that our strategic situation would be seriously—possibly even fatally—damaged in the Western Pacific if we should lose Formosa to the Communists."[11]

During 1958, when discussing his upcoming talks with Chiang Kai-shek, Dulles even emphasized to the British that if the Japanese thought the

7 John Foster Dulles Papers, Princeton University, Reel 212/213, March 6, 1956, 94964.

8 Letter from Major General Claire Lee Chennault to John R. Steelman, June 10, 1949, PHST, Official File, OF 150, Box 759, File O.F. 150 Misc. (1947–48) [2 of 2], HSTPL; underlining in original.

9 Letter from Hollington K. Tong to Harry S. Truman, January 4, 1950, PHST, Official File, OF 150, Box 759, File O.F. 150 Misc. (1947–48) [1 of 2], HSTPL.

10 John Foster Dulles Papers, Princeton University, Reel 212/213, November 22, 1955, 94355.

11 Eisenhower Letter to L. W. Douglas, Personal and Confidential, March 9, 1955, DDE Diary Series 10, DDE Diary March 1955 (2), DDEPL.

United States was weaker than China, "they would go over to the Chinese Communists just as quickly as they could."[12] However, due to Japan's World War II experience with the A-bomb, using atomic weapons to prove American strength could be equally dangerous, and Ambassador MacArthur in Tokyo warned that the consequences of using atomic weapons "could range from denial by the Japanese Government of continued use of our bases in Japan, either for operations or logistical support, to a strike by Japanese labor on the bases, which would make them virtually inoperable."[13] This complex situation tied Washington's hands; it had to support Taiwan militarily but try its best to avoid using atomic bombs while doing so.

It was widely believed that the best interest of all Asian countries could be furthered by forming a Pacific Pact, similar to NATO in Europe. However, as Douglas MacArthur told Truman at their October 15, 1950, meeting at Wake Island, "due to lack of homogeneity of the Pacific nations" these countries did not want to cooperate together but wanted "assurance of security from the United States."[14] America's Asian alliances and coalition partners looked to Washington to protect Taiwan. As Dulles freely admitted, aiding the Nationalists might end up involving the United States in a "civil dispute." But China was not the only case of a divided country. Other examples included "Korea, Germany, Austria, Vietnam and Laos." According to Dulles: "If there were armed attacks from the Communist portions of these countries against the non-Communist portions, we would aid the latter and in fact did so in Korea."[15]

In January 1950, President Truman was warned: "If we lose Formosa we will have lost not only a perfect military base for Army operations, but the controlling link between China, the Philippines, Indo China, Siam, Burma and all of India; and it is a well known fact that the Philippines will go Communist within a short period after the fall of Formosa."[16] Therefore, letting the PRC take the offshore islands would eventually lead to Chinese pressure against Taiwan sufficient to "bring about a government which would

---

12 Telegram from Foreign Office to UK Embassy, Washington, October 22, 1958, The National Archives, Kew, PREM 11/3738.

13 Taiwan Straits: Issues Developed in Discussion with JCS, TOP SECRET, September 2, 1958, DDE AWF, Int. Series 11, Formosa (2), 3, DDEPL.

14 Substance of Statements made at Wake Island Conference, TOP SECRET, October 15, 1950, PHST, President's Secretary's File, Box 208, P.S.F. Korean War File, Wake Island Talk: Conference—Statements, HSTPL.

15 John Foster Dulles Letter to Lew Douglas, PERSONAL, March 19, 1955, DDE Ad Series 12, Douglas, Lewis W. (3), DDEPL.

16 Letter from Edward C. Spowart to Harry S. Truman, January 5, 1950, PHST, Official File, OF 150-G, Box 761, Formosa, HSTPL.

eventually advocate union with Communist China and the elimination of US positions on the islands."[17]

Should this happen, Truman was told, then it would "seriously jeopardize" the anti-communist island barrier composed of Japan, South Korea, Taiwan, the Philippines, Thailand, and Vietnam. Other Southeast Asian states, including Indonesia, Malaya, Cambodia, Laos, and Burma, would "probably come fully under Communist influence." Finally, US bases on Okinawa would become "untenable" and Japan would "probably fall within the Sino-Soviet orbit." Although all of these losses would happen gradually, over many years, this estimate concluded: "The consequences in the Far East would be even more far-reaching and catastrophic than those which followed when the United States allowed the Chinese mainland to be taken over by the Chinese Communists, aided and abetted by the Soviet Union."[18]

One method to dissuade the PRC from invading Taiwan was to provide the Nationalists with a dependable source of military equipment and training to defend themselves, even while not giving them sufficiently advanced equipment to allow Taiwan to attack the PRC. According to a US intelligence advisory committee report from April 1957, in the near term the "Nationalists are very unlikely to launch an invasion or, in the absence of Chinese Communist provocation, to initiate other major military action."[19] Due to the Chinese on Taiwan displaying "a degree of cooperation and intelligent effort scarcely equaled elsewhere in American experience," this partnership proved to be a "strategic bargain" for Washington since the "creation of United States military bases has been rendered unnecessary by the size and effectiveness of the Chinese military establishment."[20] This helped to relieve tensions. After a particularly bad incident in Taiwan, Eisenhower told Dulles: "The President thinks we must have a very serious look at these Asiatic countries, and decide whether we can stay there. It does not seem wise, if they hate us so much."[21] Later, on June 4, 1957, Eisenhower told Senator Wiley that stationing troops in foreign countries "should only be done when impossible to avoid it," and

17 Summary, Estimate of Factors Involved in the Taiwan Straits Situation, TOP SECRET, September 4, 1958, DDE 36, Staff Notes September 1958, 3–4, DDEPL.
18 Summary, Estimate of Factors Involved in the Taiwan Straits Situation, TOP SECRET, September 4, 1958, DDE 36, Staff Notes September 1958, 3–4, DDEPL.
19 John Foster Dulles Papers, Princeton University, Reel 216, April 5, 1957, 97367.
20 Report on Foreign Economic Policy Discussions Between United States Officials in the Far East and Clarence B. Randall and Associations, SECRET, December 18, 1956, DDE U.S. Council on For Econ Policy, Randall Series, Trips Subseries, Box 2, Far East Trip [December 1956], Final Report, 7, DDEPL.
21 Phone Calls, May 24, 1957, DDE Diary 23, May 1957, Phone Calls, DDEPL.

that while he was doing what he "could to get our troops out, but of course it would be risking the collapse of our position in the Far East if we were to pull out of Formosa and Korea."[22]

The Chairman of the JCS posed Washington's dilemma in the following terms: "Are we to risk loss of U.S. prestige and influence in world, through loss of the Offshore Islands occasioned by failure to exert a maximum defense; or are we to risk loss of prestige and influence, through limited use of nuclear weapons to hold the Islands." Given these two options, the JCS reached a "consensus that we should take the second risk." They told President Eisenhower: "If we were to decide not to, we would have to recast our whole philosophy of defense planning. If we do not decide to take the second risk, each succeeding crisis and its concomitant decisions will become increasingly difficult for us."[23]

Secretary of State Dulles's stance on the use of atomic weapons was clear, and he once even told General Twining: "There was no use of having a lot of stuff and never being able to use it."[24] During a meeting with Eisenhower, Dulles reminded him that "we have geared our defenses to the use of these [atomic weapons] in case of hostilities of any size, and stating that, if we will not use them when the chips are down because of adverse world opinion, we must revise our defense setup."[25] But just because Washington was committed to protecting the offshore islands and Taiwan, it did not mean the US government advocated initiating an attack on the mainland. On June 25, 1962, during a third Taiwan incident, Rusk even reminded the British Foreign Secretary, Lord Home, that "Chiang Kai-shek would have no United States support if he attempted to attack the mainland," and it was agreed that the British chargé d'affaires would tell PRC leaders that the "United States had done and were doing everything possible to restrain the Nationalists from provocative action."[26]

In the midst of a life-or-death Cold War struggle, appeasement of communism was not considered to be an option. This left only two alternatives: "In the fullness of time either the communists will cease to be communists, whether by

---

22 Legislative Leadership Meeting, June 4, 1957, Supplementary Notes, Confidential, DDE Diary 24, June 1957 Misc. (2), DDEPL.

23 Taiwan Straits: Issues Developed in Discussion with JCS, TOP SECRET, September 2, 1958, DDE AWF, Int. Series 11, Formosa (2), 3–4, DDEPL.

24 Telephone Call to General Twining, September 2, 1958, Dulles, J.F., Tel Conv. Box 9, August–October 1958 (4), DDEPL.

25 Memorandum of Conference with the President, SECRET, September 4, 1958, DDE 36, Staff Notes September 1958, DDEPL.

26 "Record of a Conversation between the Foreign Secretary and Mr. Dean Rusk on Monday, June 25, 1962," The National Archives, Kew, PREM 11/3738.

revolution or evolution, or the United States and its friends will have to fight them, whether in global or local wars."[27] Truman was accused of giving up on China, thereby losing "to our country most of the fruits of the victory won by our fighting men in the Pacific theatre."[28] However, evolution was clearly the preferred option over a global war. Eisenhower argued that it was necessary to "wage the cold war in a militant, but reasonable, style whereby we appear to the people of the world as a better group to band with than the Communists." If done correctly, "we have got a real fighting chance of bringing this world around to the point where the Communist menace, if not eliminated, will be so minimized it cannot work."[29]

While an extremely long-term policy, therefore, and not one that brought immediate benefits, the US-sponsored strategic sanctions and the Nationalist blockade were highly successful in forcing evolutionary change on the PRC. While about half of China's trade was at that point being conducted overland, mainly with the USSR, an estimated 1,000 foreign ship arrivals per year accounted for the rest of her foreign trade. With American training, equipment, and financial backing, it was hoped that "the blockade of war goods, partially effective now, will grow more effective as the naval and air forces of Nationalist China are built up with U.S. aid."[30]

A prime goal of the economic sanctions and blockade was to break up the Sino-Soviet alliance. Chennault warned in 1949 that it might take "decades or centuries" to subvert the "Communist dynasty in China."[31] But Secretary of State Acheson told Governor Dewey in a April 10, 1950, telephone conversation that the only flicker of "hope in the Far east is to drive a wedge between Peking and Moscow," a policy that it would be "unwise" for Dewey to ever mention in a public speech.[32] As early as December 1954, the NSC paper entitled "Policy toward the Far East" stated that a major objective was:

27 Report on Foreign Economic Policy Discussions Between United States Officials in the Far East and Clarence B. Randall and Associations, SECRET, December 18, 1956, DDE U.S. Council on For Econ Policy, Randall Series, Trips Subseries, Box 2, Far East Trip [December 1956], Final Report, 3, DDEPL.
28 Letter from William C. Bullitt to President Truman, February 9, 1948, PHST, Official File, OF 150, Box 759, File O.F. 150 Misc. (1947–48) [1 of 2], HSTPL.
29 Conversation between the President and Senator Styles Bridges, May 21, 1957, DDE Diary 24, May 1957 Misc. (2), 1, 7, DDEPL.
30 "China Blockade: How It Works; Ships by the U.S.—Sailors by Chiang Kai-shek," *U.S. News and World Report*, February 20, 1953.
31 Letter from Major General Claire Lee Chennault to John R. Steelman, June 10, 1949, PHST, Official File, OF 150, Box 759, File O.F. 150 Misc. (1947–48) [2 of 2], HSTPL.
32 Memorandum of Conversation, Dean Acheson and Governor Dewey, SECRET, April 10, 1950, Dean G. Acheson Papers, Box 67, HSTPL.

"Disruption of the Sino-Soviet alliance through actions designed to intensify existing and potential areas of conflict or divergence of interest between the USSR and Communist China."[33] In May 1955, Senator Mundt congratulated Eisenhower for keeping the "Communists guessing," since "it creates much uneasiness among Communist high echelon in Russia and China."[34]

On the surface, the US and UK economic policies with the PRC differed dramatically, but they in fact sought the same goal: splitting the Sino-Soviet alliance apart and bringing the PRC into the Western "camp." In 1955, Eden even told Eisenhower that "the British government would always hope to be on the American side in every quarrel."[35] But rather than following the US lead by cutting China completely off from international trade, the British countervailing view was that it was better to leave the door open by conducting some trade, just in case China decided to turn to the West. This difference caused significant friction in Anglo-US relations. In private communications, however, Selwyn Lloyd reassured John Foster Dulles during September 1958 that "Your troubles are our troubles," and he even asked "is there any way in which we can help?"[36]

The Anglo-American "carrot-and-stick" diplomatic approach had the desired long-term impact on China, in particular since the end result of these two countries' economic policies contributed to Beijing's decision to turn more to the West. Although Eisenhower was a firm supporter of the Republic of China on Taiwan, on April 17, 1955, he told Dulles "that in the long run, unless the unexpected happened, it might be necessary to accept the 'Two China' concept. He spoke of '5–10 or 12 years'."[37] Dulles, in a conversation with Molotov a month later, explained that rather than letting the Taiwan Strait start a world war, "surely the situation could continue another decade or longer if the alternative was the risk of war within a year."[38]

---

33 NSC 5429/5, "Policy toward the Far East," TOP SECRET, December 22, 1954, DDE WH Office, OSANSA, NSC Series, Policy Paper Subseries, Box 12, 3, DDEPL.

34 Memorandum to the President regarding Senator Mundt's letter, May 12, 1955, DDE Papers 5, ACW Diary May 1955(5), DDEPL.

35 Notes dictated by the President regarding his conversation with Sir Anthony Eden, held Sunday, July 17, in the afternoon, July 19, 1955, DDE Diary Series 11, DDE Diary July 1955 (1), DDEPL.

36 Letter from Selwyn Lloyd to John Foster Dulles (Top Secret), September 11, 1958, The National Archives, Kew, CAB 21/3272.

37 Memorandum of Conversation with the President, Augusta, Georgia, April 17, 1955, TOP SECRET, April 18, 1955, Dulles, J.F., W.H. Memo No 3, Meet Press 1955 (5), 2, DDEPL.

38 Conversation at Ambassador's Resident, Vienna on May 14, 1955, TOP SECRET, May 17, 1955, DDE Subject Series Box 70, State, Dept. of (May 1955), 2, DDEPL.

Clearly, Washington was in no rush to solve the problem; over 60 years later, the U.S. government is still 'kicking the can'. By the late 1950s, only one decade after the creation of the PRC, tensions between China and the Soviet Union had reached a breaking point. In order to try to begin to pay off China's enormous foreign debt to the USSR, Mao Zedong adopted economic policies, such as the 1958 Great Leap Forward, that produced a nationwide famine.[39] Some historians have argued that the resulting Sino-Soviet rift took Washington by "surprise" and that the US government did not adopt policies to "expedite the estrangement."[40] But, others have confirmed that Dulles "sought to split the Chinese and Russians by driving them ever closer together."[41] The Sino-Soviet monolith's collapse during the late 1950s proves that Truman's and Eisenhower's strategic objectives were fully achieved. During the next decade, Mao Zedong gradually turned China's relations further away from the USSR and closer to the West. Beginning in 1969, 14 years after Eisenhower's and Dulles's evolutionary statements, President Richard Nixon—Eisenhower's vice president—began the process of recognizing the PRC.

Even while the PRC was facing economic collapse, with US assistance Taiwan took a completely different development path. British officials reported during 1955 that "Formosa is prosperous (with United States aid) and the people, whose standard of living is much higher than that of most Oriental countries, seem contented."[42] Eschewing a simple military solution to China's unification, Chiang Kai-shek prophetically told an Australian newspaper that Taiwan would focus on economic development: "We shall continue to build up Taiwan as an example of what free men can do."[43] US support for Taiwan was absolutely crucial to its economic success, often referred to as the "Taiwan miracle." As Eisenhower put it: "The vigorous and skilled population on Taiwan, the record of growth in investment and output, the very real potential for acceleration, offer a prospect for a convincing demonstration that under free institutions a pace and degree of

---

39 Lawrence C. Reardon, *The Reluctant Dragon: Crisis Cycles in Chinese Foreign Economic Policy* (Seattle: University of Washington Press, 2002), 103–4.

40 Shu Guang Zhang, *Economic Cold War: America's Embargo against China and the Sino-Soviet Alliance, 1949–1963* (Stanford: Stanford University Press, 2001), 237.

41 Marilyn Young, *The Vietnam Wars, 1945–1990* (New York: HarperCollins, 1991), 309–10.

42 Report from UK Consulate, Tamsui, to Foreign Office (Confidential), February 24, 1955, PREM 11/879.

43 John Foster Dulles Papers, Princeton University, Reel 214/215, August 29, 1956, 96035.

achievement can eventually be obtained in excess of that resulting under totalitarianism."[44]

In December 1956, the importance of this miracle to the rest of East Asia was emphasized: "Taiwan is becoming a show window of the free world, which impresses friends and foes alike with the constancy and success of American policy."[45] The NSC's policy for Taiwan, called NSC 5723, also emphasized the need for the Taiwan miracle to include greater democracy: "An increasingly efficient Government of the Republic of China (GRC), evolving toward responsible representative government, capable of attracting growing support and allegiance from the people of mainland China and Taiwan, and serving as the focal point of the free Chinese alternative to Communism."[46] Successful examples like Taiwan were called by James W. Riddleberger the "reverse-domino effect." Once these "islands of development" were formed, they could "give assistance and inspiration in their turn to other underdeveloped countries which are further behind in the growth process." By 1960, Taiwan was already at the stage where it could help other developing countries by extending "technical assistance to free Vietnam."[47]

Defeating global communism was Eisenhower's primary challenge, with the defense of Taiwan one major component of this larger strategy. On January 26, 1955, Eisenhower met with Senator Knowland and said: "Co-existence is the absence of killing each other. I don't say it is satisfactory or that I like it. It simply means you and I are not killing each other off." With regard to Formosa and China, the "most we could ever have would be dual recognition of Nationalist China and Red China," but "at present neither side would accept it." For this reason, Eisenhower concluded: "Times seems to be the final arbiter of history."[48]

---

44 Hearings Before the Committee on Foreign Affairs House of Representatives, March 1, 1960, DDE U.S. Council on For Econ Policy, Randall Series; Agency Subseries, Box 2, Int. Cooperation Adm (1), 1, DDEPL.

45 Report on Foreign Economic Policy Discussions between United States Officials in the Far East and Clarence B. Randall and Associations, SECRET, December 18, 1956, DDE U.S. Council on For Econ Policy, Randall Series, Trips Subseries, Box 2, Far East Trip [December 1956], Final Report, 8, DDEPL.

46 NSC, U.S. Policy toward Taiwan and the Government of the Republic of China, TOP SECRET, October 4, 1957, White House Office, Office of the Special Assistant for National Security Affairs: Records 1952–61, NSC Series, Policy Papers Subseries, Box 22, 1, DDEPL.

47 Hearings Before the Committee on Foreign Affairs House of Representatives, March 1, 1960, DDE U.S. Council on For Econ Policy, Randall Series; Agency Subseries, Box 2, Int. Cooperation Adm (1), 3, DDEPL.

48 Eisenhower's Meeting with Senator Knowland, January 26, 1955, DDE Papers 4, ACW Diary, January 1955 (1), DDEPL.

As Eisenhower acknowledged to his friend Lew Douglas: "The central fact of today's life is that we are in a life and death struggle of ideologies. It is freedom against dictatorship; Communism against capitalism; concepts of human dignity against the materialistic dialectic." America's opponents in this life-or-death struggle were playing by new rules: "They have complete contempt for any of those concepts of honor, decency and integrity which must underlie any successful practice of international law and order as we have always understood it." Eisenhower pessimistically concluded: "I have come to the conclusion that some of our traditional ideas of international sportsmanship are scarcely applicable in the morass in which the world now flounders."[49]

By 1958, the small offshore islands located in the Taiwan Strait, most of which an average American could not have named or pointed to on a map, had helped to exacerbate Sino-Soviet relations, resulting in a split. This outcome was no accident but was the result of measured and carefully thought out policies enacted by the Truman and Eisenhower administrations. For example, the strategic embargo adopted by the Truman administration in 1950, plus the 10-year Nationalist blockade lasting from 1948 to 1958, had such a huge impact on China's economy that by the mid-1950s over 50 percent of China's foreign trade was being conducted with the USSR, which became a source of enormous friction. Rising military, political, and especially economic tensions eventually resulted in the Sino-Soviet split. Even though Harry S. Truman's successor, Dwight D. Eisenhower, is usually credited for bringing these policies to fruition, a wide variety of documents prove that these nonpartisan Cold War policies were successfully adopted and supported by both President Harry S. Truman and President Dwight D. Eisenhower.

With the first live round discharged in Hong Kong during the prodemocracy demonstrations of spring 2020, the world has woken up to find a resurgent and imperialistic China. Like Imperial Japan in its heyday, which misjudged its sea power position and adopted a failed continental strategy, China seems intent on subjugating its neighbors and poorest trading partners. Domestically, it is applying a continental assimilate-or-die strategy against its ethnic minorities, with a campaign of genocide targeting Uighurs and Tibetans. For the rest of the population, it is imposing a 24-hour surveillance state coupled with political reliability scores that limit job and travel prospects and threaten jail terms. This conjures parallels not with Imperial Japan but with Nazi Germany.

---

49 Eisenhower Letter to L. W. Douglas, Personal and Confidential, March 29, 1955, DDE Diary Series 10, DDE Diary March 1955 (1), 1–2, DDEPL.

Simultaneously, China has pivoted to the sea, starting with Hong Kong, its traditional maritime gateway, and is projecting power abroad by building overseas bases in the South China Sea, in the India Ocean, and as far away as Djibouti, on the African coast. The world's great trading nations must recognize this maritime quest as dangerous and work to counter this new phase of China's imperial expansion. For thousands of years, China has been a continental power based on its military prowess. Emperors and dynasties would come and go. Most were Han Chinese but some were Mongol, Manchu, and Soviet-trained Communist, but one factor remained constant: the imperative to ward off landward invasions. Protected by natural barriers, like the Himalayas, the vastness of Xinjiang, and the Gobi Desert, Chinese leaders exerted maximum effort to close the gaps, most notably with the Great Wall.

With the 2013 Belt and Road Initiative (BRI), the Chinese government has sought to use money, rather than military might, to buy the fealty of its many land neighbors, plus selected countries abroad. It has provided them with surveillance-state technology to keep their dictators in power and presumably millions, if not billions, of dollars in bribes, to keep the dictators flush. But such economic efforts are doomed to fail, since local economies challenged by COVID and other difficulties simply cannot pay back the enormous BRI investments. Woe to those underdeveloped countries that cannot repay their debts. Sri Lanka has just handed over a treaty port to China with a 99-year lease for Hambantota, a copycat of the nineteenth-century British treaty ports that the Chinese so revile.

On the high seas, the Chinese Navy is protecting the all-important sea lines of communication bringing essential petroleum back from the Persian Gulf. Not since the fifteenth-century Ming Navy, which sponsored seven Treasure Fleets to the south and west, has China exerted such influence over the seas. The People's Liberation Army Navy (PLAN) has grown exponentially, first with American help in the 1980s to be turned as a weapon against the USSR, and then with Russian help in the 1990s and beyond to be turned against the United States. Vladimir Putin's lifeline out of his own fiscal and military mismanagement would be a Sino-American war, a war that would benefit his kleptocracy alone by bringing world living standards crashing down to his own country's low level.

The US maritime strategy since 2010 has been called the "pivot to Asia," with 170 ships—including the most powerful nuclear aircraft carriers ever built plus a fleet of attack submarines second to none—to contain the China threat. But the conundrum of the Taiwan Strait has continued down to the present time, when the PRC has purportedly tried to use the COVID-19 outbreak to

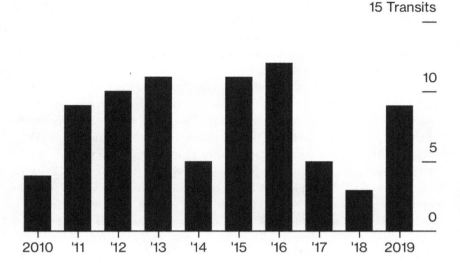

Figure C.1 Passing Through Taiwan Strait.

U.S. warship transits through the Taiwan Strait increases last year.
Source: U.S. Pacific Fleet.
https://www.bloomberg.com/news/articles/2020-01-17/u-s-warship-sails-taiwan-strait-after-trade-deal-election.

apply pressure on Taiwan to reunify. Even prior to the COVID pandemic, however, tensions were arguably on the rise due to tensions in Hong Kong. In January 2020, for example, the US warship *Shiloh* transited the Taiwan Strait soon after Tsai Ing-wen won a landslide reelection bid. Rather than being an anomaly, Figure C.1 shows that during 2019 there were nine transits, the most since President Barack Obama's last year in office. There were a record thirteen transits in 2020. President Joseph Biden has already had three transits as of May 11, 2021.

The United States also has allies and coalition partners to consider. On Christmas day, a top Japanese defense official urged US President-elect Joe Biden to "be strong" in supporting Taiwan in the face of an aggressive China, calling the island's safety a "red line."[50] This was in response to China's decision to sail both of its aircraft carriers through the Taiwan Strait at the same time on December 20, right after the Arleigh-Burke-class guided missile

---

50 Ju-min Park, "Japan Official, Calling Taiwan 'Red Line,' Urges Biden to 'Be Strong'," December 25, 2020, Reuters.com; https://www.reuters.com/article/us-japan-usa-taiwan-china-idUSKBN28Z0JR.

destroyer, the USS *Mustin*, had transited on December 19. This had "strong
political implications," according to *Duowei News*, adding that by sending its two
aircraft carriers through the Taiwan Strait simultaneously, Beijing is issuing "a
clear declaration of its intention to unify the island" with the mainland and is
sending a clear "warning to the U.S."[51]

Taiwan is not just standing idling, however, having just launched its first
missile corvette, the *Tuo Chiang*—the first of five planned missile corvettes.
Called an "aircraft carrier killer" by the Taiwanese press, these ships are
armed with "Sea Sword II anti-aircraft missiles, eight subsonic Hsiung Feng
II (HF-2) anti-ship missiles, eight supersonic Hsiung Feng III (HF-3) medium-
range missiles, one Phalanx close-in weapons system (CIWS), two 12.7 mm
Browning M2HB machine guns and two Mark 32 Surface Vessel Torpedo
Tubes."[52]

Meanwhile, on the diplomatic front, Taiwanese supporters in the United
States convinced Congress in May 2019 to enact the Taiwan Assurance Act
(TAA) reaffirming the 1979 Taiwan Relations Act (TRA). The TAA states
that the US Congress believes Taiwan is a vital part of the US' "Free and
Open Indo-Pacific Strategy" and as such the government should support
Taiwan's continued pursuit of asymmetric capabilities: "The US should
conduct regular sales and transfers of defense articles to Taiwan in order
to enhance its self-defense capabilities, particularly its efforts to develop and
integrate asymmetric capabilities, including undersea warfare and air defense
capabilities, into its military forces."[53] After Trump signed the TAA into law
on December 27, 2020, China's Foreign Ministry Spokesman Zhao Lijian told
a news conference in Beijing that the US move was an "interference in China's
internal affairs": "China firmly opposes US' Taiwan Assurance Act, and the
US should stop interfering in China's internal affairs by using the Taiwan
question."[54]

---

51 Duowei News, "Beijing's sending both its aircraft carriers through the Taiwan Strait is a
   'clear declaration of its intention to unify the island' with the Mainland and 'a warning
   to the U.S.'," December 29, 2020, Memri.com; https://www.memri.org/reports/
   chinese-duowei-news-beijings-sending-both-its-aircraft-carriers-through-taiwan-strait-
   clear.

52 Sam Cohen, "Water Wars: Flirting in the Taiwan Strait," December 23, 2020,
   Lawfareblog.com; https://www.lawfareblog.com/water-wars-flirting-taiwan-strait.

53 "Trump Signs Taiwan Assurance Act," December 29, 2020, Taipei Times; https://
   www.taipeitimes.com/News/front/archives/2020/12/29/2003749564.

54 Ovunc Kutlu and Riyaz ul Khaliq, "Trump Signs Taiwan Act into Law, Angering Rival
   China," December 28, 2020, aa.com; https://www.aa.com.tr/en/americas/trump-
   signs-taiwan-act-into-law-angering-rival-china-/2090720.

This is not good news for China. PRC leader Xi Jinping could face additional trouble as perceptions increase that his "Mandate of Heaven" is slipping. Traditionally, comets and earthquakes show heaven is displeased. Dynasties can fall as a result. Revolutions are timed with these events. In addition to Taiwan's continued resistance to Chinese reunification attempts, there are four other serious indicators, including the recent UN censure on China's Uighur policy, the ongoing repression of Hong Kong democracy, difficult trade talks with the United States, and most importantly the global COVID pandemic, which was identified in Wuhan almost two months before it went public, but anyone who tried to warn people was thrown in jail. Therefore, Xi Jinping is simultaneously facing five major Mandate of Heaven crises—diplomatic, ethnic, political, trade, and health—which is unprecedented. It is a perfect storm. Can the already weakened Communist Party survive? Or, is Xi's mandate slipping for good?

Why should the world care about Taiwan? In times of domestic stress, like now, Chinese leaders sometimes lash out, such as during 1954–55, 1958, 1962, and 1995–96 along the Taiwan Strait. The US Navy is on the front lines of trying to keep tensions from boiling over. But the world should expect the unexpected. Democratic Taiwan has valiantly fought off all such bullying attempts by an autocratic one-party dictatorship, as the all-too-overlooked Taiwan Strait acts as the one reliable bulwark against invasion of one of the first true Asian democracies. Only time will tell if this "English Channel" of the Far East will uphold its namesake.

APPENDIX

NAVAL TERMS AND ACRONYM LIST

ASW	Anti-Submarine Warfare
BRI	Belt and Road Initiative
CCF	Chinese Communist Forces, or PLA
CHINCOM	Chinese Communists; Chinese Committee
CIA	Central Intelligence Agency
CinCPac	Commander-in-Chief, US Pacific Command
CinCPacFlt	Commander in Chief of the Pacific Fleet
CNAF	Chinese Nationalist Air Force
CNO	Chief of Naval Operations
CO	Commanding Officer
COCOM	Coordinating Committee for Multilateral Export Controls
DDC	Dachen Defense Command
DDCAT	Dachen Defense Command Advisory Team
DOD	Department of Defense
EEZ	Exclusive Economic Zone
GIMO	Generalissimo
GNP	Gross National Product
GRC	Government of the Republic of China
JCS	Joint Chiefs of Staff
LCM	Landing Craft Mechanized
LST	Landing Ship, Tank
MAAG	Military Assistance Advisory Group
NDB	Nuclear Depth Bomb
NGRC	Nationalist Government of the Republic of China
NHHC	Naval History and Heritage Command
NSC	National Security Council
NWC	Naval War College
ONI	Office of Naval Intelligence

PLA	People's Liberation Army
PLAAF	People's Liberation Army Air Force
PLAN	People's Liberation Army Navy
PRC	People's Republic of China
R&D	Research and Development
RCN	Republic of China Navy
ROC	Republic of China
ROE	Rules of Engagement
SAR	Search-and-Rescue
SLOC	Sea line of communication
SRBM	Short-Range Ballistic Missile
TAA	Taiwan Assurance Act
TRA	Taiwan Relations Act
UN	United Nations
USN	United States Navy
USTDC	United States Taiwan Defense Command
WEI	Western Enterprises Incorporated
ZPG	Zhejiang Provincial Government

SELECTED BIBLIOGRAPHY

Books and articles

Anderson, George W., *Reminiscences of Admiral George W. Anderson, Jr.*, Oral History 42.

Bouchard, Joseph F., *Command in Crisis: Four Case Studies*. New York: Columbia University Press, 1991.

Chang, Gordan H., *Friends and Enemies: The United States, China, and the Soviet Union, 1948–1972*. Stanford: Stanford University Press, 1990.

Chang, Jung, and Jon Halliday, *Mao: The Unknown Story*. New York: Alfred A. Knopf, 2005.

Chen Jian, *Mao's China & the Cold War*. Chapel Hill: University of North Carolina Press, 2001.

Chen Ming-tong, *The China Threat Crosses the Strait: Challenges and Strategies for Taiwan's National Security*, trans. Kiel Downey. Taipei: Dong Fan Color, 2007.

Chiu, Hungdah, *China and the Taiwan Issue*. New York: Praeger, 1979.

Christensen, Thomas J., *Useful Adversaries: Grand Strategy, Domestic Mobilization, and Sino-American Conflict, 1947–1958*. Princeton, NJ: Princeton University Press, 1996.

Clough, Ralph N., *Island China*. Cambridge, MA: Harvard University Press, 1978.

Cohen, Warren I., ed., *New Frontiers in American-East Asian Relations*. New York: Columbia University Press, 1983.

Dikötter, Frank. *Mao's Great Famine: The History of China's Most Devastating Catastrophe, 1958–1962*. New York: Walker, 2010.

Durkin, Michael F., *Naval Quarantine: A New Addition to the Role of Sea Power*. Maxwell Air Force Base, AL; Air University: Air War College, 1964.

Elleman, Bruce A., *Modern Chinese Warfare, 1795–1989*. London: Routledge, 2001.

———. *High Seas Buffer: The Taiwan Patrol Force, 1950–1979*. Newport, RI: US Naval War College Press, 2012.

———. *Taiwan Straits: Crisis in Asia and the Role of the U.S. Navy*. Lanham, MD: Rowman & Littlefield, 2015.

———. *China's Naval Operations in the South China Sea: Evaluating Legal, Strategic and Military Factors*. Folkestone, UK: Renaissance Books, 2018.

———. *Taiwan's Offshore Islands: Pathway or Barrier?* Newport, RI: U.S. Naval War College Press, 2019.

Elleman, Bruce A., and S. C. M. Paine, eds., *Naval Blockades and Seapower: Strategies and Counter-Strategies, 1805–2005*. London: Routledge, 2006.

———. *Naval Power and Expeditionary Warfare: Peripheral Campaigns and New Theatres of Naval Warfare*. London: Routledge, 2011.

Elleman, Bruce A., and James Bussert, *People's Liberation Army Navy (PLAN) Combat Systems Technology, 1949–2010*. Annapolis, MD: Naval Institute Press, 2011.

Elleman, Bruce A., and Stephen Kotkin, eds., *Manchurian Railways and the Opening of China: An International History.* Armonk, NY: M.E.Sharpe, 2010.

Gallagher, Rick M., *The Taiwan Strait Crisis.* Newport, RI: Strategic Research Department, Research Report, 1997.

Garver, John W., *China's Decision for Rapprochement with the United States, 1968–1971.* Boulder, CO: Westview Press, 1982.

———. *The Sino-American Alliance: Nationalist China and American Cold War Strategy in Asia.* Armonk, NY: M.E. Sharpe, 1997.

Gibert, Stephen P., and William M. Carpenter, *America and Island China: A Documentary History.* Lanham, MD: University Press of America, 1989.

Glass, Sheppard, "Some Aspects of Formosa's Economic Growth," in Mark Mancall, ed., *Formosa Today.* New York: Praeger, 1964.

Hickey, Dennis Van Vranken, *United States-Taiwan Security Ties: From Cold War to Beyond Containment.* Westport, CT: Praeger, 1994.

Hinton, Harold C., *China's Turbulent Quest.* New York: Macmillan, 1972.

Holober, Frank, *Raiders of the China Coast: CIA Covert Operations during the Korean War.* Annapolis, MD: Naval Institute Press, 1999.

Hugill, Paul D., *The Continuing Utility of Naval Blockades in the Twenty-first Century.* Fort Leavenworth, KS: U.S. Army Command and General Staff College, 1998.

Khrushchev, Nikita Sergeevich, and Sergei Khrushchev, *Memoirs of Nikita Khrushchev: Statesman, 1953–1964.* College Park: Penn State Press, 2007.

Kissinger, Henry, *White House Years.* Boston, MA: Little, Brown, 1979.

Lasater, Martin L., ed., *Beijing's Blockade Threat to Taiwan: A Heritage Roundtable.* Washington, DC: Heritage Foundation, 1986.

Lilly, James R., and Chuck Downs, eds., *Crisis in the Taiwan Strait.* Washington, DC: American Enterprise Institute for Public Policy Research, 1997.

Liu, Ta Jen, *U.S.-China Relations, 1784–1992.* Lanham, MD: University Press of America, 1997.

Lüthi, Lorenz M. *The Sino-Soviet Split: Cold War in the Communist World.* Princeton, NJ: Princeton University Press, 2008.

Mancall, Mancall, ed., *Formosa Today.* New York: Praeger, 1964.

Marolda, Edward J., and Oscar P. Fitzgerald, *From Military Assistance to Combat, 1959–1965,* Volume Two in the series *The United States Navy and the Vietnam Conflict.* Washington: Naval Historical Center, 1986.

———. *A New Equation: Chinese Intervention into the Korean War. Proceedings of the Colloquium on Contemporary History.* Washington, DC: Naval Historical Center, 1991.

———. *By Sea, Air, and Land: An Illustrated History of the U.S. Navy and the War in Southeast Asia.* Washington, DC: Government Printing Office, 1994.

———. "Wall of Steel: Sea Power and the Cold War in Asia," in David Stevens, ed., *Maritime Power in the Twentieth Century.* St. Leonards, Australia: Allen & Unwin, 1998, 103–18.

———. "Hostilities along the China Coast During the Korean War," in Robert W. Love Jr., Laurie Bogle, Brian VanDeMark, and Maochun Yu, eds., *New Interpretations in Naval History.* Annapolis, MD: Naval Institute Press, 2001, 351–63.

———. "Confrontation in the Taiwan Straits," in M. Hill Goodspeed, *U.S. Navy: A Complete History.* Washington, DC: Naval Historical Foundation, 2003.

———. *The Approaching Storm: Conflict in Asia, 1945–1965.* Washington, DC: Government Printing Office, 2009.

Marolda, Edward J., "The U.S. Navy and the Chinese Civil War, 1945– 1952," PhD Diss., The George Washington University, 1990.

Muller, David, *China as a Maritime Power*. Boulder, CO: Westview Press, 1983.

Paine, S. C. M, *The Wars for Asia, 1911–1949*. New York: Cambridge University Press, 2014.

Park, Chang-Kwoun, "Consequences of U.S. Naval Shows of Force, 1946–1989." University of Missouri-Columbia, PhD Diss., August 1995.

Reardon, Lawrence C., *The Reluctant Dragon: Crisis Cycles in Chinese Foreign Economic Policy*. Seattle: University of Washington Press, 2002.

Ryan, Mark A., David M. Finkelstein, and Michael A. McDevitt, *Chinese Warfighting: The PLA Experience since 1949*. Armonk NY: M.E. Sharpe, 2003.

Smoot, Vice Admiral Roland N., "As I Recall … The U.S. Taiwan Defense Command," *Proceedings*, September 1984, volume 110/9/979, 56–59.

Szonyi, Michael, *Cold War Island: Quemoy on the Front Line*. New York: Cambridge University Press, 2008.

Tkacik, John J., Jr., ed., *Reshaping the Taiwan Strait*. Washington, DC: Heritage Foundation, 2007.

Tucker, Nancy Bernkopf, ed., *Dangerous Strait: The U.S.-Taiwan-China Crisis*. New York: Columbia University Press, 2005.

Wang, Gabe T., *China and the Taiwan Issue: Impending War at Taiwan Strait*. Lanham, MD: University Press of America, 2006.

Yang Zhiben [杨志本], ed., *China Navy Encyclopedia*, [中国海军百科全书], vol. 2. Beijing: Sea Tide Press [海潮出版社], 1998.

Young, Marilyn, *The Vietnam Wars, 1945–1990*. New York: HarperCollins, 1991.

Zhang, Shu Guang, *Economic Cold War: America's Embargo against China and the Sino-Soviet Alliance, 1949–1963*. Stanford: Stanford University Press, 2001.

Zhao Suisheng, ed., *Across the Taiwan Strait: Mainland China, Taiwan, and the 1995–1996 Crisis*. New York: Routledge, 1999.

Internet Sources

Bob Bublitz, "To Speak of Many Things," http://www.centurum.com/vq/pdf/VQ%20 Winter-Spring%202006%20News3.pdf.

"CINCPAC Command History, 1974," http://oldsite.nautilus.org/archives/library/ security/foia/japanindex.html.

First Taiwan Strait Crisis: Quemoy and Matsu Islands, http://www.globalsecurity.org/military/ ops/quemoy_matsu.htm.

"Intelligence for Economic Defense," Sherman R. Abrahamson, CIA Historical Review Program, https://www.cia.gov/static/5803efc7ba6c6412056efd616bfea01c/Intel-for-Economic-Defense.pdf.

Robert Keng, "Republic of China F-86's in Battle," at http://www.aircraftresourcecenter. com/Stories1/001-100/021_TaiwanF-86_Keng/story021.htm.

The Nuclear Information Project, "USS Randolph and the Nuclear Diplomatic Incident," http://www.nukestrat.com/dk/randolph.htm.

Policy and Direction: The First Year, Chapter XX "The Relief of MacArthur," U.S. Army Center of Military History, http://www.history.army.mil/books/pd-c-20.htm.

ROCAF F-104 Retirement, http://www.taiwanairpower.org/history/f104ret.html.

"Taiwan Strait: 21 July 1995 to 23 March 1996," http://www.globalsecurity.org/military/ ops/taiwan_strait.htm.

INDEX

CPSIA information can be obtained
at www.ICGtesting.com
Printed in the USA
BVHW040031300422
635410BV00001B/1